Sex & Gender

Sex & Gender

Christian Ethical Reflections

MARY JO IOZZIO AND PATRICIA BEATTIE JUNG
Editors

Georgetown University Press/Washington, DC

The publisher is not responsible for third-party websites or their content. URL links were active at time of publication.

Library of Congress Cataloging-in-Publication Data
Names: Iozzio, Mary Jo, editor. | Jung, Patricia Beattie, editor.
Title: Sex and gender : Christian ethical reflections / Mary Jo Iozzio and
    Patricia Beattie Jung, editors.
Description: Washington, DC : Georgetown University Press, 2017. | Includes
    bibliographical references and index. | Description based on print version record
    and CIP data provided by publisher; resource not viewed.
Identifiers: LCCN 2017009231 (print) | LCCN 2017011975 (ebook) | ISBN 9781626165304
    (pb : alk. paper) | ISBN 9781626165298 (hc : alk. paper) | ISBN 9781626165311 (eb)
Subjects: LCSH: Sexual ethics—Religious aspects—Christianity. | Sexual ethics. | Christian
    ethics. | Sex—Religious aspects—Christianity.
Classification: LCC HQ32 (ebook) | LCC HQ32 .S395 2017 (print) | DDC
    176/.4—dc23
LC record available at https://lccn.loc.gov/2017009231

This book is printed on acid-free paper meeting the requirements of the American National Standard for Permanence in Paper for Printed Library Materials.

18 17   9 8 7 6 5 4 3 2 First printing

Printed in the United States of America

Cover design by N. Putens.

We dedicate this work to our contributors and the many colleagues in the Society of Christian Ethics who challenge us to think critically and creatively about the construction of sexual norms and their ethical reconstruction in ways illustrative of the best insights of the Christian traditions of love, justice, and God's call to delight in pied beauty.

Contents

Introduction

MARY JO IOZZIO AND PATRICIA BEATTIE JUNG

This anthology offers a snapshot of recent work by the members of the Society of Christian Ethics (hereafter the SCE) on matters of sex and gender. These essays were first presented and vetted at annual meetings of that society, and then reviewed by and chosen for publication by the co-editors and editorial boards of the *Annual of the Society of Christian Ethics* (1981–2003, hereafter the *Annual*) and the *Journal of the Society of Christian Ethics* (2004–present, hereafter the *JSCE*). We limited our choices to essays from the *Annual* and *JSCE* for several reasons. They offer scholarship from among the finest in our guild. They have been previously reviewed with criteria (and publication rates) on par with the most competitive journals in the field. They were edited prior to their publication in the *JSCE* in light of discussions that followed their presentation at SCE annual meetings. All these factors support this editorial choice.

Building a Community That Fosters Moral Deliberation

The *Annual* and its successor publication, the *JSCE*, have published ethical arguments on a wide range of subjects of critical concern to both church and society in North America and across the globe. From its inception in 1959 the SCE tested and critically analyzed many controversial lines of moral argument during its annual meetings. And yet, during its first few decades there was very little formal consideration on anything related to sexual ethics. In hindsight the absence of such early deliberations about sexual issues is easy to understand. In the years immediately following World War II, society at large was silent about the traditions that fortify predominantly patriarchal attitudes on sex and gender. Not surprisingly, that silence was not broken in the SCE, given the homogenous character of its membership during its fledgling years. But two intertwined factors may have led to more forthright explorations of sexual issues by Christian ethicists: key developments in the SCE's growth as an academic society accompanied by important moments in what has been called "the sexual revolution" in North America.

Social retrenchment and political conservatism typified the postwar era during the 1950s. Yet with the emergence of widespread access to "the pill" early in the 1960s and the increase of students (especially women) in colleges and universities, the so-called sexual revolution began in North America. During this time the intersections between sexism and hetero-sexism, along with militarism, racism, and classism, began to be exposed and named, however hesitatingly. The Civil Rights Movement and sub-sequent legislation raised consciousness of the structural disadvantages minorities faced. The Stonewall Riots in 1969 and the inception of the Gay Pride Movement brought that tumultuous decade to a close. These events bookend a decade marked by explosive cultural change, igniting in subsequent decades a series of challenges to traditional racial and class as well as sex and gender narratives that continues to burn.

Ensuing decades saw the Women's and Lesbian, Gay, Bisexual, Trans-gender, Intersex, and Queer (hereafter LGBTIQ) Liberation Move-ments grow through various phases. New insights into the dangerous realities of gender and sexual discrimination emerged along with more comprehensive psychosocial, anthropological, and biological data on the family, marriage, domestic violence, pornography, prostitution, LGBTIQ realities, sexual and gender bullying, rape cultures, and the HIV/AIDS pandemic. Greater access to and utilization of this research made it clear that vigorous ethical exchange on and faithful theological thinking about these issues was urgent and, in many instances, a matter of life and death.

Corresponding to these widespread cultural changes, the member-ship and structures of the SCE itself underwent dramatic transformation during these same decades. When the society was first founded in 1959, SCE membership consisted largely of white, male, (mainline) Protes-tant clergy. As Edward Leroy Long Jr. and Christine E. Gudorf recount, only one woman and six African Americans could be counted among its members in 1960; Catholics first attended in 1963.[1] There was little room in SCE ranks for the serious consideration of experiences or perspectives that had not already been privileged and arguably proved to be normative in traditional Protestant views of sex and gender.

Not surprisingly, before volume 1 of the *Annual* was published in 1981, there had been only one concurrent session devoted to the subject of sexual ethics during all the previous annual meetings of the SCE. In his 1976 presentation, responding in part to the midcentury "sexual revolution," John Giles Milhaven critically reviewed three of the standard approaches to sex and their assessments of pleasure shared between spouses and commended a fourth approach that recognized the intrinsic value of conjugal sex and the mutual delight spouses enjoyed. In "Christian Evaluations of Sexual Pleasure," Milhaven argued that when such pleasure is authentically personal and interpersonal, it can become a personal communion uniquely shared with one's spouse.

Though Milhaven's essay was well received and certainly groundbreaking for its time, further serious deliberations about sexual and gender issues once again stalled within the SCE. A review of its programs shows that it would be another seven years before the subject of sexuality was broached again as the formal focus of an academic discussion at an annual meeting of the society. No single factor broke this silence, but over the course of the society's fifty-plus years, much has changed within the membership of the SCE. Unquestionably, many more women and scholars of color can be counted among the society's membership and leadership. Additionally, in accord with the 1998–2000 recommendations of the Twenty-First Century Committee, programmatic funding for the initiatives of related working groups raised the profiles of African American and African (2003), Latino/a (2007), and Asian and Asian American (2009) scholars within the society.

Moreover, the membership has become far more diverse in terms of sexual orientation, gender, and sexual lifestyle. The membership of the SCE now includes people who are married, divorced, widowed, single, as well as vowed celibates; some are (great grand, grand, and first-time) parents, and others are childless or child-free. The SCE now includes not only clergy persons but many lay theologians as well. Some members of the SCE are from sexually diverse groups that until relatively recently had been denied access not only to civil marriage but also to the basic public rights to housing and public accommodations, and even in some instances to safety in public places and to police protection. Other members have been previously (or may still be) denied access to formal theological education, especially but not exclusively in religiously affiliated programs.

Even if they were not excluded from the classroom outright, many might well have been denied an opportunity to give theological voice to their reflections on sexuality from lecterns or pulpits. Just as the composition of the SCE has slowly changed, so has the makeup of the theological and pastoral leadership of some Christian denominations. While we recognize that there is no positive right to ordination or employment in an institution of higher learning, respect for the dignity of all human persons requires that the preemptive exclusion of anyone from serious consideration for appointment to a pulpit or lectern for whatever reason inclusive of sexual diversity requires serious moral justification.

Currently at the SCE's annual meetings members have many opportunities to test their approaches to and perspectives on questions in the field of Christian sexual ethics in rigorous academic and wide-ranging ecumenical exchange. Along with greater denominational diversity in the SCE, there is enhanced opportunity for interreligious and/or comparative ethical deliberation. Following another recommendation of the Twenty-First Century Committee, the SCE began meeting simultaneously, often cosponsoring sessions, with two sister societies: the Society of Jewish Ethics (since 2003) and the Society for the Study of Muslim Ethics (since 2010). Consequently, there is great opportunity for vigorous interfaith exchange of theo-ethical ideas about sexual orientation and intimacy, gender identity, and human relationality, and so on.[2]

These welcome changes to what had been previously a homogenous body brought many new perspectives and encouraged considerably more debate within the SCE about many subjects, including gender roles, the adequacy of the gender binary, heterosexual normativity, homophobia/heterosexism, divorce, "traditional" and digital pornography, and even commercial sex work. We believe these many demographic changes generated a particularly propitious environment for the construction of many finely reasoned Christian arguments about what makes for virtuous sex and about the public policies and church teachings that will promote such just love in intimate sexual relationships.

Developing Christian Traditions about Sexuality

Many Christians, including Roman Catholics, hold that ethically normative church teachings can develop and that these teachings can even be substantively reversed. This kind of development is evidenced in the dramatic reformation of many church teachings on issues like the persecution of heretics, the permissibility of usury (known more commonly today as the practice of lending money at interest), and the practice of slavery. These shifts do not simply reflect a more nuanced pastoral application of moral norms by church leaders (important as that is); rather, these shifts reflect substantive normative changes that flow from the ongoing work of the Spirit among the people of God guiding us into truly new and ever deeper understandings of the gospel's call to justice, peace, and love.

As we combed the pages of the *Annual* and the *JSCE* in search of essays that might both reflect and nurture such developments, we found more than ninety texts related to sexual ethics published over the past thirty-three years. Six of those texts offered bibliographies, pedagogical suggestions, or syllabi focused on sex and gender, which served to help SCE members meet the increasing demands for new courses on these subjects in both undergraduate and graduate programs and/or help the churches they served to affirm, develop, and/or revise their teachings on sexuality. The remaining essays offered clear theo-ethical arguments in response to the dramatic changes in sex and gender scripts embodied in North America and across the globe.

As you might expect, from this field of plenty it was very difficult to decide which essays might best stimulate clear and vigorous thinking about sexual ethics into the future.[3] We wanted to put together an anthology that faithfully and critically engaged Christian scriptures and traditions, that displayed the extensive scope of the current conversation, and that made clear the urgency and import of the issues under consideration. We are delighted to introduce you briefly to our selections.

The Essays

We believe conditions for human flourishing within the LGBTIQ community were much improved when on June 26, 2015, the US Supreme Court ruled in *Obergefell v. Hodges* that it was unconstitutional for states to ban same-sex marriage.[4] Still, this increased protection under the law is not yet equivalent to widespread moral approval or even general social acceptance. In the 2016 survey of incidents, twenty-one murders and three other suspicious deaths in the United States have been officially identified as transgender hate crimes.[5] As the shooting at the Pulse nightclub, a gay bar in Orlando, Florida, that same summer made clear, the LGBTIQ community and its allies are still often the victims of vicious criminal attack. The dis-ease with sexual minorities expressed by a significant number in our culture remains persistent because it is undergirded by deeply held, yet largely unrecognized and thereby unexamined, ideological convictions about heteronormativity. It is important to understand that this intolerance is not rooted in purely irrational emotions. Though they contribute to them, homophobia and other (most frequently male heterosexual) anxieties alone do not account for the hate crimes related to sexual orientation and gender. While the ongoing debate about access to public bathrooms for trans- and omnigender folk looms large on the cultural screen at the moment, it is important to recognize that the fundamental question of whether such variations represent differences or defects is often a matter of life and death for some.[6]

Perhaps not surprisingly then our collection opens with moral arguments about various forms of sexual diversity, focusing in particular on the impact of Christian traditions and scriptures on debates about homosexuality and heterosexism. The first two essays in this volume look critically at the rational (though in our judgment mistaken) foundations for systematic, institutionalized expressions of the conviction that only persons and partnerships that are heterosexual can be normatively good. Though they happen to focus on homosexuality, the structure (if not the details) of the arguments developed within them model approaches that could be applied to the much wider range of issues associated with sexual diversity, such as those associated with transgender and intersex.

In her essay, "The Natural Law and Innovative Forms of Marriage: A Reconsideration," Jean Porter explores the implications for the contemporary debate about same-sex marriage of the traditional scholastic approach to natural law reasoning. Faithfulness to this great tradition does not necessarily require that we confirm what was undoubtedly their unanimous condemnation of homosexual acts, nor that we refuse to entertain the possibility of same-sex marital unions. Instead, Porter suggests, it requires that we uncover the multiple lines of thought and practical reasoning that make up the scholastics' ideas about the purposes of marriage. Their ideas about what sex is for framed their identification of what was rightly ordered and what was morally defective.

For example, among the most important of the scholastics' arguments for marriage was their discernment that marriage, generally speaking, serves to establish and maintain a stable home for the care and education of children. As heirs to their concept of natural law, Porter argues that we are called not only to understand their reasoning but also to explore how the trajectory of their thought might well be developed in light of the many subsequent centuries of experience with and reflection on marriage and sexuality we now have at our disposal, including the growing data about how well children flourish in households headed by same-sex couples. Among other conclusions, Porter identifies developments in natural law reasoning that could fully support, rather than rule out, the civil recognition of same-sex marriage.

In his essay, "Reconciling Evangelical Christianity with Our Sexual Minorities: Reframing the Biblical Discussion," David P. Gushee details the many alienating consequences that follow from the traditional conclusion that "homosexuality" is irreconcilable with submission to biblical authority. Gushee, himself an evangelical Christian, both accepts the authority of the Bible and offers his community a progressive, alternative view of sexual diversity. He entertains several criticisms of traditional evangelical sexual norms and proposes alternative approaches to the interpretation of key biblical texts. He describes the changing attitudes about this among some evangelical Christians in North America, noting that the evangelical community in general had paid insufficient attention to the experiences of their LGBTIQ brothers and sisters in Christ. He names and repents as well of the harms that evangelical churches have inflicted on nonheterosexual folk "beginning with their own children." He concludes with a normative proposal deeply rooted in both evangelical convictions about the inspiration and crucial role of the whole Bible looking beyond the standard scriptural passages invoked against nonheterosexual intimacy, and in Christian discernment about the lived realities experienced by, with, and among faithful sexual minorities.

In chapter 3 readers will find an argument about violence in North American households originally sketched over twenty-five years ago by Karen Lebacqz in her presidential address to the SCE. Although her focus in "Love Your Enemy: Sex, Power, and Christian Ethics" was on what responses Christians might best endorse when domestic and sexual violence intersect, her analysis demonstrates how naive is the still commonplace presumption that intimacy is accompanied by equal power and safety for sexual partners. Since the 1990s there has been a decline in the United States in all forms of violence, including intimate partner violence (hereafter IPV). Nevertheless, according to the 2010 Executive Summary of "The National Intimate Partner and Sexual Violence Survey" published by the CDC, "nearly 1 in 10 women in the United States (9.4%) has been raped by an intimate partner in her lifetime, and an estimated 16.9% of women and 8.0% of men have experienced sexual violence other than rape by an intimate partner at some point in their lifetime."[7] Lebacqz's attention in her essay to the reflections of African Americans on "living with the enemy" underscores a point still morally relevant today: the Christian call is to love the neighbor—who might often be quite hostile and with whom one might well share a bed—as the self. The Christian moral tradition has long recognized the legitimacy of self-defense and the value of survival, as well as the call to love the enemy and practice forgiveness. Lebacqz makes clear that these moral axioms are as relevant to a Christian sexual ethic and to the domestic sphere as they are to more public spaces and international arenas.

As was dramatically publicized in a variety of contexts in the 2016 presidential campaign, sexual harassment remains well and alive in the United States. Though such behavior was made illegal under Title VII of the Civil Rights Act of 1964, it continues to plague corporate offices, the military, the halls of government at all levels, religious institutions, the academy (including the SCE[8]), and public arenas of all kinds. The US Equal Employment Opportunity Commission (known as the EEOC) defines sexual harassment as follows: "Unwelcome sexual advances, requests for sexual favors, and other verbal or physical conduct of a sexual nature constitute sexual harassment when this conduct explicitly or implicitly affects an individual's employment, unreasonably interferes with an individual's work performance, or creates an intimidating, hostile, or offensive work environment."[9] In 1999 the *Annual* published brief reflections from a "Special Plenary: Panel on Sexual Harassment" discussion on the topic.[10] While those reflections and other essays from the 1999 SCE meeting remain insightful, because sexual harassment is not a trivial concern, chapter 4 continues the trajectory Lebacqz initiated with an essay by Traci C. West.[11] In "The Harms of Sexual Harassment," West focuses on the particular vulnerability that African American women face in light of this predatory behavior. She illumines the immediate negative consequences of sexual harassment in the workplace and other public settings. Lurking under such behavior West finds (not always subtly veiled) the threat of rape. As she notes, racism and the residue of structures that offer unqualified support for especially white male expressions of dominance leave those harassed (especially African American women) burdened with both shame and the fear that the harassment will escalate to rape.[12] She notes that harassment continues beyond the original offense when the experience is trivialized through derisive attitudes that further traumatize the victims' self-understanding and confidence.

In chapter 5, through her ethnographic fieldwork,[13] Katherine Attanasi describes the experience of women in South Africa with sexual violence. Though "Biblical Ethics, HIV/AIDS, and South African Pentecostal Women: Constructing an A-B-C-D Prevention Strategy" is specifically attentive to conditions current in many South African Pentecostal congregations, readers should be wary of jumping to the (false) conclusion that this circumscribed focus makes her analysis irrelevant to analogous situations in other parts of the globe. Indeed, Attanasi's essay extends and sharpens the considerations of sexuality and power begun by Lebacqz and West. Attanasi's focus on the experience of women demonstrates how an unqualified pastoral commendation of forgiveness and/or of remaining steadfast leaves many spouses and their children trapped in abusive marriages. Further, while the promise of fidelity always carries with it a certain degree of risk, she demonstrates how in today's world marriage can become a very dangerous venture, especially if a sexual double standard leaves only one spouse practicing sexual exclusivity. When not mutually embodied, steadfastness can leave the one partner practicing fidelity at extreme risk of HIV infection and other sexually transmitted diseases.

The pastoral guidance and public health policy Attanasi commends recognize that both abstinence and fidelity understood as sexual exclusivity must be practiced by both partners if those strategies are to be effective at all. Her essay illustrates the ways that naive pastoral recommendations—which "idealize" the unilateral practice of abstinence and sexual exclusivity, recommend the avoidance of condoms because they are contraceptive, and/or emphasize steadfastness regardless of the situation—in fact threaten the very survival of many spouses. She further uncovers the ways in which a selective reading of (often mistranslated) biblical passages about divorce frequently results in its absolute prohibition, again, requiring faithful spouses to remain in dangerous, abusive relationships. She suggests instead that genuinely faithful interpretations of scripture recognize that under some circumstances divorce may well be biblically permissible. Her principal concern, which we might well imagine Jesus shares, is with the health and well-being of those most at risk.

The sixth essay in this volume examines in culturally specific detail one way that gender is socially constructed in modern life. In his essay,

"Brothers in Arms and Brothers in Christ? The Military and the Catholic Church as Sources for Modern Korean Masculinity," Hoon Choi considers not just the deep historical roots in Confucianism of patriarchal views about masculinity but also the modern forces of militarism that perpetuate its expression of authoritarianism and gender inequity in contemporary South Korea. He details the dangerous consequences of this construction of masculinity for men and women alike, for family life, and for Korean society at large. Choi identifies the ways in which the compulsory military service of young Korean men and the practices commonplace within South Korean Catholic parishes perpetuate this unhealthy, militarized script for manhood.

For example, Choi notes how the draft instills in young Korean men patriarchal patterns of uncritical, absolute obedience in nonwar situations. During their time in military service, they learn that "real" men endure abuse and accept authoritarian expressions of power. Moreover, as they become accustomed to these patterns, they learn to desire this kind of power and to express it by adopting attitudes demonstrating hegemonic authority in social situations, business affairs, and personal relationships. To support and reinforce their personal sense of command, these young recruits learn to belittle women. They are frequently encouraged to engage in practices that degrade women when off base.

In their turn, Choi continues, local Roman Catholic churches sanctify such patriarchal patterns in two ways. Priests (themselves also subject to military conscription and so formed in this patriarchal pattern) adopt and model authoritarian leadership styles. They require obsequious and material (frequently monetary) expressions of loyalty and respect from their ecclesial "troops." Also, so that their lower "rank" in this system is clear and reinforced, in most Korean parishes women are still required to wear head coverings (a requirement that was lifted for the most part in Western Catholicism following the Second Vatican Council). Only the silent passive submission of women is permitted in church. Though the polity of Catholicism is far from democratic, much in the Second Vatican Council challenged this sort of hegemonic, patriarchal style of leadership.

In chapter 7, Karen Peterson-Iyer wrestles with the question of what a Christian ethic for sexting might look like in "Mobile Porn? Teenage Sexting and Justice for Women." Though she argues that for the most part sexting has been misclassified as child pornography, Peterson-Iyer raises hard questions about whether such behavior is merely a new form of playful flirtation, especially when practiced by adolescents outside committed relationships. In this essay, Peterson-Iyer suggests sexting is something more dangerous. Her reasons are several. In the first place, she questions how free a choice to sext really is in our culture. Despite the claims to the contrary of other teens who sext, a full 20 percent of those teens who sext report that they feel pressured into doing so, either directly by an existing or hoped-for sexual partner or more subtly in order to feel popular or attractive. It is not clear that sexting is freely chosen, an expectation relevant to the assignment of moral responsibility, at least not for all.

Among other questions, Peterson-Iyer argues it is also important to ask: with whom does the sexter seek to communicate so erotically? Certainly respect for the autonomy of others requires that we presume the original recipient of a sext is its only intended recipient. Thus, if a sext has been forwarded, secondhand recipients should at least recognize that the sexter's freedom of choice has been violated and immediately conclude that continuing to pass this sext forward is unethical. Moreover, when the intended original recipient forwards a sext to others, such behavior should be minimally recognized as a form of bullying, the negative consequences of which, especially for young women given the double standards in many cultures, are grim. If it "goes viral," even a single sext can elicit scorn from peers and punishments from parents and school officials, as well as prompt the threat of legal prosecution if one or more involved in sexting is underage. The "permanent" nature of digital footprints means their potential to harm career choices can extend across decades, if not a lifetime.

Moral questions about sexting must explore issues beyond those associated with the immoral practice of forwarding such sexual images to unintended recipients. Sexting, Peterson-Iyer argues, may be morally problematic for other reasons as well, not the least of which is that it takes place in a popular culture that positively endorses sexual exhibitionism. She suggests that, ironically, this sexualized culture disparages sexuality's capacity to increase emotional as well as physical intimacy. A sexualized culture demeans naked bodies just as much as the so-called purity culture that treats all expressions of desire and pleasure outside heterosexual marriage as pathological (again, especially regarding young women). In addition to commending respect for the autonomy of others, a Christian sexting ethic must avoid both demonizing and trivializing sexual pleasure. Instead a sexual ethic must find ways to promote healthy body images. It must avoid depersonalizing sexuality and disintegrating our bodies from ourselves. A Christian sexual ethic asks tough questions about whether sexting fosters in beautiful and powerful ways the mutuality, equal regard, emotional intimacy and trust that sexual relationships are intended to embody.

In chapter 8, "Christian Ethics and Human Trafficking Activism: Progressive Christianity and Social Critique," Letitia M. Campbell and Yvonne C. Zimmerman delineate perhaps the most controversial argument in this volume. They suggest that, instead of pressing for its legal abolition, Christian feminists should more carefully consider the pragmatic case for decriminalizing sex work consenting adults engage in while exploring alternative macro-level educational and economic strategies for curtailing its practice. Mounting evidence about the positive public health benefits associated with the full decriminalization of consensual sex work among adults has led organizations like Human Rights Watch, and more recently Amnesty International, to propose the decriminalization of commercial sexual activity.

To set the debate between prosecution and decriminalization in context, it might be worth comparing the impact of two different strategies. In New South Wales, Australia, and New Zealand the decision was recently made to decriminalize prostitution among adults. Studies of the impact of this change in public policy suggest that while "supply and demand" numbers stayed about the same, condom use among those involved rose a stunning 99 percent. Recently the Swedish policy approach has been to make it a crime to buy (but not to sell) sex; even so, buy-ing sex is usually punishable only by a fine, if only adults are involved. Research on this strategy suggests, however, that though public streets were cleared of those soliciting sex work, the "trade" simply moved in-doors via e-marketing. To protect and maintain their clientele, many prostitutes feel "forced" into more isolated areas or into their private homes, which puts them at greater risk.[14] Neither strategy adequately addresses the familial and socioeconomic factors that make prostitution seem, if not attractive, at least better than the available alternatives.

Campbell and Zimmerman suggest that when the experiences of young folk, queer people, and immigrants are carefully attended to, it becomes clear that what some of them call "sex work" may not always be dramatically coercive or uniquely exploitive. Though few among them may be truly empowered, it is also the case that not all "sex workers" find prostitution to be incomparably brutalizing. For many, commercial sex work is far from the worst harm they have suffered. In fact, they fre-quently identify "abuse in families, harassment by police, and failures of the foster care system" as far more oppressive than this, the world's old-est "profession." Many choose sex work because they prefer it to the al-ternatives they believe to be realistically available to them.

Listening to these voices indicates that in certain circumstances pros-titution may be a more complex and diverse reality than labels like "hu-man trafficking" or "sex slavery" suggest (although genuine expressions of both do exist). While not all would say they were forced into pros-titution, it is also true that many would not say they "freely chose" it. Many prostitutes describe themselves as "bruised" in spirit and broken-hearted by the work. Many report that they find it necessary to disassoci-ate themselves from their work. Many speak of it as an escape route; yet most do not believe they have "jumped from the frying pan into the fire." Given these ambiguities, Campbell and Zimmerman conclude from their study that the current focus of some on "trafficking" is too narrow. It takes the spotlight off the oppressive macro-level structures—famil-ial, economic, and social—that deny many prostitutes realistic alterna-tives to such work.

This position, that other structures are at work influencing these "choices," is highly contested. In fact, the conclusions reached by all our contributing authors are highly debatable. For that reason, we have chosen to close this volume with an essay that addresses the question of how to negotiate communal disagreements over moral issues. Passions run high among us about moral matters because for the most part we intend to lay down our lives (insofar as possible) in service to what we really value. Usually this service does not occur in dramatic life and death choices but more incrementally over the course of our everyday lives and in ordinary choices. We slowly spend our capital (of time, energy, resources, etc.) in accord with our deepest convictions about what makes for the good life. In her essay, "The Ethics of 'Recognition': Rowan Williams's Approach to Moral Discernment in the Christian Community," Sarah Moses offers guidance on how to think about and respond to differences in moral judgment.

For Christians the call into life in communion and fellowship—church membership and participation—has always been understood as part of God's invitation into discipleship. Further, if public discourse is to remain civil in our society, then learning to avoid the tactics associated with "culture wars" will prove important. So, we need to figure out a way to stay in conversation with one another, even when we disagree. Moses argues that Christians can find such a path through the critical adoption of suggestions made by Rowan Williams, a former Archbishop of Canterbury and leader of the worldwide Anglican communion.

Moses labels Williams's approach an "ethics of recognition." Only by recognizing that our membership in community is a matter of grace can we view disagreements as potential occasions of growth and edification. The fact is that discord is the norm for most communities, and consensus is more often than not only a momentary experience within them. Only by recognizing that community is the prerequisite for, not a result of, agreement can we see that neither ecclesial nor civil unity is predicated on unanimity. Only by recognizing in each other common habits of the heart and disciplines—for example, a steadfast commitment to corporate worship might be such for Christians—are we able to give up the absolute certainty with which we hold our own positions and wait for others to see the truth (even if only partial) of our perspective in light of these commonly held criteria. Citing the critical reflections of Kathryn Tanner, Moses concludes her review and commendation of Williams's "ethics of recognition" by noting some of its as-yet-to-be-resolved practical limitations.

Additional Pedagogical Resources

Each of these nine essays is followed by a set of reflection questions and suggested readings. These questions can be used in a variety of ways. They could serve as reflection paper assignments or small group discussion starters. The suggested readings do not aim to be comprehensive but intend merely to provide students and interested readers with some additional resources should they wish to dig more deeply into a particular topic.

Notes

1. See the Society of Christian Ethics, "History of the SCE," reprinted from the *CSSR Bulletin* 32, no. 2 (2003); https://scethics.org/history-sce.

2. See, for example, the panel discussion of Eliot N. Dorff, David Novak, and Aaron L. Mackler, "Homosexuality: A Case Study," *JSCE* 28, no. 1 (Spring/Summer 2008): 225–235; or Jan M. Jans, "Just a Piece of Cloth? The European Debate on 'the Islamic Headscarf' as a Case Study and Paradigm for Emergent Intercultural Ethics," *JSCE* 28, no. 1 (Spring/Summer 2008): 25–43.

3. Many fine essays in the *Annual* and the *JSCE* from the likes of Gloria H. Albrecht, Barbara Hilkert Andolsen, Katherine D. Blanchard, Lisa Sowle Cahill, Katie Geneva Cannon, James M. Childs, Miguel A. De La Torre, Erin Dufault-Hunter, Margaret A. Farley, Christine E. Gudorf, Mary E. Hunt, David F. Kelly, William McDonough, Julie Hanlon Rubio, Emilie M. Townes, and Cristina L. H. Traina (to name just a few) could not be included owing to size limitations.

4. The best conservative argument against such changes can be found in Dennis P. Hollinger's "The Purposes of Sex," in *The Meaning of Sex* (Grand Rapids, MI: Baker Academic, 2009), 93–115.

5. See Human Rights Campaign, "Violence against the Transgender Community in 2016," http://www.hrc.org/resources/violence-against-the-transgender -community-in-2016" (no date, accessed March 26, 2017).

6. Karen Lebacqz, in a seminal essay on "Difference or Defect? Intersexuality and the Politics of Difference," scrutinized the reasoning behind medical and/or surgical forms of intervention to assign a child born with intersex genitalia to a particular sex within the male-female binary. Until recently this was considered standard medical practice. Her analysis exposed this practice as unwarranted, as expressing concern not for the genuine health of the patient but for the commonly unexamined cultural preference for maintaining a simple binary. She argued in favor of viewing intersex as a "difference," concluding that no medical, developmental, or psychological evidence supported the presumption that it was "defective."

Lebacqz's essay illustrates with startling clarity the ethical impact of the growing awareness within the scientific community of the inadequacy of binary frameworks for the many biological variations now recognized within the human sex spectrum. Recognition of these variations raises critical ethical questions about the complex palette that is human sexuality. This leads to several important interrogations. For example, on what basis might what is descriptively unusual be judged normatively defective instead of merely diverse? How should ethical deliberations about sexuality be framed? Should discriminatory public policies and ecclesial practices based on a binary framework be considered prima facie illegitimate? Or, conversely, should the identities and preferences of sexual minorities who fall outside that frame be considered prima facie defective, if not sinful? Which perspective bears the burden of proof? Many, both in the academy and the public at large, have still not carefully examined their convictions about heteronormativity. Karen Lebacqz, "Difference or Defect? Intersexuality and the Politics of Difference," *Annual of the Society of Christian Ethics* 17, no. 1 (1997): 213–229.

7. Michele C. Black, Kathleen C. Basile, Matthew J. Breiding, Sharon G. Smith, Mikel L. Walters, Melissa T. Merrick, Jieru Chen, and Mark R. Stevens, *The National Intimate Partner and Sexual Violence Survey: 2010 Summary Report* (Atlanta, GA: National Center for Injury Prevention and Control, Centers for Disease Control, 2011), 2, http://www.cdc.gov/violenceprevention/pdf/nisvs_executive_summary-a.pdf.

8. See David C. Cramer, Jenny Howell, Paul Martens, and Cat Ngac Jonathan Tran, "Theology and Misconduct: The Case of John Howard Yoder," *Christian Century* 131, no. 17 (August 20, 2014): 20–23.

9. EEOC, "Facts about Sexual Harassment," https://www.eeoc.gov/eeoc/publications/fs-sex.cfm (no date, accessed November 24, 2016).

10. A significant catalyst of this concern was exposure in 1998 of the 1995 sexual affairs committed by then US president Bill Clinton with then twenty-two-year-old White House intern Monica Lewinsky.

11. The other essays on this subject in that volume were Richard H. Hiers, "Sexual Harassment: Title VII and IX Protections and Prohibitions—The Current State of the Law," *Annual of the SCE* 19, no. 1 (1999): 391–406; Judith W. Kay, "Why Procedures Are Important in Addressing Sexual Harassment," *Annual of*

the SCE 19, no. 1 (1999): 383–389; and Anne E. Patrick, "Sexual Harassment: A Christian Ethical Response," *Annual of the SCE* 19, no. 1 (1999): 371–376.

12. In a later issue of the *JSCE* Angela D. Sims extends these insights into the ways that racial and sexual vulnerabilities intersect in "Nooses in Public Spaces." Here Sims examines the hypersexualized phenomenon of lynching and its effective control over black men, as well as black women; she locates the still lethal combination of racism and sexism in the symbolic lynching that menaces racialized minorities in the States yet today. Angela D. Sims, "Nooses in Public Spaces: A Womanist Critique of Lynching—A Twenty-First Century Ethical Dilemma," *JSCE* 29, no. 2 (2009): 81–95. See also Angela D. Sims, *Lynched: The Power of Memory in a Culture of Terror* (Waco, TX: Baylor University Press, 2016).

13. Since 2009 the SCE has required that members who propose research that involves human subjects confirm that their research protocols have been approved by a recognized institutional review board so as to ensure the protection of their research subjects from harms that may arise over the course of their participation in the study. That confirmation assures the concern that the examination and investigations of moral issues respects the dignity of persons whose practices and positions members study. See the Society of Christian Ethics, "Publication Criteria and IRB Regulations," *Journal of the Society of Christian Ethics* (2009), https://scethics.org/journal-sce/publication-criteria-and-irb-regulations.

14. Emily Bazelton, "Should Prostitution Be a Crime?," *New York Times Magazine*, May 8, 2016, 34–43, 55–57. We note also that prostitution is legal in Canada and the State of Nevada, each with restrictions designed to protect the sex worker.

2

The Natural Law and Innovative Forms of Marriage

A Reconsideration

Jean Porter

This essay explores the implications of a natural law account of marriage for the gay marriage controversy, starting from the concept of the natural law developed by scholastic jurists and theologians in the twelfth and thirteenth centuries. Certainly, the scholastics themselves unanimously condemned homosexual acts, and probably never entertained the possibility of same-sex marital unions. Yet this fact taken by itself does not mean that their overall concept of the natural law and the approach to marriage developed out of that concept must necessarily rule out gay marriages. We are the heirs of several centuries of further experiences with and reflection on marriage, and through this process our own conceptions of both marriage and sex itself have changed—leading to perspectives very different from the scholastics yet recognizably products of a trajectory of thought that they initiated. In this essay I argue that the scholastic concept of the natural law, when developed and applied within a contemporary context, does not rule out gay marriage but on the contrary gives us reasons to support the legal recognition of such unions.

During the summer of 2005, an attempt was made to pass an advisory referendum to the Illinois Constitution stating that marriage between a man and a woman is the only kind of union that will be valid or recognized in that state. In their statement "Protecting Marriage," the Catholic bishops of Illinois affirmed this initiative, remarking that "while it seems redundant to define in civil law what already exists in nature, it is necessary to do so in the face of efforts to reduce marriage to a question of individual civil rights."[1] They go on to say that "seeking the truth about this

This essay was published originally in the *Journal of the Society of Christian Ethics* 30.2 (2010): 79–97.

issue requires thinking about the meaning of marriage, its purposes, and its value to individuals, families, and society," and conclude that such reflection, drawing on both reason and faith, will bring us to "the appropriate starting point: the fact that the institution of marriage is based on human nature. In other words, neither the state nor the Church invented marriage, and neither has the right to change its nature."

This is a familiar line of argument. Yet it is by no means obvious that a natural law account of sexual experience would necessarily rule out same-sex unions. Some authors have argued, to the contrary, that such unions are themselves natural in the normative sense of expressing positive human potentialities. To mention one widely influential example, Andrew Sullivan argues that homosexuality is a legitimate expression of interpersonal love, and what is more, it can serve as a kind of affirmation for the centrality of heterosexual love. Seen from this perspective, gay men and lesbians fulfill their own nature

> in a way that doesn't deny heterosexual primacy, but rather honors it
> by its rare and distinct otherness . . . The homosexual person might
> be seen as a natural foil to the heterosexual norm, a variation that
> does not eclipse the theme, but resonates with it. Extinguishing—or
> prohibiting—homosexuality is, from this point of view, not a virtu-
> ous necessity, but the real crime against nature, a refusal to accept
> the variety of God's creation, a denial of the way in which the other
> need not threaten, but may give depth and contrast to the self.[2]

It is telling that proposals for gay marriage have been both condemned and defended through appeals to naturalness or a natural law. But what exactly does this fact tell us? For many of our contemporaries, it confirms what they suspected all along: namely, that the idea of a natural law is at best a reflection of an outmoded worldview, if not a bit of outright propaganda. Yet this response would be too quick. To be sure, the diversity of views defended on natural law terms reflects the complexity of this idea and the tradition of reflection it has engendered. This complexity should in turn at least raise doubts that we know in advance what an appropriate "natural law perspective" on contemporary debates over gay marriage would be. At the same time, the complexity of a moral and legal tradition need not be a sign of its vacuity or incoherence. Under most circumstances, we are more inclined to take complexity as a strength, a reflection of intellectual seriousness and a sensitivity to practical complexities. So it is in this case, as I will suggest in what follows.

More specifically, I will reflect on the implications of a natural law account of marriage for the gay marriage controversy, taking as my starting point the concept of the natural law developed by scholastic jurists and theologians in the twelfth and thirteenth centuries.[3] This line of argument might seem to be of interest only to those who are already persuaded of the validity, or at least the attractiveness, of traditional Catholic natural law arguments. Although the scope of this essay does not allow for a full defense of the scholastic concept of the natural law, it will at least indicate its plausibility and illustrate why our contemporaries might find it attractive.

The scholastics' analysis of the purposes of sex and marriage is subtle and complex. In particular, they distinguish between the purposes of the sexual function itself and the purposes of marriage and do not simply assume that the latter follows straightforwardly from the former. This distinction introduces complexity and ambiguity into their accounts of both sex and marriage. By the same token, this distinction also opens up the possibility that our understanding of sex itself, as well as marriage, can change and develop in accordance with our ongoing experiences with and reflections on the latter. Certainly, the scholastics themselves unanimously condemned homosexual acts and probably never entertained the possibility of same-sex marital unions. Yet this fact taken by itself does not mean that their overall concept of the natural law, and the approach to marriage developed out of that concept, must necessarily rule out gay marriages. We are the heirs of several centuries of further experiences with and reflection on marriage, and through this process our own conceptions of both marriage and sex have changed—leading to perspectives very different from those of the scholastics, yet recognizably products of a trajectory of thought that they initiated. Seen from this perspective, a natural law defense of gay marriage may not be so far-fetched as we might initially assume. In what follows, I argue that the scholastic concept of the natural law, when developed and applied within a contemporary concept, does not rule out gay marriage but on the contrary gives us reasons to support the legal recognition of such unions.

Locating a Trajectory in Early Scholastic Views on Natural Law, Sex, and Marriage

The ancient traditions of reflection on the natural law offer a wide range of perspectives on nature and its normative significance.[4] The early scholastics, with their penchant for systematic analysis, quickly set about bringing order out of this diversity, relying on the newest findings of natural philosophy and systematic theology—both flourishing and widely influential disciplines at this point—as well as earlier perspectives on human nature and the natural order more generally. As they recognized, almost any originating principle of human life can be regarded as "nature," corresponding to the "law" embodied—actually or ideally—in social conventions. These include both reason and the inclinations or orderly processes that we share with nonrational creatures as well as more general metaphysical principles and even (for some) revealed divine law, or widely shared social conventions such as the so-called law of nations. At the same time, the scholastics shared a broad orientation inherited from the philosophy of nature that emerged in the late eleventh and early twelfth centuries, including especially its emphasis on the intelligibility and goodness of the created world as exhibited through its intrinsic causal structure. While this perspective by no means excluded a belief in God as Creator and Provident governor of the world—the scholastics were, after all, Christians, even if they were not all theologians—it did emphasize the intrinsic intelligibility and goodness of the world and its creatures precisely as expressions of teleologically ordered processes.

We see a good illustration of this approach, developed specifically with respect to sex and marriage, in the *Summa de Bono* of the mid-thirteenth-century theologian Philip the Chancellor:

Since the natural law is so called from nature, that is, it is that which natural reason directs and that which is written in the natural reason, since according to this way of speaking, reason is itself nature, so in the same way, it is possible to take nature as nature, or nature as reason. Nature, insofar as it is nature, directs the rational creature, that is, the human person, to have sexual relations with another, that is, for the well-being of the species, that is, for the preservation of the well-being of the species itself; and for this purpose, there is the command, "do not commit adultery," and so on; just as for the preservation of the individual there is the command, "do not kill." Nature as reason directs that one have sexual relations with one and not many; but reason as reason directs that this be one who is united to oneself. For I say "united" as regards nature, insofar as it is reason.[5]

Even though these remarks reflect Philip's distinctive perspectives and concerns, they are nonetheless broadly representative of early scholastic views on sex and marriage and the place of each in human life. Most fundamentally, in spite of lingering suspicions that sexual desire is in some way shameful or even mildly sinful, the scholastics clearly affirm that sex is a natural function to be understood and valued in light of its evident purpose of procreation. This affirmation emerged within the context of deep theological commitments to the goodness of creation, and correlatively to the value and intelligibility of created nature—commitments that were at that time under attack, and thus attracted polemical defense.

By Philip's time (that is, the early thirteenth century), the scholastics' analysis of the purposes of sex was more immediately shaped by a broadly Aristotelian philosophy of nature, according to which living creatures in particular can only be understood through a teleological analysis tracking the ways in which the structures, functions, and organs of a given creature contribute to its overall well-being, or to the existence and well-being of the kind itself.[6] It is important to note that this analysis does not presuppose an externally imposed ordering of functions or purposes, as if a living creature were a watch or a clever bit of software. Nor does it rest on an analysis of organs or functions seen in isolation from the overall life of the organism, or much less on a "statistical" judgment about the frequency of correlation between sexual intercourse and babies. Rather, it rests on a judgment—surely plausible enough, as far as it goes—that whatever else may be said, seen in light of the overall form of life proper to the human animal, the sexual act serves the purpose of propagating the species, just as it does in all other higher animals. Thus, as Philip says, "nature as nature"—in this context, our intelligible functioning as animals of a certain kind—prompts us toward sexual union.

At the same time, we are not simply generic animals; we are rational animals whose most fundamental inclinations are conditioned by, and experienced in terms of, a social life informed by discursive reflection and communication. As Philip goes on to say, "nature as reason"—that is to say, rationality as the defining characteristic of the human animal— prompts the individual to mate with one and only one other individual. It might seem that this is the point at which the inclination to mate gives rise to the institution of marriage, but in fact Philip associates marriage itself with a further aspect of human existence, namely, "reason as reason." In context and taking account of the usages of other scholastics, "reason as reason" seems to indicate those processes of rational social deliberation giving rise to institutional forms of social life.[7]

It is somewhat surprising to read that Philip regards adultery as a violation of human nature at the level of nature as nature. That is to say, he regards it as a distortion of the human inclination toward reproduction, and not only or most fundamentally as a sin at the level of nature as reason (a sin against the monogamous union of man and woman) or reason as reason (a sin against the social and juridical institution of marriage). His analysis points to a critical presupposition about the natural law as he and his interlocutors understood it. Even considered in its preconventional aspects, human reproduction can only be understood within a context set by the characteristic way of life of the human animal.[8] Thus, it is naturally aimed toward bringing forth human children who will mature into rational agents and members of society. Correlatively, the process of reproduction, considered in its properly human form, involves not only biological reproduction but also the care, nurture, and socialization of the child. The specific ways in which this socialization takes place and the ideals informing it will of course be conventional, but the necessity for some kind of socialization stems from aspects of our nature, including in this case our fundamentally social way of life and the relative weakness and lack of development of human children. Hence, because adultery transgresses and undermines the kinship structures necessary for the formation of children into fully functioning adults, it can be said to be contrary to the inclination to reproduce, even considered prior to qualifications introduced by rational reflection and institutional formulation.

The scholastic view that human reproduction is a social process, presupposing a kinship structure for its proper and complete expression, leads directly to a consideration of the purpose of marriage, which on their view provides the stable structures and the social identity necessary for the successful care and education of human children. To this extent, at least, the purpose of marriage stems directly from a natural purpose of the sexual function. This does not mean that marriage stems immediately and unreflectively from the sexual impulse. On the contrary, Philip and his interlocutors assume that marriage is, at least in some respects, a conventional expression of a natural purpose devised through the processes of communal reflection summarized as "reason as reason." Seen from this perspective, marriage is itself a social convention or, at the very least, its concrete shape in a given society is determined to some extent by the contingent conventions within which it appears.[9] These conventions are themselves constrained by and evaluated in the light of the fundamental purpose of marriage.

We thus have the beginnings of an analysis of the institution of marriage in terms of its objective purposes, as these appear when the institution is regarded as an expression of human nature. Thus understood, the institution of marriage is not just a social construct, open to serving whatever purposes and taking whatever forms we might choose to give it. However, this line of analysis does not presuppose that marriage as we experience it represents a direct expression of human nature, nor does it commit us to the view that there is one and only one "natural" form of marriage. In fact, it would be odd if the scholastics did regard marriage in these ways. Not only were they well aware of the existence of diverse forms of marriage in other times and places, they themselves were heirs to the thoroughgoing reforms of marriage in the late eleventh and early twelfth centuries, and were themselves engaged in debating fundamental questions over the necessary conditions for the existence of a marriage.[10] For them, marriage is not a necessary, organic expression of human nature but a complex and in many ways contested set of institutional practices—albeit practices that stem from and give expression to the intelligibilities of our shared nature.

It is important to keep this latter point in mind in order to appreciate the considerations that motivated and informed the scholastics' natural law analysis of marriage. In contrast to many of our own contemporaries, they did not attempt to defend the marital practices of their own societies as immediate, direct, or much less necessary expressions of human nature, nor were they much interested in developing a natural law analysis of the social and sexual practices of other societies. They were, however, very interested indeed in the marital practices of their own societies, which were currently in flux, and the natural law as they construed it offered criteria by which to appraise, defend, or reform these practices.[11] The eleventh-century reforms of marriage and their aftermath challenged the scholastics to develop a doctrine of marriage that would be legally workable as well as theologically satisfactory, and that would therefore incorporate criteria for determining the validity of a marriage. The scholastics responded to this challenge by arguing that the ideal form for a marital union is a permanent union between one man and one woman. These norms have scriptural warrant, of course, but they are also defended on the grounds that this arrangement provides the best possible framework for the care and nurture of children, and also that this arrangement is the most equitable form of relation between husband and wife—both considerations falling within the scope of the natural law.

The scholastics are well aware that indissoluble, monogamous marriage is by no means the universal form of the institution. Even apart from the practices of Muslims or the scholastics' own ancestors, the Old Testament recorded the polygamous marriages of the saints of the Old Covenant, and the Old Law made provision for divorce. These tensions did not lead them to abandon their view that monogamy and indissolubility are tenets of the natural law, but it did prompt them to elaborate the ways in which different forms of marriage are more or less compatible with the natural law. As Aquinas puts it, there are some kinds of marriage—polygamy, for example—that undermine or foreclose the attainment of one of the secondary purposes of marriage, for example, mutuality between the spouses, but that are nonetheless legitimate from a natural law perspective because they do at least allow for the expression of the primary purpose of marriage, namely, the care and proper education of the young.[12]

At this point the contours of the scholastic analysis of marriage in natural law terms begin to come into focus. This analysis presupposes that we are always presented in the first instance with conventions of marriage, and natural law analysis requires us to discern which elements of those conventions can be construed as expressions of human nature. This analysis will be teleological because the causal structures of human life (and of all created existence) are themselves intrinsically teleological. This teleological structure in turn both motivates our analysis of marriage and makes it possible. We (as a community) have a stake in formulating conventions of marriage because we (collectively) have a stake in reproducing ourselves in a certain way, taking into consideration that human reproduction involves a lengthy process of socialization as well as biological procreation. As we become reflectively aware of the place that marriage serves in human social life, we come to see that we have good reason to try to distinguish those kinds of relations that serve this basic purpose from those that do not. Similarly, we are given a criterion by which to begin to distinguish marriages from other kinds of sexual relations. That is, in order to count as marriage, an institutionalized practice must at the least serve in some way to facilitate human reproduction, broadly construed to include processes of educating children and placing them in a kinship structure. Ideally, it will also serve other purposes and reflect a wider set of values and ideals, including many that can also be grounded more or less directly in what is natural, appropriate, and praiseworthy for creatures of our kind.

This line of analysis thus both depends on and serves to clarify a paradigmatic notion of what marriage is.[13] This notion is not a formal definition and does not yield either necessary or sufficient conditions for counting particular unions as marriages. Rather, it is a general notion meant to capture the central features of an institutional practice, not to determine criteria for inclusion in a class. Yet it amounts to something more than a set of family resemblances among putative marriages. What this paradigmatic notion of marriage captures, I suggest, are the natural purposes served by the conventions of marriage as we experience it. Given this kind of notion, we do not need an exhaustive set of necessary and sufficient conditions to make reasoned judgments about which kinds of unions count as marriages and which do not; this notion gives us a framework for evaluating these in the light of the purposes informing our paradigms.

However, if it is to be persuasive, this line of analysis cannot be merely stipulative. To be plausible, it will also need to give weight to actually existing ideals and practices of marriage. It is especially important to take this into account in the present context because marriage as the scholastics experience it is a complex institution that cannot be understood solely in terms of its function in human reproduction, even broadly construed to include socialization. This fact has important implications for the scholastics' understandings of the purposes of sex because, in their view, sexual ethics is fundamentally an ethic of marriage. For this very reason, the logic of their teleological analysis does not go in one direction only. Their assessment of the purpose of sex is foundational for their account of marriage, as we would indeed expect. That assessment was developed within a context of ongoing experiences with actually existing practices of marriage, together with long-standing theological perspectives on these experiences. These experiences and perspectives on marriage led them back to their starting points in such a way that they began to reevaluate the purposes of sex itself.[14]

The scholastic theology of marriage took its starting points from a doctrine, inherited from Augustine and affirmed by Peter Lombard, according to which the institution of marriage exemplifies and preserves three central values, namely, the faithfulness of the spouses, fruitfulness as expressed through progeny, and the sacramental bond between the spouses.[15] While the third of these is of course unique to Christian marriages, the first two are characteristic of marriage as such and can be attained in any human society. Augustinian theology thus offers rich possibilities for developing an account according to which marriage is (at least potentially) both a natural and a sacramental bond, serving a range of purposes within both civil society and the church, and the scholastics exploited these possibilities in their complex theological and juridical accounts of marriage. Peter Lombard mentions two further *causae honestae* —honorable purposes—for marriage, that is, to reconcile enemies and to restore the peace, in addition to some that are less honorable but do not invalidate the marriage bond, including sexual desire and the pursuit of wealth.[16] But the very richness and complexity of the emerging doctrine of marriage inevitably generated tensions, not least with respect to its implications for the scholastics' developing analysis of sex itself.

As is well known, the scholastics were profoundly ambivalent toward sex and marriage, so much so that some early scholastics regarded sexual desire and union as venially sinful even within the context of marriage. Yet ambivalence should not be confused with an unconditionally negative judgment. On any coherent natural law analysis, sexual function cannot really be construed as anything other than a good, indeed necessary, component of the way of life natural to animals of our kind. By the same token, the goodness of sexual desire came to be defended on the grounds that a natural desire cannot be fundamentally bad or shameful, however distorted it may be by the pervasive realities of sin.[17] Initially the scholastics' positive appraisals of sex and sexual desire were tied to a narrow and restrictive account of the purpose served by the sexual function, namely reproduction. At the same time, they also held that sexual expression finds its proper context within a marriage relationship, which itself serves purposes going beyond reproduction. In this context, the affirmation that the sexual function is fundamentally natural and good opened a space for a more expansive appraisal of sex and sexual desire, corresponding to the diverse values that came to be associated with the institutions and practices of marriage. The purposes of marriage, as the scholastics understood them, led them gradually to extend and develop their sense of the values exemplified by the "marital act," even though they did not take the further step of incorporating these more positive judgments explicitly into a natural law analysis of sex. Nonetheless, this appears to be the trajectory of their thought.

It would have been possible to insist that, even within marriage, sexual acts are morally legitimate only when the spouses intend procreation. But the scholastics were not fools—they did not expect married couples to be quite so restrained in their calculations, and at any rate, Paul's remark that it is better to marry than to burn implied that at the very least, it is legitimate to have sex in order to satisfy one's desires within the framework of marriage (I Cor. 7:9). From Paul's remarks, it was only a short step to the claim that marriage serves as a *remedium*, a provision for the human need for sexual satisfaction in a decent and controlled way, and to the corresponding obligation, held equally by each spouse over against the other, to provide sex on demand. This, the "marriage debt," was held to bind on pain of mortal sin and could be claimed in a court of law if necessary.[18] These considerations do not in themselves amount to a reconsideration of the proper purposes of the sex act, but they do open up the possibility that individuals might legitimately act to satisfy sexual desire without any positive intention to pursue the natural purpose of the sex act so long as they do nothing to frustrate that purpose. We may feel that the actual scholastic view on this matter is still stringent enough, but the main point now is that their doctrine of the purposes of marriage led them inevitably to develop a more expansive view of the purposes that might legitimately justify particular acts of sexual union between marriage partners.

So far the scholastics' appraisals of marriage would seem to reflect Augustine's analysis of the values secured by marriage in most human societies. They also take his further affirmation of the sacramental value of marriage very much to heart, and they are capable of expressing warm enthusiasm for marriage as a sacramental bond and a way of life that can foster great holiness on the part of the spouses.[19] These affirmations create a context within which the scholastics begin, however tentatively, to reassess the purpose of the sex act. The most striking such reassessment occurs near the beginning of the period we are considering in the work of the monastic theologian Hugh of St. Victor, who asserts that the bodily union between the spouses is a sacrament of the relation between Christ and the church, just as the agreement between the spouses—that is, their mutual consent to marry—is a sacrament of the love between God and the soul.[20] He goes on to say that just as husband and wife are joined in one society and one love through marriage (which is established through the mutual consent of the parties), they are joined in one flesh through the conjugal act. The latter is not added to marriage in vain, he adds, because it offers both an occasion for obedience and virtue, and tangible fruit in the form of offspring).[21] These remarks are not quite equivalent to a claim that the sexual act serves as an expression of love. Nonetheless, they do imply that the mutual love and society established by marriage sets the proper context within which the purposes of sex are to be understood, and they imply that sexual union between the spouses is itself a direct expression of one component of the sacramental significance of marriage. Seen within this context, the sex act potentially serves at least two purposes, namely to provide an occasion for obedience and virtue and to provide for the continuance of the species. Hugh's analysis was passed on to the scholastics by Peter Lombard, even though its impact was perhaps muted by Peter's more pessimistic view that, even at its best, sexual desire is somewhat sinful.[22] Nonetheless, we do find later scholastics repeating Hugh's claim that the sex act between spouses can be an act of virtue.[23] At the very least, a way has been cleared for a fuller affirmation that the sex act can serve as an expression of love.

I will return to this point, but first let me summarize what this brief look at the scholastic natural law doctrine of marriage has taught us so far. First, the scholastics do analyze marriage in teleological, natural law terms. Second, their analysis depends on the claim that the primary purpose of marriage, in terms of which existing marital practices are to be understood and regulated, is the reproduction of children in a way consonant with our nature as a rational, social species. Third, they do not claim that this exhausts the legitimate purposes that marriage can serve. These other purposes become apparent both through communal experience with the exigencies of married life as it takes shape within the conditions of a given society, and through theoretical reflection in the light of broader convictions and ideals, especially, in the scholastics' case, the emerging framework of sacramental theology. Finally, the recognition that marriage can serve more than one purpose was then applied to the evaluation of the purposes of the sex act itself, which can be construed as serving one or more of the extended purposes of marriage, in addition to—perhaps even apart from—its fundamental natural purpose of reproduction.

A Contemporary Natural Law Account of Sex and Marriage

I suggested earlier that a natural law analysis of marriage developed from the scholastic conception of the natural law might serve to illuminate current controversies over same-sex marriage. Like the scholastics, we are living through a period of rapid social change and corresponding institutional breakdown and reformation, including extensive and far-reaching changes in the practice of marriage. Like them, again, we are confronted with the twofold need to understand these changes and to direct and regulate them through social and legal mechanisms. How might the scholastics' complex account of the purposes of sex and marriage serve to illuminate our own efforts to address these issues? Let me try to answer this question by setting out, in what will admittedly be a brief and preliminary way, what a natural law analysis of marriage, developed in continuity with the trajectory set by the scholastics, might look like today.

This analysis begins at the same point as the scholastics did—namely, that whatever else we may say, we should recognize that both the sexual function and the conventions of marriage serve the purpose of procreation, broadly construed to include the education and socialization of children as well as their physical reproduction. Admittedly, this kind of appeal raises a host of philosophical issues that would need to be addressed in more detail than I can attempt here. Nonetheless, unless we are to completely discount the fact that we are mammals and complex social primates, it is difficult to see how a plausible analysis of sexuality and marriage could fail to take account of the role that these play in the human reproductive process. As theologian Lisa Sowle Cahill remarks, the claim "that sex in humans has no intrinsic connection to reproductive physiology is more rhetorical than factual. Such a claim could only be maintained on the basis of an abrupt break between humanity and other mammalian species."[24]

What is more, I would argue that a theological commitment to the goodness of creation implies that we as Christians have a particular stake in affirming the value of procreation and giving this value a central place in the interpretations and practices surrounding sex and marriage. Admittedly, this is a controversial claim, and it would go beyond the scope of this essay to defend it in detail. Nonetheless, it does seem that the fundamental values associated with children, family life, and the succession of generations would be widely, if not universally, shared across a wide spectrum of theological positions. At any rate, a theological commitment to the fundamental value of procreation was one of the key factors that set the scholastic trajectory of reflection on these questions in motion, and it continues to play a central role in theological reflections on human sexuality across a wide spectrum of approaches today.[25]

Yet we can acknowledge the vitally important procreative purposes served by the sexual function and marriage without thereby committing ourselves to the view that these are the only or necessarily even the most admirable or highest purposes associated with the institution of marriage. By affirming the vital link between marriage and a procreative purpose, we acknowledge that this is the one purpose that must be successfully pursued if a society is to have any future at all. Correlatively, the procreative purpose offers a touchstone for identifying diverse forms of institutional practices as forms of marriage, as they appear in diverse societies or in the contested practices of a complex, pluralistic society such as our own. That is why procreation, broadly construed, informs our paradigms of what marriage is—that is to say, it provides a touchstone for identifying a range of examples of marital practice in terms of an initial idea of the purposes served by these institutional forms. As such, it generates starting points for further reflection and analysis together with touchstones for determining the adequacy of our accounts of what marriage is and should be. On this basis we can (usually) say with some confidence that an analysis that would not count this or that seemingly straightforward instance as a true marriage should be, at least, seriously reexamined. (To take an example from a related set of controversies, traditional Roman Catholic theologies of marriage would seem to imply that the enduring, fruitful, and mutually supportive union of a man and woman, one of whom has a surviving spouse from a first marriage, should not count as a real marriage at all. Dissatisfaction with this conclusion has done a great deal to undermine the credibility of such views.) By themselves, our initial paradigms of marriage will generally not rule out seemingly anomalous institutions and practices as forms of marriage. Paradigms of marriage are not in themselves the stuff of formal definitions and necessary and sufficient conditions—that is precisely why they offer a fruitful starting point for genuine, open-ended inquiry.

More specifically, this line of analysis leaves open the possibility that the institution of marriage can also serve other purposes, legitimate and worthy of promotion so long as they do not undermine the orientation of the institution toward procreation, comprehensively considered to include the extended processes of education and socialization. Indeed, it would be surprising if such a centrally important institution, shaped by a complex history and responsive to diverse social exigencies, did not serve a wide range of purposes both for individual participants and for society as a whole. To a very considerable extent, these purposes will be recognizably analogous to those informing medieval marriage—to provide for the decent regulation and expression of sexual desire and to sustain a network of social relations. As one expression of the latter purpose, marriage provides a framework for establishing claims for mutual personal and financial support and for securing society's recognition of these claims by enforcing demands for care and sustenance, recognizing that each spouse has a primary right to make health care decisions for the other and the like. Finally, marriage serves what many today would regard as a centrally important function of providing a framework for the public expression and support of interpersonal love. These purposes are secondary, seen from the vantage point of a natural law analysis that takes its starting points from the paradigmatic notion of marriage as an institution directed toward sustaining the physical and social life of humankind. But that need not imply that they are secondary in the sense of being lesser in value or somehow less admirable or worthy—indeed, for some couples and in some social contexts, these secondary purposes may well be more centrally important, desirable, and admirable than the primary purpose of procreation. What is more, this diverse range of purposes will in practice transform, and be transformed by, changing perspectives on what it means to bring forth children, to sustain a family system, and to be fruitful in the complex processes of caring for young life and passing on the inheritance of the past to future generations.

These observations suggest the possibility of a natural law account of marriage that does not tie the teleological analysis of marriage narrowly to the purposes of the sex act but, on the contrary, enables us to expand and develop our understanding of the latter in light of our experiences with marriage. At the same time, if this is to be plausible as a natural law analysis, we need an account of the ways in which the diverse purposes of sex and marriage fit within a general teleological account of the life and functioning of the human organism. The critical point here is that sex and marriage need to be seen within the context of an overall pattern of life, one that we share with the other primates to some extent, even though it both informs and is transformed by our capacities for rationality. Certainly, on any plausible account of the place of sexuality in a mammalian species such as our own, sex will serve a reproductive purpose, but the fact that we are social primates as well as mammals points to a more complex account of the overall purposes of sex. That is to say, we are not only animals that reproduce sexually but social animals for whom sexual exchange and interaction serve to express and cement social and personal bonds—indeed, to forge personal bonds and, hence, to some extent and with many qualifications, to shape and to form personal identity. At the social level, these purposes are expressed in structures of sexual and familiar relations, including the institutions of marriage, kinship, and family structure (which can, of course, take very diverse forms), even as they also inform the more comprehensive structures of social interactions. The key point is that institutions and practices of marriage that place a high premium on marriage as an interpersonal bond will give prominence to the ways in which sex and the complex dynamics of sexual attraction, pursuit, and fulfillment take on personal meanings to express interpersonal relations of attachment, commitment, and love.

How might we bring this line of analysis to bear on the proposed recognition of same-sex marriages? First, it seems clear that if someone were to suggest that same-sex unions should constitute the only or the paradigmatic form of marital union, this would be ruled out by a natural law analysis of marriage according to which both sex and marriage are paradigmatically oriented toward reproduction. But no one is proposing that; what is envisioned, rather, is the extension of the institutional claims and restrictions of marriage to a class of unions that cannot fulfill the reproductive purpose of marriage but that may well embody other aims served by that institution. This, it seems to me, is a very persuasive claim. We already extend the institution of marriage to include heterosexual couples who are incapable of reproduction. It might be said that even in such cases, the paradigmatic link between marriage and procreation is preserved by the symbolic weight of the male-female bond, and I would agree that this symbolism is real and important. Nonetheless, we do extend marriage to heterosexual couples whose incapacity is manifest and public, as is the case when both partners are elderly. These extensions are justified, it will be said, because for us marriage represents more than just a framework for sustaining reproduction and kinship bonds; it also provides a framework for expressing and supporting the mutual love of two people, and it would be cruel and perhaps even unjust to deny that support to those who are incapable of reproduction. For the same reason, refusing to extend this framework to same-sex couples appears to be arbitrary and therefore unjust, given the purposes of marriage as we understand and practice it today.[26] We as individuals and as a society have a particular stake in promoting the reproductive functions of marriage, whatever else we do, but that does not rule out the possibility of recognizing and promoting other purposes, as our traditions and current conditions may suggest. To the extent that we do so, we also have grounds for extending the institution of marriage to include those couples who, for whatever reason, cannot pursue the paradigmatic purpose of procreation (at least not directly) but who legitimately hope to fulfill some range of its other purposes, including perhaps some of greater value to the couple themselves and even in some ways to the community at large.

The key word here is "legitimately." It might be objected that this line of argument is indeed compelling with respect to the elderly and other heterosexual couples who are incapable of having children. But there is something intrinsically immoral about a homosexual union, and that is why we should not recognize these unions as marriages—or so the argument would go. In response, let me say first that it does not strike me as obvious that we should necessarily refuse to recognize immoral unions as marriages just because they are immoral. But it is not clear to me why, on natural law grounds, we should characterize same-sex unions as immoral per se. This is, of course, a complex and contentious issue, and I will not attempt to address it in any detail here. Nonetheless, I do want to indicate in a summary way three considerations in support of the view that same-sex relations are not intrinsically unnatural in a pejorative sense.

The first of these considerations has already been the object of widespread discussion. The classical natural law argument against same-sex unions rests on the claim that homosexual acts represent a perversion of the sexual faculty because they are intrinsically sterile—that is to say, they are acts of a kind that cannot result in procreation, in contrast to heterosexual intercourse that happens for some accidental reason to be sterile in some case. By this argument, these acts are wrong for essentially the same reasons as masturbation and the use of contraceptives are wrong. That is, these kinds of acts call for an intentional engagement of the sexual faculties in such a way that the natural capacity for procreation is foreclosed, either in virtue of the kind of act itself or through the deliberate suppression of one's procreative capacities. This line of argument gains much of its plausibility from the assumption—certainly shared by the early scholastics, and only slowly and hesitantly questioned—that the sexual function can serve only two aims, procreation and pleasure, the first of which is good and the second of which is at best suspect if not actually sinful. However, if the sexual function can credibly be seen as serving other natural purposes, then arguably, these can legitimately be pursued independently of one another, even through sexual acts that are structurally or deliberately non-procreative. In other words, if the sex act can serve more than one natural purpose, we cannot just conclude that a kind of act that forecloses one of these is necessarily perverse or unnatural so long as it can serve other legitimate purposes. We are touching here on one of the most contentious issues in recent theological ethics, and I do not intend to try to resolve it here. Let me simply say that I would side with those who argue that sexual acts that are intrinsically or deliberately sterile can nonetheless be legitimate and worthy expressions of other natural purposes, including the expression of interpersonal love.[27] The reproductive purpose of sex sets a paradigm for understanding sexuality and giving it institutional expression, but that does not necessarily mean that this purpose must be expressed, or even retained as a possibility, in each and every sex act.

What about the claim that same-sex relations are intrinsically unnatural because they represent a violation of the natural complementarity of man and woman? The difficulty with this claim is that it moves too quickly from the recognition of the naturalness of the distinction of the sexes, with its innate orientation toward reproduction, to the assertion that the gender roles through which we construe masculinity and femininity are immediate and inevitable expressions of our nature as a two-sexed species. But this does not follow any more than the natural origins of marriage necessarily imply that our practices of marriage represent the only possible framework within which human reproduction can take place. Indeed, to a very considerable extent (although of course not completely) the conventions of marriage will determine the conventions of gender in any given society—that is to say, the ideals and practices shaping masculine or feminine roles will be largely shaped by our expectations about the proper ways in which men and women relate to one another in marriage. To the extent that this is so, ideals of the complementarity of the sexes will depend on a particular view of marriage, one in which clearly marked sex differences are central to the formation and strength of the marriage relation. These ideals cannot provide an independent argument for the claim that marriage must consist in a heterosexual bond. An extension of the marriage relation to same-sex unions would imply greater flexibility in the construal of gender roles, but that would not necessarily be a bad thing.

At most, these arguments will serve to clear away long-standing objections to same-sex relations, but they still leave open the question of whether and in what ways same-sex acts might embody and promote at least some of the natural purposes of sex. (Lest this seem too chilly a formulation, I should add that exactly the same question can—and should—be asked about foreseeably sterile sexual relations between heterosexuals.) In this case, I want to suggest that the obvious, popular answer to this question is right—that is to say, such acts can serve as an expression of deep interpersonal love and deserve respect to the extent that they do. I think there can be no real doubt that same-sex couples can and do experience deep interpersonal love, which they are moved to express sexually. The real question that arises at this point is whether we have good grounds, in natural law terms and theologically considered, for affirming and seeking to protect this love. I argue that we do. This, it seems to me, is one point at which ongoing reflections on the purposes of marriage have significantly altered our understanding of the purposes that sex itself can serve in human life. More specifically, I suggest that the Christian conception of marriage as an expression of a sacramental bond between two persons has transformed our sense of the value of the personal bond itself—and eventually of the value of the sex act as an expression of that bond.[28]

My observations here will again be brief, but let me indicate what I have in mind. First, once we grant that sex serves more than one purpose in human life, including the formation and expression of personal bonds, it is apparent that the expression of interpersonal erotic love can readily be interpreted as a natural purpose in these terms. This does not mean that romantic love is necessarily a cultural universal; like many other natural aspects of human existence, this phenomenon may well require a particular set of social conditions in which it can emerge and flourish. This brings me to a further point. As far as I have been able to determine, the scholastics do not include the expression of personal love as one of the purposes of sex. Yet their overall account of the spiritual significance of sex and marriage suggests that our modern views may not be as foreign to them as we might think. We noted earlier that at the beginning of the scholastic period, Hugh of St. Victor clearly asserts that the sacrament of marriage constitutes one society and one love. Not all the scholastics were equally affirming of mutual love, but they did agree on the centrality of mutual consent—a union of wills between the parties—as an essential component (some would say the very substance) of marriage.[29] This emphasis on the volitional and spiritual dimensions of marriage, taken together with the scholastics' tentative yet clear recognition that sex within marriage can serve purposes other than the strictly procreative, points in the direction of affirming the value of interpersonal love and of the sex act as an expression of that love. At any rate, it seems overwhelmingly probable that modern ideals and practices of romantic love were given legitimacy and decisively shaped by the theological ideals and ecclesial practices of marriage that took shape in the period we are considering.

In my view, a natural law analysis of the purposes of sex and marriage does not foreclose the possibility of recognizing unions that are by their nature non-reproductive but that allow for the expression of the mutual fidelity and interpersonal love of the partners—indeed, we have good theological as well as natural law reasons for doing just that. At the same time, a natural law analysis would rule out an interpretation of marriage according to which the expression of love should be the primary and regulative purpose of marriage as a social institution, to the neglect or detriment of its paradigmatic purpose as a framework for reproduction. There is a good case to be made that a current tendency to regard romantic love as the sole and sufficient basis for a marriage reflects the exigencies of a capitalist society in which family structures stand in the way of the processes of production and the accumulation of wealth.[30] To the extent that this is so, we have good reason to resist these processes, or at least to try to hold them within due bounds. This is the decisive front on which the battle for marriage and family must be waged, not legislative and court battles over same-sex unions, which are at any rate unlikely to have a significant impact on the overall shape of the institution of marriage.

Questions for Reflection

1. Scholastics understood the purpose of marriage to be the proper education of children. Other ideas—such as romantic notions of interpersonal love, as evidenced in medieval courtly poetry—were also "in the air." What do you think is the dominant conception of the purpose(s) of marriage in North America currently? What else is "in the air"?
2. Considering the historically bound nature of all human thinking, the scholastics could not have imagined the sea change that has occurred in the human understanding of what our sexuality might be for beyond strictly procreative purposes. How might Porter's findings support other initiatives promoting and protecting equality along the spectrum of sexual diversity as well as along the spectrums of gender, race, and ability?
3. Taking a cue from the seemingly infinite diversity of God's creative will in the environment and its ecosystems, and in all creatures big and small on land, in sea, and in air, how may scientific evidence demonstrate sexual diversity as another revelation of God's preference for pied beauty writ on human parchment?

Suggestions for Further Reading

Alison, James. "A Letter to a Young Gay Catholic." In *Concilium International Journal of Theology* (2008.1): *Homosexualities*, Marcella Althaus-Reid, Regina Ammicht-Quinn, Erik Borgman, and Norbert Reck, eds., 109–117. London, UK: SCM Press, 2008.

Fehige, Joerg, and Hermann Yiftach. "Sexual Diversity and Divine Creation: A Tightrope Walk between Christianity and Science." *Zygon* 48.1 (2013): 35–59.

Jones, Stanton L. "Same-Sex Science: Assessing the Current Research." *First Things: A Monthly Journal of Religion & Public Life* 220 (February 2012): 27–33.

Larsen, Sean. "Natural Law and the 'Sin against Nature.'" *Journal of Religious Ethics* 43.4 (2015): 629–673.

Salzman, Todd A., and Michael G. Lawler. "Deconstructing and Reconstructing Complementarity as a Foundational Sexual Principle in Catholic Sexual Ethics: The (Im)Morality of Homosexual Acts." In *Moral Theology for the Twenty-First Century: Essays in Celebration of Kevin Kelly*, Julie Clague, Bernard Hoose, Gerald Mannion, eds., 120–132. New York: T&T Clark, 2011.

Stiegmeyer, Scott. "Robert George's Natural Law Argument against Same-Sex Marriage." *Concordia Theological Quarterly* 78.1 (2014): 129–153.

Notes

An earlier version of this chapter was delivered at the Spring 2006 Natural Law Colloquium at Fordham University School of Law, February 2, 2006. I am indebted to those present for many stimulating questions, comments, and suggestions. I especially want to thank Charles Reid and Eduardo Peñalver for their perceptive and very helpful responses. I read a letter version of this essay at the annual meeting of the Society of Christian Ethics in San Jose, California, on January 10, 2010. I am indebted to the comments and suggestions offered by those present and especially to helpful remarks by the anonymous readers for the *Journal of the Society of Christian Ethics*. Finally, thanks to Adam Clark for his assistance in preparing the references.

1. Catholic Bishops of Illinois, "Protecting Marriage" (2006), David John Diersen, "Catholic Citizens," News Clips, GOPUSA Illinois (January 1, 2006), www.campaignsitebuilder.com/templates/displayfilesrrmp!13.asp?siteid=524&pageid=8510&trial=false&blogid=725; see also Illinois Bishops' Statements, May 27, 2009, www.catholicconferenceofillinois.org/bishopsstatements.asp.

2. Andrew Sullivan, *Virtually Normal: An Argument about Homosexuality*, 2nd ed., with new Afterword (London: Picador, 1996), 47; for the overall argument, see 19–55.

3. My purpose here is primarily constructive rather than interpretative; I attempt to draw out the contemporary implications for the early scholastic conception of the natural law and scholastic perspectives on sex and marriage. For

that reason, I presuppose, rather than defending in detail, the main lines of an interpretation set forth in my *Natural and Divine Law: Reclaiming the Tradition for Christian Ethics* (Ottawa: Novalis; and Grand Rapids, MI: Eerdmans, 1999), and *Nature as Reason: A Thomistic Theory of the Natural Law* (Grand Rapids: Eerdmans, 2005). My overall interpretations of the scholastics' perspectives, together with more extensive textual support, are developed there; for a more detailed examination together with exploratory reflections on the contemporary significance of the scholastics' views on sex and marriage, see *Natural and Divine Law*, 187–244.

4. For further detail on the scholastics' views on nature, reason, and natural law, see my *Natural and Divine Law*, chapter 2, 63–120, and *Nature as Reason*, 68–82.

5. Text excerpted in Latin by Odon Lottin, *Le droit natural chez saint Thomas d'Aquin et ses predecesseurs*, 2nd ed. (Bruges, Belgium: Beyart, 1931), 112–13. The translation is my own.

6. See my *Nature as Reason*, 68–82; I defend an Aristotelian teleological biology in 82–125.

7. See, in particular, Albert the Great, *De bona* V 1.2, *Alberti Magni Opera Omnia ad Fidem codicum manuscriptorum* 28 (Munster: Aschendorff, 1951).

8. See my *Natural and Divine Law*, chs. 4 and 5, especially 199–206.

9. For example, Albert explicitly says that even though marriage was instituted by God, it has subsequently been shaped by both divine and human law; see *De sacramentis* 9.6, *Opera omnio* 26. The canonists, as well as the theologians, generally acknowledged that marriage always occurs in some conventional form, implying a range of more or less legitimate forms; see my *Natural and Divine. Law*, 199–206.

10. For an overview of the significance of the reforms of marriage and the far-reaching institutional and social changes associated with them (as both cause and effect), see my *Natural and Divine Law*, 206–12. James Brundage provides a richly detailed and nuanced account of the context and impact of these reforms in *Law, Sex, and Christian Society in Medieval Europe* (Chicago: University of Chicago Press, 1987), 176–228.

11. For further details and references, see my *Natural and Divine Law*, 199–206.

12. Thomas Aquinas, *Scriptum super libros IV sententiarum*, *opera omnia* 30 (Paris: Ludovicum Vives), 33.1.1.

13. I take the idea of a paradigmatic notion from Ronald Dworkin, *Law's Empire* (Cambridge, MA: Belknap/Harvard University Press, 1986), 72–73, although I may be developing it in a way that he did not intend. I am also here indebted to Julius Kovesi's analysis of the formal element of a moral notion in *Moral Notions* (New York: Routledge and Kegan Paul, 1967).

14. I owe this insight to John Gallagher, who makes a similar point with respect to magisterial teachings on marriage and sexual ethics from 1918 to the present. See his "Magisterial Teaching from 1918 to the Present," originally published in 1981, reprinted in *Readings in Moral Theology No. 8: Dialogue about Catholic Sexual Teaching*, ed. Charles E. Curran and Richard A. McCormick (Mahwah, NJ: Paulist Press, 1993), 71–97.

15. Peter Lombard, *Libri IV sententiarum* (Florence: College of St. Bonaventure, 1916), 26.1–2.

16. See ibid., 30.3.

17. Aquinas is particularly clear on this point; see his *In IV sent* 41.2 *ad* 3, and the *Summa theologiae* I–II 153.2 (*Opera omnia jussa edita Leonis XIII PM.*, 4–12, Rome: Ex Typographia Polyglotta S.C. de Propoganda Fide 1886–1906). However, he is by no means the first to defend the goodness of sexual desire in terms of its naturalness; see, for example, William of Auxerre, *Summa aurea* IV 17.1 (Paris: Centre National de la Recherche Scientifique, 1985). See also my *Natural and Divine Law*, 194–96.

18. See Brundage, *Law, Sex, and Christian Society*, 282–84.

19. For an especially striking example of scholastic enthusiasm for the married life, see Bonaventure's *Quaestiones disputatae de perfectione evangelium*, 3.1, *Opera omnia* 5 (Florence: College of St. Bonaventure, 1891); this is all the more remarkable because it occurs in the midst of a treatise devoted to the defense of the religious life as practiced by the mendicant orders.

20. Hugh of St. Victor, *De sacramentis* I 8.13, in P. Minge, *Patrologia latina* 176: 314–18 (Paris: 1844–1865).

21. Ibid.

22. See Lombard, *Libri IV sententiarum*, 26.4 and 2–3.

23. Again, see Bonaventure, *Quaestiones disputatae*, 3.1.

24. Lisa Sowle Cahill, *Sex, Gender, and Christian Ethics* (Cambridge: Cambridge University Press, 1996), 111.

25. I argue for this conclusion in more detail in *Natural and Divine Law*, 212–34.

26. This line of argument plays a critical role in defense of gay marriage as an implication of our commitments to equality and nondiscrimination; for a good, forcefully developed example, see David Cole, "The Same-Sex Future," *New York Review of Books* 56, no. 11 (July 2, 2009): 12–16.

27. For a good recent summary of the complex and acrimonious debate over this question, see Todd A. Salzman and Michael G. Lawler, *The Sexual Person: Toward a Renewed Catholic Anthropology* (Washington DC: Georgetown University Press, 2008), 172–91.

28. This process is already under way in the early scholastic period, as Hugh's remarks discussed earlier illustrate; Gallagher sets out the stages of a similar transformation of attitudes in magisterial teachings in "Magisterial Teaching from 1918 to the Present." For a broader overview of the ways in which theological commitments and broad cultural attitudes have mutually shaped and conditioned our views of marriage, see Cahill, *Sex, Gender, and Christian Ethics*, 166–216.

29. See Charles Reid, *Power over the Body, Equality in the Family: Rights and Domestic Relations in Medieval Canon Law* (Grand Rapids, MI: Eerdmans, 2004), 25–68.

30. For a good overview of the relevant issues, see Don Browning, *Marriage and Modernization* (Grand Rapids, MI: Eerdmans, 2003), 1–29.

2

Reconciling Evangelical Christianity with Our Sexual Minorities

Reframing the Biblical Discussion

DAVID P. GUSHEE

Most evangelical Christians have understood their faith, rooted in a high view of biblical authority, to be irreconcilable with "homosexuality." This has meant that devoted LGBT people raised as evangelical Christians must choose between their sexuality and their faith/religious community. This creates enormous psychic distress, turns LGBT Christians and their allies away from (evangelical) Christianity, and contributes to intense alienation between the gay community and evangelicals all over the world. But traditional evangelical attitudes on LGBT people and their relationships are beginning to change. This paper offers a description of the state of the conversation in the North American evangelical community on this issue, and summarizes my own normative proposal.

Arguments in the Western Christian world over lesbian, gay, bisexual, and transgender persons (LGBT) have now leaped the gap between mainline Protestantism and evangelicalism.[1] Evangelicals largely looked on from a distance over the past four decades as the gay rights movement advanced in Western and US culture and as mainliners began writing their scholarship and undertaking their long, often stalemated denominational debates. In evangelical circles, however, until the past few years, everyone who raised a challenge to "traditionalist" views immediately experienced some form of exclusion.

The space for conversation in evangelicalism is still very fragile and almost exclusively confined to the Western/Northern Christian world.[2]

This essay was published originally in the *Journal of the Society of Christian Ethics* 35.2 (2015): 141–158.

However, a number of new books have been written and organizations founded by avowed evangelicals attempting to open up conversational space, plead for better treatment, reframe the issues, or revise the traditionalist posture. The landscape is changing dramatically. And if even part of the vast evangelical community softens its stance, it could presage (even more) dramatic cultural and legal changes in the United States and other lands where evangelicals are a large part of the population.

Pro-LGBT evangelical forerunners go back decades, such as Ralph Blair and his group, Evangelicals Concerned.[3] The first blockbuster memoir from within the evangelical world was by Mel White, a gay man who once served in the Christian Right.[4] In the late 1990s Fuller Seminary ethicist Lewis Smedes suggested a more accepting posture toward gay couples in a well-known essay and video.[5] Evangelical psychologist David Myers, alone and working with others, has been making his faith- and science-grounded plea for full LGBT acceptance for over a decade.[6] Andrew Marin shocked many in 2009 when he called for dialogue rooted in well-informed love in a book triggered by his three best friends coming out as gay (*Love Is an Orientation*).[7]

But now the call for "generous spaciousness" has been expanded.[8] Senior evangelical pastor and ex–Vineyard Church leader Ken Wilson has called for a full "embrace" of LGBT Christians "in the company of Jesus," though he attempts to frame his approach as a "third way," emphasizing Christian unity rather than moral approval.[9] No such distinctions, though, have been accepted by the Vineyard Church, as Wilson has suffered rejection and the loss of the church he founded decades ago. In December 2014 he launched a new evangelical congregation.

Memoirs are surfacing in increasing numbers, including by gay evangelicals. These have considerably increased evangelical understanding of the gay Christian experience.[10] The first memoir by a (formerly) evangelical lesbian has appeared—musician Jennifer Knapp's *Facing the Music*.[11] The transgender issue, meanwhile, is just beginning to surface.[12]

The six most widely cited purportedly antigay Bible passages—I will call them the Big Six here—and the scholarship undergirding their traditional interpretation are being challenged directly by some evangelical scholars. In 2014, for example, biblical scholar James Brownson published a significant treatment of the relevant textual issues in his book *Bible, Gender, Sexuality*.[13] It is a rigorous work of scholarship.

Most visibly, also in 2014, young prodigy Matthew Vines, a Harvard dropout of great intelligence and vision, came out with a memoir-plus-biblical-excavation called *God and the Gay Christian*.[14] Vines has also launched a national evangelical movement called the Reformation Project.[15] This effort began as a training seminar and is growing into the most prominent LGBT activist platform in evangelicalism.

Full disclosure: I now know almost all of these people and have made my own contribution in my recent book *Changing Our Mind*.[16] I have realized over the last few years that this issue demands my attention—and my repentance, because what little I had said about LGBT-related issues until recently had been inadequate, and because evangelical churches and families are still doing an awful lot of harm to gay people, beginning with their own children.

This essay offers a description of the state of the conversation in the North American evangelical community, summarizes my own normative proposal, and reflects on the broader significance of this conversation for Christian ethics.

The State of the Evangelical Conversation

For purposes of this essay I distinguish between the US evangelical community as a *discrete, self-conscious subculture of theologically conservative white Protestants* over against evangelicalism as naming certain theological tendencies and convictions, much as one might name neo-orthodoxy or post-liberalism. This distinction draws on earlier work I have done that describes US evangelicalism beginning as a Protestant renewal movement but settling into a religious community with its own ethos, leaders, and institutions that are self-consciously distinct from mainline Protestant, Catholic, and other religious communities.[17]

This is true even though some members of the latter groups share what might be described as evangelical methodological, theological, or ethical commitments.

Sociologists of religion further distinguish white evangelicals from black Protestants and Latino/a Protestants as distinctive religious communities, even though many black and Latino/a Protestants are also "evangelical" in theology.[18] Therefore, although the LGBT/conservative Protestant interaction carries similarities across racial lines, the differences are sufficient to dissuade me from straying outside the white evangelical situation with this essay.[19] I will further focus on the US setting.

Mainline Protestantism has had an LGBT debate for decades, and often the traditionalist side of these debates self-identifies as evangelical.[20] But mainline Protestants live in a different religious subculture than evangelical counterparts. It is one thing for Wesley Seminary, the Presbyterian Church (USA), and Fortress Press to discuss LGBT issues; it is something else for Fuller Seminary, the National Association of Evangelicals, and Baker Books to do so. There has not been—until now—a full-fledged LGBT conversation in the evangelical world. That is because "everyone knew" that evangelical Christianity ruled out any acceptance of non-heterosexual sexual relationships—and everyone knew that accepting or not accepting such relationships was the sum total of the LGBT controversy. This is now changing.

How Evangelicals Think: Sola Scriptura

Despite centuries of historical-critical methodology and more recent challenges to the way evangelicals tend to read and use the Bible, a majority of my religious tribe still tend to narrow the (explicit) grounds for their religious knowledge claims to the Bible as the premier, if not the sole, authority.[21] This is sometimes called evangelical biblicism.[22] With variations, most evangelicals still believe that the (Protestant) Bible is divinely inspired, the truthful and authoritative Word of God to humans, and the only sure guide for Christian faith and practice. Most evangelicals have been deeply shaped by a sometimes productive, sometimes destructive biblical populism in which it is believed that any literate, reasonably devout Christian can read an English translation of the Bible and receive a clear understanding of God's Word and will.[23] This creates a chronic authority problem because there is no universally recognized authority to adjudicate competing evangelical interpretations of the Bible.[24] Every religious tradition has its own epistemological and authority repertoire, with its own limits and problems, and this has been ours.

Evangelical biblicism means that rarely if ever will an evangelical claim that a biblical text or writer is inaccurate, erroneous, or harmful. More often they will subtly move problematic texts into the background, where they gradually recede from view along with thousands of other ignored texts. Evangelicals will rarely if ever allow a claim from science, experience, or tradition to challenge what they believe to be a claim from the "plain sense" of scripture (often with little or no reference to social context), though they sometimes will cite other sources to buttress or supplement their "biblical" claims.[25] Claims to "what the Bible says" must generally be met within evangelicalism by stronger counterclaims to what the Bible (really) says, not to externally grounded claims.

Evangelicals also tend to be suspicious of intra-scriptural moves that would offer any kind of explicit trumping or relativizing of specific scriptural texts to resolve disputed issues. For example, a common move of Christian reformists on issues as diverse as slavery, women's roles, and sexuality has been to appeal to broader biblical themes, motifs, or threads as trumping problematic specific passages, which are often set aside as culture-bound or erroneous. Conservative evangelicals, at least, have tended to resist this move vigorously, especially if the trumped texts offer clear moral rules and the trumping move is seen as weakening them.[26]

In general, those evangelicals who define the texts that are to be viewed as most relevant to an issue dominate the discussion of that issue. This is true especially because evangelicals are rarely self-conscious about interpretive traditions in relation to scripture; no one has suggested that the very texts we treat as relevant to an issue are themselves a product of earlier choices and their transmission through some kind of ecclesial tradition.

Evangelicalism has fragmented in recent decades, and what I am saying about evangelical knowledge claims applies more to conservative evangelicals than to progressive evangelicals, who are methodologically more open to liberal or post-liberal approaches. Progressive evangelicals are also much more open to hearing criticisms about the difficulties inherent in our particular way of grounding normative knowledge claims; sometimes they are so open that they abandon evangelicalism altogether.

Especially as a result of brutal disputes in evangelical life in recent decades, the conservative side has tended to heighten its claims about biblical inspiration, truth, and authority. It is hard to question the authority of a book treated as God-breathed, completely inerrant, and utterly supreme in its authority.[27] Such claims tend to rule out conversation other than in the form of a heavily cognitive exchange of exegetical claims.[28]

The Traditionalist LGBT and Scripture Paradigm

The essentials of the traditionalist (often but not exclusively evangelical) reading of scripture in relation to what might generically be called the LGBT issue can be rendered by this formula:

> Genesis 1–2 +
> Genesis 19 (cf. Judges 19) +
> 1 Leviticus 18:22/20:13 +
> Matthew 19:1–12/Mark 10:2–12 +
> Romans 1:26–27 +
> 1 Corinthians 6:9 (cf. 1 Timothy 1:10) +
> All biblical references to sex and marriage that assume male + female
> = A clear biblical ban on same-sex relationships.

Sometimes traditionalists simply assemble some or all of the words, phrases, and sentences in these texts into a cumulative condemnation of gay people and their relationships. Other times they attempt something like a broader theological-ethical rendering of the issue, rooted in these biblical texts.

Here I summarize these references:

Genesis 1–2 offers creation accounts in which (1) God makes humanity in the divine image as male and female and commands (blesses) that they be fruitful and multiply and have dominion, and (2) God responds to the man's loneliness by creating a suitable helper-partner, woman, then giving her to the man, with the narrator connecting this primal divine act to marriage. These stories have been understood traditionally by Christians as establishing an exclusively male–female gender and marital sexual-ethical paradigm. The most coherent broader theological-ethical rendering of a traditionalist position argues that the Bible's message on sexuality is consistently gendered, complementarian, procreative, and marital, with all of these dimensions grounded in God's design in primeval creation and all ruling out same-sex relations for all time.

Genesis 19 and Judges 19 tell stories of perverse local city men seeking to sexually assault male guests receiving hospitality in local households but instead being offered defenseless women. This long has been understood as a condemnation of "homosexuality."

Leviticus 18:22 commands men not to lie with men as with women, presumably sexually; *Leviticus 20:13* prescribes the death penalty for this offense. The Hebrew word *"toevah"* used in these passages has generally been translated "abomination" to describe God's abhorrence. These passages still are cited in evangelical circles, even where Leviticus has otherwise disappeared from use.

Matthew 19:1–12 / Mark 10:2–12 depict Jesus responding to questions about the morality of divorce. He appeals to Genesis 1–2 to ground his rigorous response setting strict limits on initiating divorce. These texts are often read as Jesus's implicit affirmation of an exclusively male–female creation design for sex and marriage and thus the broader theme in Genesis 1–2.

Romans 1:26–27 is part of an argument Paul is making about why everyone needs the salvation offered in Jesus Christ. In an apparent effort to illustrate the idolatry and sinfulness of the Gentile part of the human community, Paul makes a harshly negative reference to "degrading" passions and "unnatural, shameless" same-sex acts on the part of men and perhaps also women; later he condemns twenty-one other debased behaviors or vices. This passage continues to function as the most important text cited for condemnation of same-sex acts and relationships.

1 Corinthians 6 and 1 Timothy 1 offer vice lists as part of moral exhortations. The Corinthians text excludes unrepentant practitioners of the vices in the list from the kingdom of God. The rare Greek words "*malakoi*" and especially Paul's neologism "*arsenokoitai*" used in these passages have recently been translated into English as "homosexuals" or related terms. These English terms have been formative for many Christians who have not been informed about the significant translation challenges involved.

If we take the most commonly cited texts on the issue from the traditionalist side, they derive from 11 of the 1,189 chapters in the Bible. This body of biblical citations is seen as settling "the LGBT issue."

Engagement with this issue and with traditionalists has led me to notice four problems:

1. The texts offer language so harsh about the perverse character and un-godly posture of those desirous of or participating in same-sex acts that they continue to fund an attitude of contempt that survives no matter how polite mainstream traditionalist leaders try to be today. Evangelical and fundamentalist preachers regularly show up in the news with contemptuous, even murderous anti-LGBT declarations.[29] These few sacred texts actually go further in their rejectionist rhetoric than many traditionalist evangelicals want to go these days.
2. The biblical texts focus on sexual acts and in one case sexual passions. This produces a continued narrow focus of traditionalists on same-sex acts to the exclusion of other dimensions of a complex human issue.[30] This might fairly be described as creating a legalistic, moralistic, and even casuistic rendering of the LGBT issue. It systematically blocks attention to the human beings who happen to be lesbian, gay, bisexual, or transgender; to relationships, not just acts;

and to the mental and emotional health of LGBT people at all developmental stages.

3. Because the biblical texts do not discuss what today is called sexual orientation and identity, traditionalists continue to struggle with these human realities. The reparative/ex-gay therapy temptation survives, attempting to grind same-sex sexual desires out of those who have them—despite clinical evidence of the ineffectiveness and harm of these efforts and including a notable abandonment by some of their most visible former practitioners.[31] Some traditionalists, as well, encourage LGBT people (and sometimes straight people) to reject the very concepts of gender identity or sexual orientation by refusing any identity other than Christian. Such efforts fail to take seriously the extent to which human beings are bearers of multiple identities, including gender identity and sexual orientation. They also disregard the part that psychosocial discovery of gender and sexuality, and formation of gender and sexual identity, plays in human growth and development.

4. In general, the fixed nature of the interpretive paradigm around the Big Six texts blocks engagement with any other data: the claims of contemporary research and clinicians, personal experiences of and with LGBT people, or alternative renderings of the biblical witness. Some conservative evangelicals are methodologically committed precisely to *not engaging* such other potential sources of knowledge.

Shaking the Consensus: A Youthful Movement of Dissent

This once-immovable posture has begun to totter. The most important factor is not external-cultural but internal-generational. It has come from a youthful movement of dissent in the evangelical world. This dissent increasingly takes institutional form among the young: in Facebook groups; gay–straight alliances; campus groups, often called ONE[School]; Christian college alumni; national groups like Level Ground and the Reformation Project; and resistance efforts such as Soulforce.[32]

In ascending order of challenge to their schools, these groups are de-

manding (a) safe space for LGBT students to gather for mutual support; (b) institutional acceptance and even sponsorship of such support
groups; (c) permission and even sponsorship of public campus dialogue
around LGBT issues; (d) reconsideration of student life, admission, and
hiring policies viewed as stigmatizing and discriminatory; and (e) an
overturning of the traditionalist view in favor of either a silent or neutral
institutional stance or full acceptance and complete equality for LGBT
persons and their marital-covenantal relationships.

Where these dissenting movements are strongest, they place real pressure on administrations caught between pro-LGBT and anti-LGBT forces.
The greatest pressure being placed on the traditionalist position and its institutional embodiments has come from these youthful dissenting voices,
which have found more success in schools than in churches.[33] The more recent scholarship noted in this essay has responded to, rather than created,
this movement of dissent, which—whether it uses this language or not—
strikes me as genuinely a liberationist-solidarity movement from below.

My Own Normative Proposal

In *Changing Our Mind,* I begin by moving early into at least brief analysis of the exegesis, cultural backgrounds, and hermeneutical issues raised
by each of the Big Six passages, even though I am less and less convinced
that this is where the real issue truly lies. Still, a summary is in order.

Genesis 1–2 / Matt. 19 / Mark 10.
I engage the claims that (a) these texts establish an eternal creation design rooted in God-given male/female genital/anatomical complementarity (sometimes also claims about the centrality of procreation for
legitimate sexuality) and that (b) these texts forever rule out the moral
legitimacy of same-sex relationships. I propose three biblically serious
alternatives for reading Genesis.[34]

1. Christians earlier had to learn to read the creation accounts of Genesis 1–2 in intelligent conversation with scientific discoveries about
   the world (e.g., a heliocentric rather than earth-centered solar sys-

tem, and an old earth versus a young earth). Perhaps the same principle applies to the issue of gender identity and sexual orientation. Not every person is clearly either male or female, not every person is heterosexual, therefore not every person's sexuality will be procreative—and this exceedingly well-documented diversity in the actual creation must be taken seriously in reading biblical creation texts that do not mention such diversity. This is a solvable faith/science problem. Scriptures about creation and sexuality need to be integrated with reasonably certain claims from science about gender- and sexual-orientation diversity, leading to the conclusion that just because creation accounts fail to mention this diversity, it does not mean that it does not exist or that such diversity is morally problematic. Perhaps we will one day conclude that such sexual diversity has as little moral significance in itself as "handedness" diversity, which also was once seen as a problematic orientation in need of correction.

2. Christian theology does better looking forward to redemption in Jesus Christ rather than gazing back into the mist of an unreachable pristine creation. Numerous Christian ethical disasters based on creation or "orders of creation" claims can be identified—such as the supposedly divinely ordained subordination of women and subjugation of earth and her creatures.[35] Perhaps the LGBT issue is best understood in this light, with the same solution—looking forward to redemption, not back to creation—as long as we don't understand redemption as some kind of return to Eden. If "redemption" is understood to mean a return to Eden, a restoration of pristine original creation, looking forward to redemption helps little. But if redemption looks more like gathering up the good-yet-broken strands of human existence and moving forward into a kingdom of forgiveness, grace, and new beginnings, that's different.

3. Perhaps we should focus not just on Genesis 1–2 but also Genesis 3. The Pauline-Augustinian-Lutheran tradition takes Genesis 3 to be the account of the entry of sin into the world (see 1 Cor. 15). A thoroughgoing understanding of the pervasiveness of human sinfulness would include every human's sexuality, which should be seen as

good-yet-fallen like every other aspect of human existence. One implication is that instead of straight people's sexual desires and acts being seen as innocent (especially if they are married), and gay people's sexual desires and acts being seen as sinful (under all circumstances), no one's sexual desires or acts would be viewed as entirely innocent. Everyone's sexuality is good-yet-fallen and needs to come under the discipline of covenant. This approach would eliminate straight Christians' sense of prideful superiority and might lead to greater acceptance of the idea that a rigorous covenantal-marital sexual-ethical norm can apply to all human beings, whom we now know come into the world with a range of sexual orientations, and also with sinful tendencies in relation to sex that need covenantal ordering.

Leviticus 18:22 / 20:13.

There is an obvious problem in focusing on two verses from the Levitical holiness code, one of which carries the death penalty, when Christians apply almost none of the rest of it to our lives today. Moreover, biblical commentators express uncertainty and considerable difference of opinion about why exactly those two verses ban male (but not female) same-sex acts. Many of these possible reasons (male superiority as penetrator but not penetrated in sex, sex-for-procreation-only, the need to distinguish Israel from pagan neighbors, etc.) are not normatively compelling for Christians today.[36]

Genesis 19 / Judges 19.

It is widely agreed by most commentators that these texts are about the attempted violent gang rape of strangers, and the Genesis text concerning not just visitors but angels. No biblical text mentions "homosexuality" among its many references to the sins of that legendarily evil city. These two texts are essentially irrelevant.

Romans 1 / 1 Corinthians 6 / 1 Timothy 1.

Paul, the only New Testament writer who addresses same-sex issues, wrote in a context where such acts were often adulterous, debauched, and exploitative, easily viewed by any conservative moralist of his day as abusive and excessive.[37] This context had to affect what he said about same-sex acts in both 1 Corinthians and Romans, the latter perhaps in connection to the debauchery of the Roman court under Caligula and Nero, which included violently abusive same-sex acts and reprisals.[38] This is relevant hermeneutically for the church today when thinking about same-sex acts that are not adulterous, debauched, exploitative, or imperial-pagan but instead covenantal and marital. It also could help account for the profound harshness of the language Paul uses when speaking about same-sex acts. And it may speak to the best way to translate vice-list terms in 1 Corinthians 6:9 and 1 Timothy 1:10. We should translate them in a manner that links them to sexual predation, abuse, and exploitation.[39]

The supposedly ironclad reading of these Big Six texts to ban any and all same-sex relationships today turns out to be very much arguable, especially when ancient contexts, modern contexts, and their great differences are taken seriously.[40]

Real Lives Matter

There is also serious attention to real contemporary human beings. A young evangelical Christian discovers he is gay. Devout parents experience their fifteen-year-old daughter coming out as a lesbian. A transgender teenager shows up for youth group. Often LGBT evangelicals and then their families move from the traditionalist at least into the "conflicted" category through these experiences. Their "heart" tells them one thing (be who you are / love your child!) and their "head" tells them something different (all same-sex attraction is sinful).

The methodological question here—indeed, a theological question—is what to make of the extraordinary power of transformative encounters with oneself or a loved one as a sexual minority.[41] Is perspective-shifting sympathy with the suffering of one's child a tempting seduction from God's Truth or is it a path into God's Truth? Do we read ourselves and other people through the lens of sacred texts that we love or do we

read texts through the lens of sacred people that we love? Or do we encounter both sacred people and sacred texts through the lens of Christ
whom we love above all?[42]

Many grassroots evangelicals who have broken with the traditionalist
posture emerge out of this conundrum. They have not figured out what
to do with the Big Six passages. But now "the LGBT issue" has become
the face of a beloved person. It's about loyalty and love for that person.
Then perhaps they make a theological move: *I have to believe Jesus stands
with my loved one, not with those who reject her, regardless of what it seems
to say in Romans 1.* I will therefore love her "beyond my theology."[43] It
may not be enough for a complete Christian ethic. But what if fierce parental love actually comes closer to the heart of Jesus and the meaning
of Christian discipleship than simply quoting the Big Six passages? The
emotional well-being of gay young people seems to depend on finding
some family and friends who will make this kind of move.

LGBT Youth Suffering and Family Rejection

The Center for American Progress did a key policy report on LGBT
homeless youth.[44] Homeless youth are defined as "unaccompanied young
people between the ages of 12 and 24 for whom it is not possible to safely
live with a relative or in another safe alternative living arrangement."
Among these homeless youth are "runaways" and "throwaways." The
center cites commonly reported estimates that there are between 2.4 million and 3.7 million homeless youth.

LGBT youth are vastly overrepresented among the homeless youth
population. "Several state and local studies from across the United States
have found shockingly disproportionate rates of homelessness among
LGBT youth compared to non-LGBT youth." For example, 33 percent
of homeless youth in New York City identify as LGBT. In Seattle it is 39
percent, in Los Angeles it is 25 percent, and in Chicago it is 22 percent.

The most common reasons that LGBT homeless youth cite for being
out of their homes are family rejection and conflict. Much of this family rejection and conflict is religiously motivated. The data are clear that

all too often when young people come out or are found to be LGBT, they are met with family rejection, especially from religiously conservative families whose faith leaves them unprepared to accept who their child has turned out to be. The indispensable Family Acceptance Project (FAP) has identified and researched dozens of different family responses to LGBT children and measured them to show the relationship between experiencing specific family-accepting and family-rejecting behaviors during adolescence and health and well-being as young adults. The higher the level of family rejection, the higher the likelihood of negative physical health, mental health, and behavioral problems.[45] The tragedy is that most devout religious parents are attempting to love and serve their children through the very behaviors that their children find emotionally devastating. They have no idea, at least at first, what their version of "religiously faithful parenting" is doing to their children. When it does become clear, sometimes the damage is impossible to reverse. And sometimes parents spend the rest of their lives grieving those damages.

FAP found a direct correlation between "highly rejecting" families and the following behaviors: LGBT youth are

- more than eight times as likely to have attempted suicide at least once,
- more than six times as likely to report high levels of depression,
- more than three times as likely to use illegal drugs, and
- more than three times as likely to be high-risk for HIV and STDs.

Looking at "the LGBT issue" from the perspective of struggling adolescents and their families, especially having seen numerous reruns of a disastrous Christian script leading to mental illness, family fractures, and even suicide, has revolutionized my entire perspective.

From the Big Six to the Bigger Six Thousand

With the faces of legions of exiled and wounded gay adolescents in mind, I have found my way from the Big Six to the Bigger Six Thousand. I have come to conclude that the most important theological and ethical themes in scripture point toward full acceptance rather than the wary distance or angry contempt that now characterizes evangelical responses to gay people so much of the time. Other evangelicals are beginning to make this move as well, believing that

1. *The Gospel is that God loves good-yet-fallen human beings* and has offered all of us needy sinners redemption in Christ Jesus. But a tragic misreading of scripture has blocked access to God's grace on the part of those considered unworthy of it, like the lepers of biblical times. This in turn has hurt the evangelistic witness of the Church in culture, with LGBT persons, and in our churches.

2. *The Church is a community of humble/grateful forgiven disciples of Jesus.* Christians are called to welcome as family all who believe in and seek to follow Jesus, and to live together in unity and shared commitment to the work of God's reign. A tragic misreading of scripture has tempted straight Christians to view themselves as superior to gay Christians (or to reject the idea that there could be gay Christians) and to exclude them from the Body of Christ (or to leave a church or denomination if perhaps gay people might actually be fully welcomed). It has created first- and second-class Christians and has damaged the unity of the Church.

3. *The great ethical imperatives of the Christian life* center on justice, deliverance, compassion, human dignity, and love. But a tragic misreading of scripture has produced a harvest of bitter fruit: injustice, oppression, mercilessness, degradation, and hatred or indifference. If, as Glen Stassen argues, you can know an ethical tradition by its historical fruits, these fruits are not appealing.[46] They are the opposite of what the Kingdom of God looks like, which is justice, peace, healing, deliverance, inclusion in community, and joy in God's presence.[47]

4. *It comes down to Jesus* and how those who claim his name understand the meaning of his incarnation, ministry, teaching, death, and resurrection. A tragic misreading of scripture, I believe, has actually taught traditionalists to deny the Jesus we meet in the Gospels, and

to do so in the name of Jesus himself.[48] It has created an unchristlike body of Christian tradition that continues to deliver damage every day, all around the world.

Transformative encounters with LGBT people in recent years have led me (and others) to fresh encounters with the Gospel, the Church, Christian Ethics, and above all Jesus. I have moved into deep solidarity with LGBT people, with a special focus on evangelical young people. In making this move, I am not setting aside scripture. I am embracing its deepest and most central meaning.

Conclusion

Many evangelical Christians have thought the LGBT issue was a sexual ethics issue. They thought our job was to draw a moral boundary line between whose desired or actual sexual acts are morally legitimate and whose are illegitimate. Because we fixated on the sexual ethics issues, we tragically failed to notice our LGBT neighbors bleeding by the side of the road, mainly bleeding because of what we Christians had done to them while not even knowing we were doing it.

The fundamental "LGBT issue" is that a misreading or at least a misapplication of six texts in scripture taught many Christians a tradition of contempt toward sexual and gender minorities. That teaching of contempt has cost many lives, fractured many families, and wounded the mental health of millions. It has driven many away from God and church. The LGBT issue is a Gospel issue, a human dignity issue, a family wholeness issue, a church unity issue, an adolescent health issue, a justice and love issue, a solidarity-with-the-oppressed issue, and a reconciliation-in-Christ issue. It is not fundamentally a sexual ethics issue.

We have labeled as sinful or as rebellion against God a form of human diversity that has shown up in every society and every era. We have done so despite the overwhelming research evidence and urgent appeals for destigmatization by our culture's leading scientists, clinicians, and mental health experts. In doing so, traditionalist Christianity still trains many of its most devout adherents to disdain and reject a small but significant minority of the human population, including their own children, church members, and fellow believers, leaving a legacy of great harm. This obvious moral blind spot on our part has deeply discredited the moral witness of Christianity.

It is time to end the suffering of the church's own most oppressed group. It is time to reconcile evangelical Christianity with our sexual minorities.

Questions for Reflection

1. In order for there to be a fruitful conversation among Christians who disagree about what the Bible has to say about homosexuality, all the participants must agree that the scriptures require interpretation and that the meaning of any particular text may not be self-evident to all who are faithful to it. How might preachers and teachers of the church prepare the faithful for such conversations?

2. Within all Christian denominations the Bible is considered God's definitive, divinely inspired Word to humankind. How might a contemporary hermeneutics of critical questioning through scriptural exegesis inform the reinterpretation of texts? What impact might such a reinterpretation have on our understanding of the authority of scripture?

3. Rigid constructions of sex and gender binaries based on particular interpretations of key biblical texts have been used to justify widespread violence against sexual minorities. On annual average, 30 percent of reported hate crimes in the United States target sexual minorities. In other countries these biblical interpretations still sacralize the criminalization of those who are queer. What biblical texts do you think are (mis)used to underwrite such instances of shaming, beating, raping, and killing? What biblical texts are ignored? How might the latter inform the reinterpretation of the former?

Suggestions for Further Reading

Carlin, Nathan. "A Pastoral Theological Reading of *Middlesex*." In *Intersex, Theology, and the Bible: Troubling Bodies in Church, Text, and Society*, Susanna Cornwall, ed., Chapter 4, 99–119. New York: Palgrave Macmillan, 2015.

Childs, James. "Eschatology, Anthropology, and Sexuality: Helmut Thielicke and the Orders of Creation Revisited." *Journal of the Society of Christian Ethics* 30.1 (2010): 3–20.

Gill, Emily R. *An Argument for Same-Sex Marriage: Religious Freedom, Sexual Freedom, and Public Expressions of Civic Equality.* Washington, DC: Georgetown University Press, 2012.

Jung, Patricia Beattie, "God Sets the Lonely in Families." In *More Than a Monologue: Sexual Diversity and the Catholic Church, Vol. 2,* Patrick Hornbeck II and Michael A. Norko, eds., 115–133. Bronx, NY: Fordham University Press, 2014.

Stiegemeyer, Scott. "How Do You Know Whether You Are a Man or a Woman?" *Concordia Theological Quarterly* 79.1–2 (January–April 2015): 19–48.

Notes

1. I mainly deploy the acronym LGBT in this paper to refer to lesbian, gay, bisexual, and transgender persons while recognizing that there is not quite consensus on the best shorthand terminology: LGBTQIA+, etc. For brevity, I do not even attempt to address parallel conversations in Catholicism or other communities.

2. Global South evangelicals are not proving friendly to any rethinking of this issue. Sometimes they are aided by US anti-LGBT evangelicals. See Alex Seitz-Wald, "Evangelicals Are Winning the Gay Marriage Fight—in Africa and Russia," *National Journal,* January 23, 2014, http://www.national journal.com/gay-washington/evangelicals-are-winning-the-gay-marriage-fight -in-africa-and-russia-20140123.

3. See the website of Evangelicals Concerned: http://ecinc.org/.

4. Mel White, *Stranger at the Gate: To Be Gay and Christian in America* (New York: Penguin, 1994).

5. Lewis B. Smedes, "Like the Wideness of the Sea?" *Soulforce,* August 13, 2004, http://abouthomosexuality.com/lewissmedes.pdf. This essay is sometimes referred to as "There's a Wideness in God's Mercy," other times "Like the Wideness of the Sea." These are of course references to two parts of one line of a classic Christian hymn.

6. David G. Myers, *Psychology,* 10th ed. (New York: Worth, 2013); and David G. Myers and Letha Dawson Scanzoni, *What God Has Joined Together: A Christian Case for Gay Marriage* (New York: HarperSanFrancisco, 2005).

7. Andrew Marin, *Love Is an Orientation: Elevating the Conversation with the Gay Community* (Downers Grove, IL: Intervarsity Press, 2009). He also founded the Marin Foundation to further this work: http://www.themarinfoundation.org/.

8. Wendy VanderWal-Gritter, *Generous Spaciousness: Responding to Gay Christians in the Church* (Grand Rapids, MI: Brazos, 2014).

9. Ken Wilson, *A Letter to My Congregation: An Evangelical Pastor's Path to Embracing People Who Are Gay, Lesbian, and Transgender into the Company of Jesus* (Canton, MI: Read the Spirit Books, 2014).

10. Wesley Hill, *Washed and Waiting: Reflections on Christian Faithfulness and Homosexuality* (Grand Rapids, MI: Zondervan, 2010); Justin Lee, *Torn: Rescuing the Gospel from the Gays vs. Christians Debate* (New York: Jericho Books, 2012); and Tim Otto, *Oriented to Faith* (Eugene, OR: Cascade, 2014).

11. Jennifer Knapp, *Facing the Music: My Story* (New York: Howard Books, 2014). Perhaps the most visible evangelical lesbian in good standing was, for a while, Wheaton College staffer Julie Rodgers. The legitimacy of her service at Wheaton even as a celibate lesbian was questioned in this piece published in December 2014: Julie Roys, "Wheaton's 'Gay Celibate Christian,'" *World*, December 11, 2014. Then, in July 2015, she abandoned both her Side B posture and her Wheaton post. See Julie Roys, "Why Julie Rodgers Is Right—and Tragically Wrong on Same-Sex Relationships," *Christian Post*, July 15, 2015 http://www.christian post.com/news/why-julie-rodgers-is-right-and-tragically-wrong-on-same-sex -relationships-141552/.

12. I find little evangelical conversation on transgender issues to this point. The only source I have found is not an evangelical one: Justin Tanis, *Trans-Gendered: Theology, Ministry, and Communities of Faith* (Cleveland: Pilgrim Press, 2003).

13. James V. Brownson, *Bible, Gender, Sexuality: Reframing the Church's Debate on Same-Sex Relationships* (Grand Rapids, MI: Eerdmans, 2013).

14. Matthew Vines, *God and the Gay Christian: The Biblical Case in Support of Same-Sex Relationships* (New York: Convergent Books, 2014).

15. See "About the Reformation Project," http://www.reformationproject .org/about/, accessed June 11, 2015.

16. David P. Gushee, *Changing Our Mind: A Call from America's Leading Evangelical Ethics Scholar for Full Acceptance of LGBT Christians in the Church* (Canton, MI: Read the Spirit Books, 2014).

17. See Dennis Hollinger and David Gushee, "Evangelical Ethics: Profile of a Movement Coming of Age," *Annual of the Society of Christian Ethics* 20 (2000): 181–203. See also David P. Gushee and Isaac B. Sharp, eds. *Evangelical Ethics: A Reader* (Louisville, KY: Westminster John Knox Press, 2015).

18. For example, see the polls of the Public Religion Research Institute, www .publicreligion.org.

19. See Kelly Brown Douglas, *Sexuality and the Black Church* (Maryknoll, NY: Orbis Books, 1999); Delroy Constantine-Simms, ed., *The Greatest Taboo: Homosexuality in Black Communities* (Los Angeles: Alyson Books, 2000); Patricia Hill Collins, *Black Sexual Politics: African Americans, Gender, and the New Racism* (New York: Routledge, 2005); Yvette A. Flunder, *Where the Edge Gathers: Building a Community of Radical Inclusion* (Cleveland: Pilgrim Press, 2005); Horace L. Griffin, *Their Own Receive Them Not: African American Lesbians and Gays in Black Churches* (Eugene, OR: Wipf & Stock, 2006); G. Winston James and Lisa C. Moore, eds., *Spirited: Affirming the Soul and Black Gay/Lesbian Identity* (Washington, DC: RedBone Press, 2006); and Traci C. West, *Disruptive Christian Ethics:*

When Racism and Women's Lives Matter (Louisville, KY: Westminster John Knox, 2006).

20. However, this too is changing. Mark Achtemeier offers a good example of a mainline evangelical changing his view on LGBT issues; see Achtemeier, *The Bible's Yes to Same-Sex Marriage: An Evangelical's Change of Heart* (Louisville, KY: Westminster John Knox Press, 2014). Similarly in the United Methodist Church one finds former Asbury professor Steve Harper. See his *For the Sake of the Bride: Restoring the Church to Her Intended Beauty* (Nashville: Abingdon, 2014). More often today mainline evangelicals vis-à-vis LGBT issues look like the Evangelical Covenant Order of Presbyterians, founded in 2012 by disaffected conservatives who left the PCUSA primarily over the LGBT issue.

21. See National Association of Evangelicals, "Statement of Faith," http://www.nae.net/about-us/statement-of-faith; Southern Baptist Convention, "Baptist Faith and Message," http://www.sbc.net/bfm2000/bfm2000.asp; and with more nuance, Fuller Seminary, "Statement of Faith," http://fuller.edu/About/Mission-and-Values/Statement-of-Faith/ (accessed December 16, 2014).

22. Carefully analyzed and pungently critiqued by sociologist of religion Christian Smith, in *The Bible Made Impossible: Why Biblicism Is Not a Truly Evangelical Reading of Scripture* (Grand Rapids, MI: Brazos Press, 2011). Interestingly enough, Dr. Smith transited right out of evangelicalism to Catholicism not long after publishing this book. A popular new book for evangelicals on the same problem is Peter Enns, *The Bible Tells Me So: Why Defending Scripture Has Made Us Unable to Read It* (New York: HarperOne, 2014).

23. Among the many who have challenged this populism/democratic perspicuity has been Stanley Hauerwas, *Unleashing the Scriptures: Freeing the Bible from Captivity to America* (Nashville: Abingdon, 1993). Not coincidentally, though Hauerwas is popular with evangelicals, his own affinity has turned Anglican. The sometimes chaotic and disastrous consequences of evangelical populist biblicism has driven many an evangelical toward Canterbury, Rome, Byzantium, and the Church Fathers.

24. See Molly Worthen, *Apostles of Reason: The Crisis of Authority in Modern Evangelicalism* (New York and London: Oxford University Press, 2014).

25. Christian Smith, among others, attributes this to an evangelical lineage going back to Scottish common-sense realism. *Bible Made Impossible*, chap. 3. I got the term from David L. Balch, ed., *Homosexuality, Science, and the 'Plain Sense' of Scripture* (Grand Rapids, MI: Eerdmans, 2000). A number of learned evangelicals, motivated in part by the weaknesses of evangelical biblicism, have been attracted to the broader Christian tradition, or Tradition, in recent decades. See D. H. Williams, *Evangelicals and Tradition: The Formative Influence of the Early Church* (Grand Rapids, MI: Baker, 2005).

26. James Brownson, for example, now a revisionist on LGBT issues, expresses dissatisfaction with the broader-theme move as a response to the Big Six passages,

though he does suggest a close attention to the "underlying moral logic" governing texts; see Brownson, *Bible, Gender, Sexuality,* 15.

27. The Southern Baptist Convention makes a good case study. Compare the 1963 Baptist Faith and Message with the 2000 revision: http://www.sbc.net/bfm2000/bfmcomparisonasp (accessed December 16, 2014).

28. The extent of this hypercognitivism in conservative evangelicalism has become clearer to me in exchanges related to the LGBT issue. I am hearing from many LGBT young people describing their efforts to dialogue with family members or church leaders. In many such dialogues the only admissible evidence is biblical exegesis.

29. Two terrible recent stories involving conservative preachers expressing public desires for gay people to die or be killed come from Arizona: Tram Mai, "Tempe Pastor Calls for Killing Gays to End AIDS," *USA Today,* December 6, 2014, http://www.usatoday.com/story/news/nation/2014/12/04/pastor-calls-for-killing-gays-to-end-aids/19929973/; and from New Zealand, Teuila Fuatai and John Weekes, "Pastor Tells Gay Christian to Commit Suicide," *New Zealand Herald,* December 8, 2014, http://www.nzherald.co.nz/nz/news/article.cfm?c_id=1&objectid=11370806.

30. The Romans 1 passage, which mentions illicit lusts and degrading passions and links these to same-sex acts, also makes it difficult for evangelicals to maintain a clear distinction between lesbian and gay sexual orientation, on the one hand, and same-sex sexual acts, on the other—as some Christian thinkers and communities have tried to do in order to make space for LGBT people in the churches. If that distinction collapses, it becomes next to impossible for any evangelical who acknowledges LGBT sexual orientation to be seen as a Christian in completely good standing.

31. See this famous renunciation: Warren Throckmorton, "Alan Chambers: 99.9% Have Not Experienced a Change in Their Orientation," *Patheos,* January 9, 2012, http://www.patheos.com/blogs/warrethrockmorton/2012/01/09/alan-chambers-99-9-have-not-experienced-a-change-in-their-orientation/.

32. A good example is OneGordon: http://www.onegordon.com; for Level Ground, begun out of Fuller Seminary, see http://onlevelground.org/; for Soulforce, see http://soulforcecom/, accessed December 11, 2014.

33. It appears that the power structures of evangelical churches more often push out LGBT Christians and their families, whereas students and alumni remain associated with evangelical colleges and have financial power in relation to them.

34. This section draws from Gushee, "Creation, Sexual Orientation, and God's Will," chap. 15 in *Changing Our Mind.*

35. See Dietrich Bonhoeffer, *Ethics: Dietrich Bonhoeffer Works,* vol. 6 (Minneapolis: Fortress Press, 2005), 388–408; see also Clifford J. Green, "Editor's Introduction to the English Edition," in ibid., 17–22. This idea was suggested to me by James M. Childs. See Childs, "Eschatology, Anthropology, and Sexuality:

Helmut Thielicke and the Orders of Creation," *Journal of the Society of Christian Ethics* 30.1 (2010): 3–20.

36. Background sources for this paragraph can be found in Gushee, *Changing Our Mind*, chap. 12, "Leviticus, Abomination, and Jesus."

37. For fuller discussion, see Gushee, *Changing Our Mind*, ch. 14, "God Made Them Male and Female," informed especially by William Loader, *The New Testament on Sexuality* (Grand Rapids, MI: Eerdmans, 2012), ch. 6.

38. Brownson, *Bible, Gender, Sexuality*, 156–57.

39. Ibid., 274.

40. An increasingly massive literature related to sexuality in the ancient world is now available, sometimes with connections to ancient Jewish and Christian texts. Few can claim to have mastered it. A leader is Australian scholar William Loader, with his five-volume series, "Attitudes towards Sexuality in Judaism and Christianity in the Hellenistic Greco-Roman Era," published by Eerdmans. See also Finnish scholar Martti Nissinen, *Homoeroticism in the Biblical World: A Historical Perspective* (Minneapolis: Fortress, 1998); Kirl Ormand, *Controlling Desires: Sexuality in Ancient Greece and Rome* (London: Praeger, 2009); Bernadette Brooten, *Love between Women: Early Christian Responses to Female Homoeroticism* (Chicago: University of Chicago Press, 1996); Sarah Ruden, *Paul among the People: The Apostle Reinterpreted and Reimagined in His Own Time* (New York: Image Books, 2010); Dale B. Martin, *Sex and the Single Savior: Gender and Sexuality in Biblical Interpretation* (Louisville, KY: Westminster John Knox, 2006).

41. For fuller discussion, see Gushee, *Changing Our Mind*, chap. 17.

42. This is an issue much-discussed online by families of LGBT Christians. A small number of books are now out as well, including Carol Lynn Pearson, *No More Goodbyes: Circling the Wagons around Our Gay Loved Ones* (Walnut Creek, CA: Pivot Point Books, 2007); and Susan Cottrell, *"Mom, I'm Gay": Loving Your LGBTQ Child without Sacrificing Your Faith* (Austin, TX: FreedHearts, 2014).

43. Larry L. McSwain, *Loving beyond Your Theology: The Life and Ministry of Jimmy Raymond Allen* (Macon, GA: Mercer Press, 2010).

44. Andrew Cray, Katie Miller, and Laura E. Durso, "Seeking Shelter: The Experiences and Unmet Needs of LGBT Homeless Youth," *Center for American Progress*, http://cdn.americanprogress.org/wpcontent/uploads/2013/09/LGBT HomelessYouth.pdf, accessed December 16, 2014. All citations in this section are from this report.

45. San Francisco State University, Family Acceptance Project, http://family project.sfsu.edu/. Some of the family rejecting behaviors documented and studied by FAP include hitting/slapping/physical harming; verbal harassment and name-calling; exclusion from family activities; blocking access to LGBT friends, events, and resources; blaming the child when he or she experiences abuse or discrimination; pressuring the child to be more masculine or feminine; threatening God's punishment; making the child pray and attend religious services to change

their LGBT identity; sending them for reparative therapy; declaring that the child brings shame to the family; and not talking about their LGBT identity or making them keep it a secret from family members and others. Everyone needs to read this document from FAP: *Supportive Families, Healthy Children,* available in English, Spanish, and Chinese at http://familyproject.sfsu.edu/publications.

46. See Glen Harold Stassen, *A Thicker Jesus: Incarnational Discipleship in a Secular Age* (Louisville, KY: Westminster John Knox Press, 2012).

47. Our list in Glen H. Stassen and David P. Gushee, *Kingdom Ethics: Following Jesus in Contemporary Context* (Downers Grove, IL: Intervarsity Press, 2003).

48. In dialogue, a traditionalist on this issue cited Matthew 10:37 to me in relation to a father rejecting and shunning his gay son for his entire adult life: "Whoever loves son or daughter more than me is not worthy of me." Therefore: loving Jesus "more" means rejecting one's gay child in Jesus's name. I don't recognize that Jesus.

3

Love Your Enemy
Sex, Power, and Christian Ethics

KAREN LEBACQZ

Dear Abby: A friend of mine was picked up and arrested for raping a 24-year-old woman he had dated twice. He had sex with her the first time he took her out. He said she was easy. The second time . . . she gave him the high-and-mighty act and refused to have sex with him. He got angry, and I guess you could say he overpowered her. Now he's got a rape charge against him, which I don't think is fair. It seems to me that if she was willing to have sex with him on the first date, there is no way she could be raped by him after that. Am I right or wrong? —A Friend of His[1]

This letter to "Dear Abby" highlights two problems. First, a young man has "overpowered" his date, forcing sexual contact on her. Second, the "friend" who writes this query is confused about whether such forced sex constitutes rape or whether it simply constitutes sex.

These two problems represent two dimensions of sexuality and violence in women's experience. First, violence in the sexual arena is a commonplace occurrence. Women are raped and experience forced sex with considerable frequency. Second, "normal" patterns of male-female sexual relating in this culture are defined by patterns of male dominance over women. Hence, "our earliest socialization," argues Marie Fortune, "teaches us to confuse sexual activity with sexual violence."[2]

In this essay I argue that an adequate Christian sexual ethic must attend to the realities of the links between violence and sexuality in the experiences of women. It must attend to male power and to the eroticizing of domination in this culture. Because domination is eroticized, and

---

This essay was published originally in the *Annual of the Society of Christian Ethics* 10 (1990): 3–23.

because violence and sexuality are linked in the experiences of women, the search for loving heterosexual intimacy is for many women an exercise in irony: women must seek intimacy precisely in an arena that is culturally and experientially unsafe, fraught with sexual violence and power struggles.

Typical approaches to sexual ethics are therefore inadequate because they presume an equality, intimacy, and safety that does not exist for women. Rather, heterosexual women need to operate out of a "hermeneutic of suspicion" that does not ignore the role conditioning or status of men and women in this culture. I will use the term "enemy" as a role-relational term to highlight the need to be attentive to the dangers built into heterosexual sexuality. The attempt to form a heterosexual relationship can then be seen as an exercise in "loving your enemy." From African American reflections on living with the enemy, I then draw two norms for a heterosexual ethic: forgiveness and survival.

Women's Experience: Sexuality and Violence

Statistics on rape are notoriously unreliable, but most observers now agree that a conservative estimate suggests that at least one out of three women will be raped or will be the victim of attempted rape in her lifetime.[3] Rape and fear of rape are realities for many if not most women. Violence is directly linked with sexuality in the experience of many women.

What is particularly troubling is the *context* in which rape occurs. Popular images of the rapist perpetuate the myth that rape is an attack by a stranger. Indeed, the myth that rape is only committed by strangers may encourage men to attack the women with whom they are intimate, since—like the "friend" from "Dear Abby"—they do not believe that they can be charged with rape for forcing sexual intercourse on someone they know.

Rape is not committed only by strangers. In a study of nearly one thousand women, Diana Russell found that only 11 percent had been raped (or had been the victims of attempted rape) by strangers, while 12 percent had been raped by "dates," 14 percent by "acquaintances," and

14 percent by their husbands.[4] Thus, while roughly one woman in ten had been attacked by a stranger, more than one woman in three had been attacked by someone she knew. Rape or attempted rape does not happen just between strangers. It happens in intimate contexts, and in those intimate contexts it happens to more than one third of women. In a study of six thousand college students, 84 percent of the women who reported being attacked knew their attackers, and more than 50 percent of the rapes occurred on dates.[5] Moreover, these rapes are often the most violent: Menachem Amir found that the closer the relationship between the attacker and the victim, the greater was the use of physical force; neighbors and acquaintances were the most likely to engage in brutal rape.[6] Thus, not only are women not safe on the streets, they are not safe in presumably "intimate" contexts with trusted friends, neighbors, acquaintances, and even spouses.

The picture is even more complicated. If we look not at the *number of women* who experience rape or attempted rape but at the *number of attacks*, the picture changes dramatically. Of the total number of rapes reported by Diana Russell, *wife rape accounted for 38 percent of all attacks.* Nearly two fifths of rape crimes are perpetrated within the presumed intimacy of heterosexual marriage.[7] Thus, it is not only in *public places* that women must fear for our safety: the nuclear, heterosexual family is not a "safe space" for many women. Moreover, while violent rape by a stranger is something that most women will not experience more than once in their lives, violent rape by a spouse is clearly a repeated crime. Some women live with the daily threat of a repeated experience of rape within the most "intimate" of contexts: marriage.

The net result is that sexuality and violence are linked in the experience, memory,[8] and anticipation of many women. Those who have experienced rape or who live with a realistic appraisal of it as a constant threat may eventually come to live with "a fear of men which pervades all of life."[9]

Beverly Harrison charges that "a treatment of any moral problem is inadequate if it fails to analyze the morality of a given act in a way that represents the concrete experience of the agent who faces a decision with respect to that act."[10] If the concrete experience of so many women facing the realities of heterosexual sexuality is an experience of violence and fear, then any adequate Christian sexual ethic must account for the realities of rape, violence, and fear in women's lives.[11] Heterosexual women must formulate our sexual ethics within the context of understanding the ironies of searching for intimacy in an unsafe environment.

Eroticizing Dominance: The Social Construction of Sexuality

The problem is not just that rape occurs or that women experience violence and fear in the arena of sexuality. A treatment of any moral problem must not only represent the concrete experience of the agent(s) involved, but must also *understand that experience in its social construction.*[12]

The problem is not just that a man raped his twenty-four-year-old date, though this is serious enough. The problem is not only that rape is common, though it is. The problem is that the rapist's friend, like many others in this culture, does not think that what happened was rape and does not understand the difference between sexual violence and ordinary heterosexual sexuality.[13] The "friend" who writes to "Dear Abby" is not alone. Of the college women whose experiences of attack fit the legal definition of rape, 73 percent did not call it rape because they knew the attacker. Only 1 percent of the men involved were willing to admit that they had raped a woman. In another survey, over 50 percent of male teenagers and nearly 50 percent of female teenagers deemed it acceptable for a teenage boy to force sexual contact on a girl if he had dated her several times or if she said she was willing to have sex and then changed her mind.[14] Thus, in circumstances similar to those reported to "Dear Abby," a large number of young people would not consider forced sex to constitute rape.

Nor is it only teenagers who think it acceptable for men to force sexual contact on women. In another study, nearly 60 percent of "normal" American men said that if they could get away with it, they would force a woman to "commit sexual acts against her will." When the vague phrase "commit sexual acts against her will" was changed to the more specific term "rape," 20 percent still said they would do it if they could get away with it.[15]

In fact, men *do* get away with rape. Forcible rape has a lower conviction rate than any other crime listed in the Uniform Crime Reports.[16] A few years ago, a jury acquitted a man of the charge of rape even though the woman's jaw was fractured in two places as a result of her resistance; the acquittal rested on the finding that "there may have been sexual relations on previous occasions."[17] The confusion as to whether it is possible to rape a woman once she has consented to sexual relations therefore seems to be reflected in the law.[18] Given the attitude "I would do it if I could get away with it" and the fact that people do get away with it, it is no wonder that one out of three women will be raped or will be the victim of attempted rape.

Thus, violence has been structured into the system itself, structured into the very ways that we experience and think about heterosexual sexuality. Sexuality is not a mere "biological" phenomenon. It is socially constructed.[19] Sexual arousal may follow biological patterns, but *what* we find sexually arousing is culturally influenced and socially constructed. In short, there is a social dimension to even this most "intimate" of experiences, and in this culture sexuality, imbalances of power, and violence are linked. As Marie Fortune so pointedly puts it, "the tendency of this society to equate or confuse sexual activity with sexual violence is a predominant reality in our socialization, attitudes, beliefs, and behavior."[20] Thus, it is not only the actual experiences of violence and fear that we must address in order to have an adequate sexual ethic. We must also address the social construction of sexuality that creates the climate of violence and fear that permeates women's lives and confuses sexuality and violence.

Why is sexuality linked with violence in our socialization and experience? *The social construction of heterosexual sexuality in this culture has been largely based on patterns of dominance and submission in which men are expected to be dominant and women are expected to be submissive.* Men are expected to disregard women's protests and overcome their resistance. When a man "overpowers" a woman, is he raping her or is he simply being a man in both his eyes and hers?

Social domination is linked to cultural patterns in which men in general have more power than women do. Men are not only physically larger

in general, but they also possess power to control social, legal, financial, educational, and other important institutions. We are accustomed
to male power because it surrounds us. However, the point of interest is
not simply that men *have* power. Rather, the key factor is that male power
has become *eroticized*. Men and women alike are socialized not only to
think that being a man means being in control but also to find male domination sexually arousing. The overpowering of a woman is a paradigm
for "normal" heterosexual relations, at least among young people and in
segments of popular literature.

Studies of pornography demonstrate the eroticizing of domination in
this culture.[21] Andrea Dworkin, Nancy Hartsock, and others argue that
pornography is a window into one of the primary dynamics of the social construction of sexuality in this culture: "we can treat commercial
pornography as . . . expressing what our culture has defined as sexually
exciting."[22] Pornography would suggest that men are socialized to find
both male power and female powerlessness sexually arousing.[23] In pornography, domination of women by men is portrayed as sexy. It is the
power of the man or men[24] to make the woman do what she does not
want to do—to make her do something humiliating, degrading, or an-
tithetical to her character—that creates the sexual tension and excitement. Dworkin puts it bluntly: the major theme of pornography is male
power, and the means to achieve it is the degradation of the female.[25]
Since power-as-domination always has at least an indirect link with violence, this means that there is at least an indirect link between sexual
arousal and violence in this culture.[26] In pornography, women are raped,
tied up, beaten, humiliated—*and* are portrayed as initially resisting and
ultimately enjoying their degradation. No wonder many real-life rapists
actually believe that women enjoy sadomasochistic sex or "like" to be
forced;[27] this is the constant message of pornography.

Pornography is big business.[28] While pornography may not reflect
the active *choices* of all men in this culture, it reflects a significant dimension of the *socialization* of both men and women.

However, it is not only men in this culture who find male power or female powerlessness sexy. Women in this culture (even feminist women,

as Marianna Valverde so devastatingly demonstrates)[29] are attracted to powerful men, whether that power is defined in macho, beer-can-crushing terms or in the more subtle dynamics of social, economic, and political power.[30] Women also link violence and sexuality. In Nancy Friday's classic study of women's sexual fantasies, "Julietta" gives voice to this pattern: "While I enjoy going to bed with some guy I dig almost any time, I especially like it if there's something in the air that lets me think I'm doing it against my will. That I'm being forced by the man's overwhelming physical strength."[31] Julietta is sexually aroused, at least in fantasy, by the thought of being overpowered. Nor is she alone. In *Shared Intimacies: Women's Sexual Experiences*, Lonnie Barbach and Linda Levine report that women's most frequent fantasies are "variations on the theme of being dominant and submissive."[32] Not all women link domination and eroticism, but the pattern is there.

Since men and women alike are socialized both to expect men to overpower women and to find the exercise of power sexually arousing, it is no wonder that the boundary between acceptable "normal" sexual exchange and rape has been blurred. The letter to "Dear Abby" exposes the confusion that arises in a culture that links dominance with eroticism and implies that sexual arousal and satisfaction involve a man overpowering a woman. The "friend" assumes that the woman secretly likes to be forced and that rape is acceptable on some level because on some level it cannot be distinguished from regular sexual contact.

Criteria for an Adequate Ethics

It is plain, then, that to be adequate, Christian sexual ethics must deal not only with the realities of rape and fear in women's lives, but also with socialization patterns in which both men and women are socialized to find male power and female powerlessness sexually arousing. It must deal with the realities of the link between violence and sexuality in this culture, and it must understand the ways in which the social construction of sexuality contributes to the lived experiences of women and men. Only in this way will we truly link the personal with the political; only in this way can we bring moral reflection on sexual behavior into line with the fact that sexual relations are political and not merely personal.

To be adequate, Christian moral reflection must begin with real experience, not with romantic fantasies about love, marriage, and the family. We must name the realities of sexual violence in women's lives. We must take account of the fact that women often experience their sexuality in a context of rape, date rape, acquaintance rape, forced sexual contact, and spousal rape. If nearly 40 percent of rapes happen within heterosexual marriage, then a sexual ethic for heterosexuals must account for this real, lived, concrete experience of women. A Christian sexual ethic must have something to say to the man who raped his twenty-four-year-old date, to the woman who was raped, and to the "friend" and everyone else who is confused about what constitutes acceptable sexual contact between men and women.

To be adequate, Christian sexual ethics must carry out cultural analysis and mount a cultural critique. We must attend not only to the differences in power between men and women in a sexist culture, but also to the distortions that such differences in power have brought to the experience of sexuality itself. An ethic based on assumptions of mutuality and consent falls short of dealing with the social construction of sexuality in terms of the eroticizing of dominance and submission.

To be adequate, Christian sexual ethics must develop a role-based model of personal sexual relations because only a role-based model is adequate to the moral complexities that are exposed when we begin to take seriously the degree to which our sexuality and our sexual interactions are socially constructed. Women are not respected in the sexual arena, but are raped, attacked, and treated as objects. At the same time, heterosexual women seek to trust, love, and be intimate with those who have the power to rape, attack, and be disrespectful.[33] The twenty-four-year-old woman who was raped by her date must now struggle to find intimacy with those who will represent for her the violence in her memory and life. Other heterosexual women will "make love" to spouses who have raped them before and will rape them again. All heterosexual women seek partners from among those who represent the power of male domination in this culture. There are ambiguities and ironies in the search for intimacy in all these contexts. An adequate Christian sexual ethics must attend to these ambiguities and ironies.

A Hermeneutics of Suspicion

The first step for such an ethic will certainly be a "hermeneutics of suspicion." The distortions of culture must be exposed for what they are. This means that we ask first whether patterns of sexual arousal based on male domination and female submission are trustworthy patterns.

To say that women eroticize domination in fantasy is not to say what happens when women actually experience sexual domination. Since the issue of forced sex came up repeatedly in her interviews, Shere Hite finally asked women whether they were afraid to say no to a man's overtures, and if so, how they felt during and after the act of intercourse. Uniformly, the women indicated that they did *not* find sex pleasurable under such circumstances and that they experienced anger and feelings of powerlessness.[34] Whatever their fantasies may be, women do not in fact like being forced and do not enjoy sex when it happens against their will. Barbach and Levine put it bluntly: "what women enjoy in fantasy and what they actually find arousing in reality are two very different things."[35]

The famous "Hite report" on women's sexuality surfaced evidence that many women who are fully capable of orgasm and frequently do achieve orgasm during masturbation do not in fact have orgasms during heterosexual intercourse. Why, Hite asked, "do women so habitually satisfy men's needs during sex and ignore their own?"[36] Her answer is that "sexual slavery has been an almost unconscious way of life for most women." One of Hite's subjects put it bluntly: "sex can be political in the sense that it can involve a power structure where the woman is unwilling or unable to get what she really needs for her fullest amount of pleasure, but the man is getting what he wants."[37] Hite concludes that lack of sexual satisfaction (perhaps better: lack of joy, pleasure, the erotic) is another sign of the oppression of women.

The first step toward an adequate Christian sexual ethics for hetero-sexual people, then, is to expose cultural patterns in which sexuality becomes a political struggle and in which domination is eroticized. The first step is an active hermeneutics of suspicion.

Power and Sex: The Need for a Role-based Morality

If the first step for such an ethic is a hermeneutic of suspicion, I believe that the second step is a recovery of the significance of role and status.

In other arenas of ethical inquiry, the significance of role or status would not be questioned. For example, in their role as pastor, ministers hold professional power. They also represent ministry, the church, and even God in the eyes of parishioners. Based on their role or status, there is a power gap between pastor and parishioner. Because of this power gap, pastor and parishioner do not come into sexual arenas as "equals,"[38] and sexual approaches by a pastor to a parishioner are problematic at best.[39] In short, the power that attaches to the pastoral role is morally relevant for determining what is ethically acceptable for a pastor to do in the sexual arena. If the power that attaches to the pastoral role/status is morally relevant in determining an appropriate sexual ethic, then the power that attaches to any role/status is *also* morally relevant. This means that the power of men in a sexist culture is morally relevant for determining an appropriate sexual ethic for men and women. If sexual contact between people is ethically problematic when one has more power than the other, then all heterosexual sexual contact is ethically problematic in a sexist society.

What we need is an approach to sexual ethics that can take seriously the power that attaches to a man in this culture simply because he is a man (no matter how powerless he may feel), the power that he has as representative of other men, and the power that he has for women as representative of the politics of dominance and submission and as representative of the threat of violence in women's lives.

I believe that many heterosexual women know this and live it in our everyday lives. Yet we have been reluctant to deal with its implications on the theoretical level. We have been leery of a sexual morality that pays attention to roles or status—with good reason: too often, paying attention to roles has meant that it is "woman's place" to please or serve the man. However, in our efforts to reject inappropriate roles for women, we are in danger of assuming that all attention to role or status in sexual morality should be taboo. Because the traditional roles assigned to men and women were sexist, there is a tendency, even among feminists, to seek a role-less or role-free morality. Thus, feminists speak of "intimacy," "mutuality," "reciprocity," and "sharing" as central to sexual ethics. Such terms assume an equality of the partners involved. This assumption may be valid in lesbian or gay circles.[40] Nonetheless, it is precisely my argument that *the partners involved in heterosexual sexuality are not equal in power or status in this culture* and that therefore a sexual ethics that assumes their equality and ignores differences in power will be an inherently flawed sexual ethics.

In a sexist culture, women do not have equal freedom, knowledge, and power with men. Their "consent" to engage in heterosexual sexual exchange is therefore circumscribed by cultural distributions of power. Until these distributions are attended to, we will not have an adequate sexual ethics.

I propose that *the man's status or role as representative of those who have power in the culture is important in the development of a sexual ethic.* The representative nature of men as people with power in this culture needs to be kept before us. Even when the individual man works hard not to be an oppressor, his representative role should not be ignored any more than the pastor's representative role and its attendant power should be ignored. In other words, we need to keep the political dimensions before us, rather than retreating to a private language of mutuality, relationality, and sharing.

I use the term "enemy" to indicate the man's role as representative of those who have power in this culture. I am aware of the dangers of labeling anyone as the "enemy." In her recent book, *Women and Evil*, Nel Noddings argues that when we label someone as the enemy, we devalue that person's moral worth.[41] It is not my purpose to return to a labeling and condemnation of men that often characterized the feminist movement a number of years ago; neither do I wish to devalue the worth of men.[42] Many men today are working hard to divest themselves of the vestiges of sexism that affect them. Not all men experience their sexual arousal along patterns defined by traditional pornography with its degradation of women. "Enemy" is a strong term, and to suggest that it can be used to designate the role of men because of the power of men in a sexist society is to run the risk of misunderstanding. Nonetheless, in the situation of the young woman who was raped, it is not unwarranted to suggest that her date has proven himself to be her "enemy," to be one who will vent his anger and use his power against her by using her for his own ends without regard for her person, her feelings, or her needs. Similarly, for the 25 percent of college women who also experience rape or attempted rape, we need a strong word. Precisely because the term "enemy" is strong, and even problematic, it will force us to take seriously the issues involved.

"Love Your Enemy": Toward a Christian Sexual Ethic

If we understand men and women to be in power positions that can be characterized by the role designation "enemy," then an examination of the meaning of "love of enemies" may contribute something to an ethic for heterosexual sexuality. While I believe that the meaning of love of enemies can usefully illumine the moral situation from both the man's and the woman's side, I will focus here on the woman's plight and on what love of enemy might mean for her.

I will frame this discussion with two words drawn from reflections of black Christian ethicists. African Americans in this country have had reason to struggle with what it is to be in relationship with those who stand in the role of enemy and to explore the meaning of "love of enemies." I will therefore take the words of a black man and the words of a black woman as each offering insight into the meaning of ethics in a context of "enemies."[43] These two words set boundaries within which a new approach to heterosexual sexual ethics as an exercise in "loving your enemy" might take place.

The first word is *forgiveness*. For the explication of this term I turn to Martin Luther King, Jr. King situates forgiveness at the heart of love of enemies: "The degree to which we are able to forgive determines the degree to which we are able to love our enemies."[44] One cannot even begin the act of loving the enemy, he argues, without prior acceptance of the necessity of forgiving, over and over again, those who inflict evil and injury upon us.

Forgiveness is a difficult word for many women to hear. What would it mean to tell the young woman who has been raped to forgive? Significantly, forgiveness does *not* mean ignoring the past or moving prematurely to reconciliation. On this, King is clear: "forgiveness does not mean ignoring what has been done or putting a false label on an evil act."[45] The Amanencida Collective puts it even more strongly: "to grant pardon, those on the receiving end must recognize their actions as being wrong, in need of pardon."[46] Hence, recognition of the injustices in the situation is part and parcel of forgiveness and hence part and parcel of love of enemies.

According to King, forgiveness means that the evil act no longer serves as a barrier to relationship. Forgiveness is the establishment of an atmosphere that makes possible a fresh start. The woman who has been raped and who then begins to date again—taking the risk that she will be able to find a safe space with a man, even though he represents the power of men and the very violence that she has experienced—is exercising "forgiveness." She is declaring her willingness to enter relationship.

In short, while forgiveness means that "the evil deed is no longer a mental block impeding a new relationship,"[47] the stress here needs to be on *new* relationship. To forgive does not mean going back to the relationship the way it was or accepting the evils perpetrated within it. Love of enemies, for King, begins in forgiveness, but forgiveness itself begins in the recognition of something that needs to be forgiven and, therefore, in the recognition of injustices that need to be redressed. Love of enemies requires justice.[48] Indeed, Paul Lauritzen argues that, in the absence of repentance, forgiveness may even be "morally objectionable" because it can involve "an unjustifiable abandonment of the appropriate retributive response to wrongdoing."[49] The stress in forgiveness is on recognition of the evil. The evil must be named for what it is, and the participants must be willing to establish a new relationship that does not incorporate that evil. Forgiveness means that we must be willing to set things right so that there can be a fresh start. Forgiveness is essentially restorative.[50] Where there is a concrete evil fact such as rape, forgiveness may require repentance; where the man is not himself one who rapes but simply one who represents the power of men in sexist society, forgiveness requires a willingness to establish a relationship based on justice.

Forgiveness, then, is not sentimentality; it requires recognition of injustice and redress of injustice. It is based on truth. Forgiveness means that the relationship is changed, but that the enemy remains the enemy.[51] Forgiveness does not mean that we recognize no one as enemy; rather, forgiveness means that we recognize that though an individual or group stands in the role of enemy, yet we can seek a relationship with that person or group that is a relationship free of injustice. While love of enemies requires forgiveness, the link between forgiveness and justice must be remembered.

This brings me to the second word, *survival*. Women who have been raped often speak of themselves as "survivors." This word then seems appropriate for a heterosexual ethics directed to women who are aware of the dynamics of male dominance and violence in their lives.

For an explication of survival, I draw on Katie Cannon's work. "Throughout the history of the United States," declares Cannon, "the interrelationship of white supremacy and male superiority has characterized the Black woman's moral situation as a situation of struggle— a struggle to survive."[52] Being sexually and socially exploited by both white and black males, black women developed skills to "prevail against the odds with integrity."[53] In a situation where freedom and choice and consent "have proven to be false in the real-lived texture of Black life,"[54] and where sex is experienced both as an act of love *and* as an act of terror,[55] ethics cannot be based on assumptions that grow out of control, power, or freedom—the prerequisites of consent or mutuality. Instead, a different ethic (and by extension, I would argue, a different sexual ethic) emerges.

Black female protagonists, argues Cannon, are portrayed in black women's literature as women for whom survival is an overriding ethical perspective. They are "women with hard-boiled honesty, a malaise of dual allegiance, down-to-earth thinking, the ones who are forced to see through shallowness, hypocrisy and phoniness in their continual struggle for survival."[56] There were things that the black woman had to tell her children even though she did not want to (e.g., to say "Sir" or "Ma'am" to those who were their sworn enemies) so that they would survive. And there were things that she wanted to tell her husband (e.g., that a white man had leered at her) but did not dare, lest it provoke her husband to an action that might cost his life. Survival was the test for how one dealt with one's sexuality and how one handled being black and female in the midst of an oppressive culture.

These qualities of hard-boiled honesty, dual allegiance, down-to-earth thinking, and seeing through hypocrisy are important for heterosexual women of all colors. We need to learn a hard-boiled honesty and a down-to-earth thinking that debunks the romantic myths that link our sexuality with dominance and submission. We need to listen to our dual allegiance that makes us both love this enemy and yet fear (justifiably) for our well-being in a sexist culture. We need to see through the hypocrisy of a culture and a religion that neglects the violence against women and urges women toward premature reconciliation or toward a "love" of men not based on justice. Perhaps above all, those of us who are white as well as female and who therefore benefit as well as suffer from the current social construction of sexuality, need to learn to "face life squarely, front and center, without reverence or protection by the dominant powers in society."[57] In short, we need skills oriented toward survival.

Cannon's perspective seems important to me because it does not postulate what Hartsock calls "an artificial community of formal equals"[58] whose sexual relations can be described in terms of consent and mutuality. Rather, Cannon recognizes that all people do not have equal power and that issues of unequal power are central to ethical decision-making.

Ethics must be done with attention to the social construction of experience and to the ongoing history of a community.

As forgiveness, with its implicit recognition of injustices that need rectification, is the first word to illumine love of enemies, so survival with its hard-nosed realism is the second. The twenty-four-year-old woman who has been raped should forgive her attacker (enemy) only if he acknowledges wrong-doing, repents, and seeks a new relationship free of power, domination, and violence. She should seek relationship with those men who are actively struggling to combat the legacy of a sexist culture. She should love her enemies, both specific and representative, but she should not lose sight of the fact that she is dealing with "enemies," understood in a role-relational sense.[59] Her survival should be central to the meaning of love of enemies.

I would therefore argue that feminist analyses of culture that intend to expose injustices are themselves an act of love for the enemy and should remain part and parcel of any heterosexual sexual relationship. Those analyses intend to help men as well as women move to the point where we can redress injustices, set things right, and have the possibility for that joyful eroticism we want to develop. Women who are heterosexual should neither give up their feminism nor mute the power of the feminist critique of the culture.

Is it possible to love the person and yet recognize and hold this feminist stance? Retaining perspective and critique is often one of the hardest things to do. Too often, we have taken love to mean putting oneself aside. Stephen Mott comes dangerously close to this when he urges that the minimal statement of Christian love is looking to the other's well-being and not to our own self-benefit and that the highest expression of love is self-sacrifice.[60] Similarly, Sam Keen argues that the first step in love of enemies is what he calls *metanoia*, the perceptual movement away from what we consider to be the center.[61]

Like most feminists, I am very uneasy about any understanding of love or forgiveness that urges a losing of the self or of the self's perspective, for this contradicts the value of survival. One of the things that happens all too often to women, particularly in abusive situations, is a tendency to lose their own perspective. The story of Alice will illustrate. When first visited in the hospital where she had nearly died from severe damage to her kidneys following a beating by her husband, Alice described being pushed into the stove and "stomped on" by her husband Mike. A week later, after Mike had brought her flowers, made apologies, and promised to mend his ways, Alice changed her description of the incident: "perhaps it was my fault. Mike says he didn't really throw me against the stove. He just pushed at me, and I fell . . ."[62] Alice gives up her own testimony that she was in fact pushed and beaten in the face of pressure from her spouse to change her story ("Mike says . . .") and because of her own desire to keep her relationship with him intact ("How could someone so kind and gentle like Mike, someone that I could love so much and who could love me so much, do this to me?"). Here, Alice lost her perspective; she exchanged it for Mike's perspective in the effort to retain relationship.

I would argue that Alice cannot genuinely love Mike if she gives up her own perspective or moves too quickly to reconciliation. Fortunately, we have also come to a better understanding of the need for self-love as a part of *agape*. There can be no *agape* if the agent loses herself; without a self, love is impossible. The agent's own integrity and "endeavor to stay with his or her own considered insights and commitments" are central to the ability to love, as Gene Outka notes.[63] Alice cannot really love Mike if she ignores the fact that he *is* her "enemy," understood in role-relational terms. "Love of enemies" cannot mean a forgiveness that ignores injustices or loses the perspective that there *are* enemies. This is probably the most important task for women. A role-based morality never ignores the fact that the other by whom I am confronted is historically conditioned by a specific culture and will represent and carry the scars of that culture, just as I do.

It is partly for this reason that I am less sanguine than some of my feminist colleagues about relational ethics. Minimally, I would argue that all of our relationships are mediated to a certain extent through roles and status and that our roles and status are culturally conditioned and socially constructed. Even as we are in the midst of attempting to change those roles, it is still important that we attend to them. We need a heterosexual sexual ethic that neither permits nor encourages loss of perspective and of self. To speak only the language of relationality, intimacy, or mutuality is to offer Alice no clues as to how to deal with the "enemy" in her own household. As much as we may love the individual, it is important to deal with that individual as standing in a role and therefore representing the cultural conditioning that attaches to that role.

Noddings argues that it is when we deal with others as representatives, rather than as concrete others, that we can do evil to them.[64] I recognize the dangers in dealing with others as representatives rather than as concrete persons, and I would not suggest that we ever ignore the concrete reality of the other. As Martin Luther King, Jr., puts it, "we must recognize that the evil deed of the enemy-neighbor, the thing that hurts, never quite expresses all that he is."[65] The man who is representative of domination and violence toward women, who stands in the role of "enemy" in that sense, is nonetheless a person with his own pains and history. By suggesting that "love of enemies" may be a helpful category for looking at heterosexual ethics, it is not my purpose to ignore the personal histories and pains of individual men, but rather to recognize the significance of social constructions and historical contingencies in ethics.

I seek a sexual ethics that does not abstract men and women from the concrete historical realities that have shaped us. Given the historical and cultural link between heterosexual sexuality and the pattern of dominance and submission, I think that an adequate sexual ethic for heterosexuals must be informed by a recognition of the representative nature of men and women and therefore by the meaning of "love of enemies."[66]

To recognize the other whom one loves as "enemy" and to deal with the enemy in terms of roles means to remember that each of us represents what Gustavo Gutiérrez would call a "class"—a group that is socialized differently and has different understandings and perspectives because of that socialization. Women's and men's experiences of the world are different. To remember that the one we love is in the role of "enemy" is to remember this fact. To recognize the one whom one loves as "enemy" is to accept the implications of the social construction of sexuality and to understand that the task is not simply to create a private haven into which one can retreat, but is to work for a new social construction of sexuality that will undo the injustices that permeate the present culture.

Heterosexual love is a very difficult task for a woman who is also a feminist. The heterosexual woman must love a concrete other who is a distinct individual with his own history. He is also a man and therefore represents the socialization of heterosexuality into patterns of domination and submission. Sexuality is not only God's marvelous gift to the human race, it is also a social construction fraught with the problems of human power relations. To love the concrete other who is also the enemy is to walk between forgiveness and survival.

Questions for Reflection

1. Karen Lebacqz argues that domination and submission have been eroticized in our culture. What evidence does she offer in support of that claim? Do you agree with her?

2. Given the commonplace nature of intimate partner violence, Lebacqz suggests it is wise to abandon romantic illusions and bring a "hermeneutic of suspicion" to our sexual partnerships. Why and how would significant differences in power and status between partners make intimacy (potentially at least) hazardous for some?

3. Lebacqz suggests that Christian sexual ethics should incorporate elements similar to those embodied by many in the African American community who practice "love of enemy." Christian forms of faithful self-love (far from selfishness) recognize the value of survival and acknowledge that genuine reconciliation requires the formation of truly new relationships that rest on authentic repentance; such self-love does not ignore injustices or risks thereof. What do you think the practice of forgiveness entails?

Suggestions for Further Reading

Davis, Tawana, Owen Strachan, Lindsey A. Holcomb, and Justin S. Holcomb. "After Domestic Violence, Why Should a Christian Wife Call the Police, Not a Pastor, First? Addressing a Sin That at Some Point Afflicts 1 in 4 US Women." *Christianity Today* 59.1 (January–February 2015): 26–27.

Dyer, Jacqueline T. "Just Social Work? Collaborating with African American Clergy to Address Intimate Partner Violence in Churches." *Social Work & Christianity* 43.4 (Winter 2016): 33–54.

Fortune, Marie. *Sexual Violence: The Sin Revisited*. Cleveland, OH: Pilgrim Press, 2005.

Mayo, Maria. "Passionate Prayer or Pastoral Pressure?: Forgiveness in Luke 23:34a and the Pastoral Care of Victims of Domestic Violence." *The Limits of Forgiveness: Case Studies in the Distortion of a Biblical Ideal*, Chapter 4, 159–206. Minneapolis, MN: Fortress Press, 2015.

Nadar, Sarojini, and Cheryl Potgieter. "Liberated through Submission? The Worthy Woman's Conference as a Case Study for Formenism." *Journal of Feminist Studies in Religion* 26.2 (Fall 2010): 141–151.

Vasko, Elizabeth. "The Difference Gender Makes: Nuptiality, Analogy and the Limits of Appropriating Hans Urs von Balthasar's Theology in the Context of Sexual Violence." *Journal of Religion* 94.4 (October 2014): 504–528.

Notes

1. *San Francisco Chronicle*, January 7, 1990, Sunday Punch section.

2. Marie Marshall Fortune, *Sexual Violence: The Unmentionable Sin* (New York: Pilgrim Press, 1983), 22.

3. The National Institutes of Health and *Ms.* magazine recently conducted a study of six thousand college students; their findings are reported in the videotape *Against Her Will: Rape on Campus*, narrated by Kelly McGillis. The study established that one out of four women had been raped or had been the victim of attempted rape on campus. These statistics reflect only those who experienced attack on campus and do not reflect child sexual abuse, marital rape, or other attacks that raise the average.

4. Diana Russell, *Rape in Marriage* (New York: Collier Books, 1962), reported in Linda A. Moody, "In Search of Sacred Spaces," *American Baptist Quarterly* 8/2 (June 1989): 109–10.

5. *Against Her Will: Rape on Campus.*

6. Menachem Amir, "Forcible Rape," *Federal Probation* 31/1 (1967): 51, reported in Diane Herman, "The Rape Culture," in *Women: A Feminist Perspective,* ed. Jo Freeman (Palo Alto, CA: Mayfield, 1979), 50.

7. Indeed, Andre Guindon notes that half the crimes in North America are perpetrated within the heterosexual family and suggests that images of man as the violent one contribute not only to these crimes but also to those perpetrated outside the heterosexual family. See *The Sexual Creators: An Ethical Proposal for Concerned Christians* (New York: University Press of America, 1986), 173.

8. It is hard to overestimate the long-term effects of rape, especially when the

victim is a young child or girl or when the rape is the victim's first sexual experience. Most rapes are in fact perpetrated on very young victims.

9. Carole R. Bonn, "Dominion to Rule: The Roots and Consequences of a
Theology of Ownership," in *Christianity, Patriarchy and Abuse: A Feminist Critique*, ed. Joanne Carlson Brown and Carole R. Bonn (New York: Pilgrim Press,
1989), 109.

10. Beverly Wildung Harrison, "Theology and Morality of Procreative
Choice," in *Making the Connections: Essays in Feminist Social Ethics*, ed. Carol S.
Robb (Boston: Beacon Press, 1985), 123.

11. Indeed, I am convinced that the treatment of sexual ethics is inadequate because it fails to represent the concrete experience of women, including both our
experiences of pain and our experiences of erotic joy. The feminist literature has
begun to reflect both of these concerns.

12. While this is not explicit in the quotation above, it is both implicit and explicit elsewhere in Harrison's work.

13. Legal definitions of rape vary from state to state. In the past, in some juris-
dictions rape has been defined in such a way that attack of one's spouse would *not*
have fit the definition of rape. Most states today have definitions along the lines of
that proposed by Fortune (*Sexual Violence*, 7): "forced penetration by the penis or
any object of the vagina, mouth, or anus against the will of the victim."

14. These statistics are reported in Fortune, *Sexual Violence*, 2. They are taken
from Laurel Fingier, "Teenagers in Survey Condone Forced Sex," *Ms.*, February
1981, 23.

15. Carol Turkington, "Sexual Aggression Widespread," *APA Monitor* 18/13
(1987): 15, quoted in Polly Young-Eisendrath and Demaris Wehr, "The Fallacy of
Individualism and Reasonable Violence against Women," in *Christianity, Patriarchy and Abuse*, ed. Brown and Bonn, 136.

16. Camille E. LeGrand, "Rape and Rape Laws: Sexism in Society and Law,"
California Law Review 61/3 (1973): 927, reported in Herman, "The Rape Culture,"
in *Women: A Feminist Perspective*, ed. Freeman, 57.

17. Herman, "The Rape Culture," in *Women: A Feminist Perspective*, ed. Freeman, 57.

18. Herman argues that this attitude reflects the clear understanding of women
as the property of men. In this regard, L. William Countryman's *Dirt, Greed, and
Sex: Sexual Ethics in the New Testament and Their Implications for Today* (Philadelphia: Fortress Press, 1988) is instructive.

19. It is often difficult to see this, because we think of the erotic dimension as
personal, private, or biological. In *Intimate Matters: A History of Sexuality in America* (New York: Harper and Row, 1988), John D'Emilio and Estelle B. Freedman
demonstrate that the assumption that sexuality is oriented toward erotic and personal pleasure is itself a modern development.

20. Fortune, *Sexual Violence*, 16.

21. While there is no single definition of pornography, I take Marianna Valverde's to be consonant with that of most other feminist thinkers. Valverde proposes that pornography is characterized by (1) the portrayal of men's social and physical power over women as sexy, (2) the depiction of aggression as the inevitable result of power imbalances, such that we expect the rape of the powerless by the powerful, and (3) the idea of sex as having a relentless power to cut across social barriers and conventions, so that people will do things to others that would not normally be expected (e.g., rape a nun). See Marianna Valverde, *Sex, Power and Pleasure* (Philadelphia: New Society Publishers, 1987), 129f. Particularly important in Valverde's analysis, however, is her recognition that pornography cannot be defined solely by the content of the material, but must also be defined by its *use*—e.g., the commercialization of sex. See also Mary Hunt, "Theological Pornography: From Corporate to Communal Ethics," in *Christianity, Patriarchy and Abuse*, ed. Brown and Bonn.

22. Nancy C. M. Hartsock, *Money, Sex and Power: Toward a Feminist Historical Materialism* (Boston: Northeastern University Press, 1985), 168.

23. The Professional Ethics Group of the Center for Ethics and Social Policy at the Graduate Theological Union has had a grant from the Lilly Endowment to conduct studies of pastors. These studies suggest that many men find a woman's tears or other signs of vulnerability very sexually arousing. We had one pastor in our study who claimed that he was addicted to pornography.

24. Pornography often depicts group attacks on a woman. Similarly, rape itself is often done by gangs or in the presence of other men. See Herman, "The Rape Culture," in *Women: A Feminist Perspective*, ed. Freeman, 47.

25. Andrea Dworkin, *Pornography: Men Possessing Women* (London: The Women's Press, 1981), 24–25. Dworkin argues (69) that pornography reveals an inextricable link between male pleasure and the victimizing, hurting, and exploitation of women: "sexual fun and sexual passion in the privacy of the male imagination are inseparable from the brutality of male history." I think that to claim that male pleasure is "inextricably" tied to hurting the other is too strong. Nonetheless, the prevalence and power of pornography in our midst demonstrates that much pleasure for both men and women has been tied to having power to make another person do what is humiliating.

26. The roots of violence need further exploration. In *Touching Our Strength* (San Francisco: Harper and Row, 1989), 13–15, Carter Heyward notes that the recent work of the Stone Center for Developmental Services and Studies at Wellesley College, Massachusetts, suggests that the roots of violent abuse lie in socialization for separation, in which we are cut off from the possibilities of mutuality and joy in our most important relationships.

27. Herman, "The Rape Culture," in *Women: A Feminist Perspective*, ed. Freeman, 47.

28. Hunt, "Theological Pornography," in *Christianity, Patriarchy and Abuse*, ed. Brown and Bonn, 95.

29. Valverde, *Sex, Power and Pleasure*, 62.

30. In *Office Romance: Love, Power, and Sex in the Workplace* (New York: Rawson Associates, 1989), 159, Lisa A. Mainiero quotes one executive woman as saying, "The combination of power and business judgment can be a real turn-on. It's sexy as hell."

31. Nancy Friday, *My Secret Garden: Women's Sexual Fantasies* (New York: Pocket Books, 1973), 110.

32. Lonnie Barbach and Linda Levine, *Shared Intimacies: Women's Sexual Experiences* (New York: Bantam Books, 1980), 123.

33. Two caveats need to be entered here. First, Mariana Valverde (*Sex, Power and Pleasure*, 47) charges that, due to the wide range of heterosexual experiences, we cannot speak confidently about heterosexuality in general. Second, Harrison and Heyward ("Pain and Pleasure," 148) charge that in the sexual arena more than in any other, feminists tend to impose their own morality on others. My intention is neither to label all heterosexual men or women, nor to impose an ethic on them, but rather to lift up dimensions of experience that have been neglected, in hopes that those dimensions might assist at least some women in the effort to create a Christian sexual ethic that takes their experience seriously. I am also keenly aware that what I will describe here is culture-bound and may not speak as helpfully to those from different backgrounds.

34. Shere Hite, *The Hite Report* (New York: Dell Publishing Co., 1976), 461–62. One woman said, "I felt like hell—angry and unhappy." Another "hated" herself for being afraid to say no. Another thought she was not "supposed" to say no since she was married; she "faked orgasms."

35. Barbach and Levine, *Shared Intimacies*, 125. The responses also make clear that women do not always feel that they can say no and that women will tend to blame themselves instead of the man—hating their own passivity or "weakness." They further make clear that women will fake orgasm rather than confront their partner with the truth of their dislike. Deception is a technique commonly used by those with little power against their oppressors.

36. Hite, *The Hite Report*, 419.

37. Ibid., 420. Whether men are in fact getting what they want is, of course, also an issue. My own interpretation would be that in an oppressive society, most men also do not get what they really want.

38. Karen Lebacqz, "Pastor-Parishioner Sexuality. An Ethical Analysis," *Explore* 9 (Spring 1988): 67–81.

39. See Marie Marshall Fortune, *Is Nothing Sacred? When Sex Invades the Pastoral Relationship* (San Francisco: Harper and Row, 1989) and Peter Rutter, *Sex in the Forbidden Zone: When Men in Power—Therapists, Doctors, Clergy, Teachers, and Others—Betray Women's Trust* (Los Angeles: Jeremy P. Tarcher, Inc., 1989).

40. Indeed, I am personally convinced that those in the "straight" community have much to learn from those who have not been confined by male-female patterns of relating.

41. Nel Noddings, *Women and Exile* (Berkeley: University of California Press, 1989), 198.

42. In *Talking Back: Thinking Feminist, Thinking Black* (Boston: South End Press, 1989), 127, Bell Hooks argues that labeling men "the enemy" in the early stages of the feminist movement was an effective way to begin the critical separation that women needed in order to effect rebellion, but that as the movement has matured, we have seen the error in such separation and have come to appreciate the need for the transformation of masculinity as part of the feminist movement.

43. In so doing, I will no doubt stretch and possibly misuse their insights; if so, I offer my most genuine apologies. Nothing could prove better how socially constructed all of our realities are than the difficulties experienced by a white person of some privilege in trying to utilize insights drawn from black experience.

44. Martin Luther King, Jr., *Strength to Love* (London: Hodder and Staughton, 1963), 43.

45. Ibid., 35. Similarly, Paul Tillich argues that in accepting someone into the unity of forgiveness, *"love exposes . . . the acknowledged break with justice"* (*Love, Power, and Justice* [New York: Oxford University Press, 1954], 86).

46. Carter Heyward et al., *Revolutionary Forgiveness: Feminist Reflections on Nicaragua* (Maryknoll: Orbis Press, 1987), 93.

47. King, *Strength to Love*, 35.

48. Ibid.

49. Paul Lauritzen, "Forgiveness: Moral Prerogative or Religious Duty?" *Journal of Religious Ethics* 15/2 (Fall 1987): 150. Lauritzen does argue (151), however, that in the context of religious belief, forgiveness *can* be given without repentance on the other's part because the forgiveness itself takes away the character of the sin.

50. Ibid., 143. Forgiveness is then akin to "jubilee justice"; see Karen Lebacqz, *Justice in an Unjust World: Foundations for a Christian Approach to Justice* (Minneapolis: Augsburg Press, 1987).

51. Victor Furnish, *The Love Command in the New Testament*, 67, quoted in Lauritzen, "Forgiveness," 150.

52. Katie G. Cannon, *Black Womanist Ethics* (Atlanta: Scholars Press, 1988), 6–7.

53. Ibid., 7.

54. Ibid., 75.

55. Ibid., 85.

56. Ibid., 89.

57. Ibid., 125.

58. Hartsock, *Money, Sex and Power*, 177.

59. In this regard, I have not found the literature on love of enemies as helpful as I wished. Most of it is focused on instances where we clearly recognize our enemy, whereas I am trying to deal with a situation where we do not recognize that we are in fact dealing with an enemy and where recognition is the first step (see Lebacqz,

Justice in an Unjust World, 108f.). Also, the literature focuses on attitudes rather than roles; its primary concern is reducing enmity (cf. Stephen C. Mott, *Biblical Ethics and Social Change* [New York: Oxford University Press, 1982], 37). If "enemy" is understood as a culturally constructed role, then the task is not to reduce hatred but to ask how one loves the person who stands in a particular role, just as one might ask about love of mother, sister, teacher, etc.

60. Mott, *Biblical Ethics and Social Change*, 42.

61. Sam Keen, *Faces of the Enemy: Reflections of the Hostile Imagination* (San Francisco: Harper and Row, 1986).

62. This story is reported in Polly Young-Eisendrath and Demaris Wehr, "The Fallacy of Individualism and Reasonable Violence against Women," in *Christianity, Patriarchy and Abuse*, ed. Brown and Bonn, 127–28.

63. Gene Outka, *Agape: An Ethical Analysis* (New Haven: Yale University Press, 1972), 35.

64. Noddings, *Women and Evil*, 211. Note, though, that *agape* itself appears to be tied to status/role issues, not to questions of personal attitude. Outka says that *agape* is regard for the neighbor that in crucial respects is independent and unalterable, implying that it is indeed given to the other not because of personal likes or tastes but because of the status of the other as person. *Agape* deals with putting others into the role of "neighbor." It is a role-relational term.

65. King, *Strength to Love*, 36.

66. The analogy may be particularly apt since there is evidence to suggest that the term *echthros* in Matt. 5:43–48 and Luke 6:27–28, 32–36 refers to a local enemy, even a member of the household. See W. F. Arndt and F. W. Gringrich, *Greek-English Lexicon of the New Testament* (Chicago: University of Chicago Press, 1957), 331, and Richard Horsley, "Ethics and Exegesis: 'Love Your Enemies' and the Doctrine of Non-Violence," *JAAR* 59/1 (Spring 1986): 17. Horsley suggests, "the phrase surely means those with whom one is in personal, local interaction."

4

The Harms of Sexual Harassment

Traci C. West

This essay exposes trivializing and derisive attitudes about sexual harassment that encourage harassers, thereby perpetuating degrading, terrorizing, and traumatizing costs for women including assaults on their dignity, violation of their trust, and disruption of their self-understandings and confidence. Sexual harassment is defined here as the exertion of power, most often in the form of male dominance over females who are treated merely as objects.

I would like to highlight the costs of sexual harassment by paying particular attention to its emotional and spiritual consequences for the women who are its victims. I will describe some of the power dynamics that foster this behavior and then offer a few concluding thoughts about the direction needed to oppose and prevent it.

The common, everyday incidence of the sexual harassment of women signifies the cultural permission it is given. A primary challenge facing those of us who actively oppose this cultural custom is overcoming the "What's the big deal?" response that remains so prevalent. The widespread trivializing and derisive attitudes about sexual harassment encourage harassers and help to ensure that this degrading treatment will continue to occur.

It may happen to you if you are an adult woman who is walking down the street and told by strangers: "Smile, for me, honey!" "Hey, whore!" "Hey, legs, what are you doin' tonight?" Sometimes this street harassment even happens to children, as it did to me when I was 13 years old. I was walking with my older sister in a predominantly black

This essay was published originally in the *Annual of the Society of Christian Ethics* 19 (1999): 377–382.

neighborhood in New York City. We were on our way to visit my grand-father. As two white police officers came toward us, one grabbed my buttocks. They both laughed and walked away.

It may happen in the home during a family holiday gathering. When the group starts to relax after eating Thanksgiving supper, you may be subjected to your adult male relatives' sexual "jokes" about women. Or, it can also happen to you as a young girl in the home, in a moment when your dad slips his hand down your shirt to fondle your breasts.

The possibility of its occurrence in the workplace is certainly not lim-ited to any particular job setting. It could be the pornography that your male colleagues at the shipyard plaster up on the wall in a room used by all of the workers. It could take the form of sexually suggestive com-ments or touching by your faculty colleague at a meeting or an informal departmental gathering. It might come from the customers you wait on at the restaurant while you try to take their order. Your harasser could be the senior partner at the law firm where you are an attorney. If you are a woman serving in the military, you could be harassed by your com-manding officer, or if a student by your professor as you consult him in his office after class. In our culture, sexual harassment is hardly an un-usual phenomenon for women; it can occur in almost any setting.

When women are sexually harassed, they undergo an assault on their dignity. Women can experience a sense of being humiliated and feel-ing disgusted. This response may be induced by the harasser's tone of voice, his jeering laughter, the sight of his leering facial expression, or the feeling of his invasive touch. Whatever form the harassment may have taken, women can feel soiled by it.

Sexual harassment also often consists of a violation of trust, espe-cially when the harasser is known by the woman or is in a position of authority or trust such as the police officer in the street or the senior fac-ulty member in her department. Women may repeatedly ask themselves, "How could he do this? Why is he doing this?" Harassment may cause a woman to be plagued by a heightened, unrelenting sense of being unsafe.

Most importantly, these feelings of trust-violation during and after the harassment can cause women to experience a fear of being raped.

This [potential] is the most significant reason why the sexual harassment by women that occurs in a minority of cases is not "just the same" as sexual harassment by men. The fear of rape is one of the most insidious features of harassment, but it is often denied or treated dismissively in so-called "mild cases." As a Supreme Court Justice noted in a landmark sexual harassment decision, "women who are victims of mild forms of sexual harassment may understandably worry whether a harasser's conduct is merely a prelude to violent sexual assault. Men, who are rarely victims of sexual assault may view sexual conduct in a vacuum without a full appreciation of the social setting or the underlying threat of violence that women may perceive."[1]

Sexual harassment can mean a violation of one's intimate self. That is, it can generate a sense of violation affecting a woman's relationship to herself. It may seem as if her physical and spiritual being has been invaded. Her reactions may involve a constant insecurity and self-consciousness about how her body moves or how she dresses. These types of concerns may extend to a much deeper alienation from her body—especially the sexual parts of her body—and can be accompanied by physical health problems. The sense of intimate violation can be manifested by awareness of an absence, a lack of psychic wholeness. She may simply "know" that a spiritual and emotional wholeness that was present before the sexual harassment exists no longer.

These impacts are filtered through the cultural kaleidoscope of women's varied social identities. Here I offer two examples, though others could be adduced. If a socio-economically middle stratum, white woman experiences an assault upon her dignity through sexual harassment, her white womanhood may significantly impact her response. The way that white womanhood is constructed in this culture may allow her to perceive her status as a "good girl"/"good woman" to have been "soiled" by the assault. The goodness that is usually culturally equated with her womanhood identifies her as the typical woman of "the heartland" Midwest, as a "soccer mom" of the Northeast, as a precious "belle" of the South, or simply as a typical "all-American" girl. "Good girls" and white women are so often conflated in their cultural meanings that this anguished reaction of being soiled can arise from the perception that a woman is not being treated in a way that she ought to be treated. The particular social construction of her white womanhood informs her interpretation of her experience.

By contrast, for black women the sense of being soiled in response to sexual harassment may reinforce a pre-existing tainted status that is culturally attached to their black womanhood. For African-American women, because blackness is already identified within the dominant culture with what is dirty, foul smelling, or tarnished, the harassment may evoke an intensified sense of being soiled. Please do not interpret this clarification about racial/gender cultural meanings as asserting that, "For black women, it's worse." Rather than making such an absurdly competitive comparison, I am describing some of the contrasting ways that identity might shape and inform women's anguish in the wake of sexual harassment.

Pamela R. Fletcher writes about the spiritual impact of being accosted by a white male stranger in a restaurant while accompanied by white friends who then reacted to the incident with complete insensitivity. Her description provides a keen, summary depiction of the emotional and spiritual injury sexual harassment can cause:

> . . . days later, I could still feel his rough grasp around my waist. My body felt so sore, I wondered if I was only imagining that the hurt was there when it was really in my soul; I felt like such a fool. That night, unlike any other time, my soul suffered a deep wound that has yet to heal.[2]

The fact that these sorts of injuries constitute the primary moral harm that results from the harassment contributes to the trivialization of sexual harassment. These injuries are too often treated with dismissive attitudes such as "How much does it really matter that individual women experience these inner 'little' dramas? Women get upset all of the time." Instead, we must recognize that these emotional and spiritual violations of women both threaten and deny human freedom in our society. Nothing less is at stake. The measure of civil society is bound to the degree that sexual harassment of women exists.

Additionally, sexual harassment is about the exertion of power, most often in the form of male dominance. It can be an expression of perceived male entitlement to women's bodies, and may also involve displaying and preserving male superiority. For example, law professor Elvia Arriola writes about instances where sexual harassment is conjoined with racism, and in some instances heterosexism, for women in the construction trades. She cites the treatment of Pam Berdebes, a lesbian ironworker and plumber, to whom her male coworkers sought to teach a lesson.

> Ten days into a new job, her partner intentionally dropped a heavy fence that they were carrying and Berdebes fell, breaking a leg. Determined not to quit, Berdebes went back to work—"cast and all"—one week later. With that, she became "one of the guys." Thereafter, her male coworkers resorted to "kinder things" like sexual teasing and jokes, grabbing her breasts, and "peeing in front of [her]."[3]

The men who are perpetrators may be sexual predators who have the habitual need to prey upon women in a harassing fashion. Or, they may be "out for a lark," seeking the rush of excitement in seeing the woman's reaction to it. Sometimes they are angrily seeking revenge for what they perceive as having been "led on" by a woman, or are vindictively reacting to an increased female presence in what had previously been an exclusive male domain. Though the specific motivation varies in the harassment of women, the harassers exercise what they perceive to be their right to dominate women. They do so because they can, that is, because of the forms of cultural permission granting this right. Of course, men exercise this right of male dominance in a vastly differentiated manner according to the other social meanings attached to their identity, such as race or socio-economic background.

The identification of many forms of sexual harassment with some of the most trivial expressions of male dominance becomes enhanced when it is defined as a private matter. The fact that male-female interaction related to sexuality is generally relegated to the private sphere within our culture helps to make this problem difficult to stem. The type of everyday, mundane interactions between men and women under which many incidents of sexual harassment fall are often not seen as appropriate spheres for public regulation. Therefore, to complain about sexual harassment is to bring private male prerogatives into public scrutiny. I believe that the greatest legal progress in addressing inappropriate behavior has occurred in the context of the workplace, mainly because it has been successfully claimed that, in this setting, these "mundane" interactions are public violations with economic consequences, and thus, should be subject to sanctions.

In many instances, the manipulation of male power that sexual harassment represents consists of a type of shame game. The harasser often implies or states, "Are you going to be a nice girl and cooperate?" He insists, "Come on, be a good girl and go along" with the joke or with the pat on your behind. This is intended to make women feel ashamed of themselves if they object to such a "little thing." He sets her up with a spurious claim that she should be ashamed of herself for failing to recognize the harassing behavior as only humor, as an "accidental" touch, or as something to which she consented. This tends to be an effective approach. Catherine MacKinnon reports in her pioneering study on sexual harassment, women's most common reaction to harassment is to attempt to ignore it.[4] She then cites evidence indicating that seventy-six percent of ignored advances intensified.

The harasser may be titillated by the woman's reaction of being embarrassed or shamed. In this sense, the shame feeds his act. This tactic of shaming may simply be an attempt to assure her submission to whatever invasion or assault he perpetrates. He may also count on her shame reaction to be able to get away with it, to deter her from complaining. Finally, shaming her can feed his state of denial: the problem is hers. In other words, as he shames her, he denies his culpability in harming her, as well as her sense of being wronged.

In conclusion, we need institutionalized responses to sexual harassment that remove the burden of solving this problem from women. I know all too well from my own work on this issue how difficult it is to get institutions to accept more responsibility. I began working on it twenty years ago as a college student supporting a student colleague who was the plaintiff in a lawsuit against my university (Alexander v. Yale—the lawsuit that established sexual harassment as a form of sex discrimination in education). I then helped to design the first grievance procedure at that institution, and I sat on the Board created by the grievance procedure. Institutions fight hard against making and sustaining these kinds of changes. Moreover, it is not an easy task to design a policy that is responsive to the realities that women face. For example, racial and sexual harassment may merge in actual incidents of harassment. In the Jean Jew promotion case at the University of Iowa, faculty colleagues apparently referred to Jew as a "chink" and "whore."[5] Institutions are usually quite unwilling or unprepared for such complexities and can become quagmired in trying to clarify whether racial harassment or sexual harassment occurred. Nonetheless, to tolerate the absence of concrete measures of support for the victims of sexual harassment and the lack of specific sanctions against the perpetrators is to take a definite institutional position on this issue. This collective silence makes it clear that harassing actions are among the behaviors that are acceptable within some segments of the organization. If such behaviors were not supported, they would not be allowed to continue. I want to emphasize that both sanctions and ongoing education are needed.

As we design appropriate responses to the problem of sexual harassment, we must not limit the focus to the workplace. If we were to accept this constraint, we would impair our ability to challenge the behavior's rootedness in systemic forms of power in our culture. We would relinquish—or at least limit too narrowly—the more general social transformation that is needed to disrupt the broad cultural acceptance of male dominance and other related forms of social power such as heterosexism, socio-economic exploitation, and white supremacy.

Therefore, it is crucial to maintain a comprehensive understanding that links sexual harassment in the workplace with the harassment of women that takes place at other sites. They are all rooted in the same systems of male dominance, which must be opposed in order to affect substantively the perpetuation of harassing behavior. This linkage maintains a holistic vision of change in our communities, rather than a fragmented one that recognizes the need to sanction sexual harassment only in certain "important" spheres. It also maintains pressure on harassers by signaling that the terrorizing and traumatizing of women are intolerable not just at work, but also on the street, at a restaurant when ordering a meal from the waitress, or at home when talking to a female relative. As Christian ethicists, we can contribute to this holistic vision and influence the legal theorists who have valiantly led the fight against sexual harassment in our society to become ever more expansive.

Questions for Reflection

1. Sexual harassment is more than an inappropriate comment or misplaced touch. It is the harasser's persistent and deliberate devaluation of the victim on the basis of sex or gender. West exposes how the culture of silence about sexual harassment tacitly permits it by denying its power to harm. Similar to the axiom that suggests we might judge a society by the way in which it treats its "least" members, how might you judge the institutions to which you belong (school, workplace, civic, government, military, church, family) in matters of their care for women's physical, psychological, social, sexual, and spiritual well-being? Consider the treatment of perhaps especially African American, Latina, Asian American, and other minoritized women in this regard?

2. The Women's Movement has been largely successful in convincing many that "the personal is political." To the extent that "sexual affairs" are understood to be private, the political dimensions of these interpersonal realities remain hidden. What might be some of the "political" harms associated with "affairs" at work? What obstacles, for example, fear of repercussions or of being "too thin-skinned," interfere with exposing the seemingly mundane nature of sexual harassment that occurs in public (e.g., commercial, recreational, and work) and in private (behind closed doors) places with impunity?

3. Many churches, universities, and other communities reveal trenchant patterns of organization that reinforce racist and/or sexist hierarchies and power dynamics that protect mostly white male dominance over others deemed objects—to use, abuse, then refuse (as in trash)—rather

than as persons. Where do you locate yourself on the spectrum of human sexual and racial diversity? What strategic actions might you take to advance justice for those harmed by the violence of systemic social structures of sin and oppression (see for example, Black Lives Matter, "Guiding Principles," http://blacklivesmatter.com/guiding-principles/)?

Suggestions for Further Reading

Avina, Claudia, and William O'Donohue. "Sexual Harassment and PTSD: Is Sexual Harassment Diagnosable Trauma?" *Journal of Traumatic Stress* 15.1 (2002): 69–75.

Cooper-White, Pamela. "Violence and Justice." In *The Oxford Handbook of Theology, Sexuality and Gender,* Adrian Thatcher, ed., 487–504. Oxford, UK: Oxford University Press, 2015.

Sanders, Cody J., and Angela Yarber. *Microaggressions in Ministry: Confronting the Hidden Violence of Everyday Church,* Part 2: "The Targets of Microaggressions," 45–97. Louisville, KY: Westminster John Knox Press, 2015.

Thistlewaite, Susan Brooks. *Women's Bodies as Battlefield: Christian Theology and the Global War on Women.* New York: Palgrave Macmillan, 2015.

Vega, Gina, and Debra R. Comer. "Sticks and Stones May Break Your Bones, but Words Can Break Your Spirit: Bullying in the Workplace." *Journal of Business Ethics* 58.1 (2005): 101–109.

Notes

1. Ellison v. Brady, 924 F 2d 872 (9th Cir. 1991).

2. Emilie Buchwald, Pamela R. Fletcher, Martha Roth, *Transforming a Rape Culture* (Minneapolis, MN: Milkweed Editions, 1993), 438.

3. Elvia Arriola, "'What's the Big Deal?' Women in the New York City Construction Industry and Sexual Harassment Law, 1970–1985," in D. Kelly Weisberg, ed., *Applications of Feminist Legal Theory to Women's Lives: Sex, Violence, Work, and Reproduction* (Philadelphia: Temple University Press, 1996), 779–796.

4. Catherine A. MacKinnon, *Sexual Harassment of Working Women* (New Haven, CT: Yale University Press, 1979), 48.

5. For a discussion of this case, see Sumi K. Cho, "Converging Stereotypes in Racialized Sexual Harassment: Where the Model Minority Meets Suzie Wong," Adrien Katherine Wing, ed., *Critical Race Feminism: A Reader* (New York: New York University Press, 1997): 203–220.

5

Biblical Ethics, HIV/AIDS, and South African Pentecostal Women

Constructing an A-B-C-D Prevention Strategy

KATHERINE ATTANASI

This essay shows how South African Pentecostal teachings about sexuality, particularly HIV prevention and divorce, constrain women's real and imagined choices. Institutional Review Board–approved fieldwork revealed the prevalence of wives remaining faithful to unfaithful husbands despite high risks of physical abuse and HIV infection. Maintaining the "ideal" of abstinence and faithfulness, male pastors actively oppose condom use and emphasize that "God hates divorce" (Mal. 2:16). In this essay I engage and resist such hermeneutics. Using scripture as source and norm, I construct an A-B-C-D prevention strategy to enhance women's freedom: Abstain, Be faithful, use Condoms, or Divorce.

Sub-Saharan Africa is home to two-thirds of the people living with HIV/AIDS worldwide.[1] Although South Africa does not have the highest infection rate, there are more people living with HIV in South Africa (5.6 million) than in any other country.[2] I center on Pentecostalism because of its prominence in South Africa.[3] Eighty percent of South Africans are Christians, and over a third of South Africans identify as Pentecostal or Charismatic, more than any other branch of Christianity.[4] I focus on women because they disproportionately bear the burdens of HIV. Women make up nearly 60 percent of HIV infections worldwide and 70 percent of adult infections in South Africa.[5] Biologically, the virus is more easily transmitted from men to women. Economically, South African women have more limited educational and employment opportunities than their

This essay was published originally in the *Journal of the Society of Christian Ethics* 33.1 (Spring 2013): 105–117.

male counterparts, which increases their financial dependence on men and results in a diminished capacity to negotiate sexual relationships. Interpersonally, for women to refuse sex, suggest condom use, or ask men about other sexual partners is seen as inappropriate—if not taboo.

In this essay I draw on the experiences of black South African Pentecostal women to construct an effective HIV prevention strategy. I first describe my research design and relate my findings regarding HIV prevention, namely, that churches endorse abstinence and faithfulness but not condoms. I then underscore the limits of this prevention strategy as it pertains to faithful wives of unfaithful husbands, the most common marriage scenario among my participants. To promote women's freedom, in the end I argue for the permissibility of condoms and divorce, which some of my participants endorsed.

Research Methodology and Key Findings

I conducted fieldwork among South African Pentecostals in 2008 in one village and one township.[6] To make initial contacts, I relied on a white South African Pentecostal man, who is a personal friend and who was formerly an official in the Apostolic Faith Mission, a South African Pentecostal denomination. My friend introduced me in advance to one pastor in each research site. Each pastor then arranged for me to pay a host for lodging and to hire a research assistant; pastors also encouraged congregants' voluntary participation in my study.[7] With these volunteers I conducted more than fifty interviews and a dozen follow-up interviews. In both sites I used a snowball sampling technique in which key informants referred me to individuals, who then suggested other participants. I strove for variation with regard to age, marital status, employment, and educational level.[8]

The congregations treated me as a religious insider because I had been formally introduced to them by their pastors and because of my own background in Pentecostalism. My experience parallels what Nancy Ammerman describes in her book *Bible Believers*;[9] that is, as a Christian familiar with the language and vocabulary of my participants, I understood Pentecostal language and vocabulary and, when asked, I could explain my own religious experiences in those terms. While conducting research I conformed to Pentecostal behavioral regulations and partici-pated in the religious life of the congregations, including the 6:00 a.m. prayer meetings.

My research methodology reflects the relatively recent emergence of fieldwork in Christian ethics, a conversation that the SCE has fostered for several years.[10] As Christian Scharen and Aana Marie Vigen high-light, an important function of ethnography is to provide a thick de-scription of a specific situation so that the particular becomes the starting point from which any general claims might be made.[11] Scharen and Vigen say, "At its best, theology and ethics represent intentional and nuanced efforts to make sense of suffering *and* to do something . . . about it."[12]

In doing fieldwork in ethics, perhaps the most challenging question that remains is how to move from thick description to making normative claims. As I see it, there are two ditches to avoid. On the one side is a sort of "show-and-tell," whereby a researcher might simply conclude, "How interesting that vulnerable South African women pray that they do not contract HIV from their cheating husbands." On the other side is a neo-colonial assertion of power on the part of a white academic, who recom-mends a "best course of action" that is not grounded in local norms or practices. I prefer a collaborative exchange so that I do not assert any-thing that has not already emerged from among my participants.[13]

To keep it between the ditches, so to speak, I draw on the work of fem-inist political theorist Brooke Ackerly, particularly what she describes as third-world feminist social criticism. Ackerly highlights three roles of the social critic, whose aim is to facilitate "society's self-examination" by facilitating critical inquiry, deliberative opportunities, and institutional change.[14] I developed an A-B-C-D prevention strategy, which emerged from the participants themselves and which has the potential to engen-der institutional change.[15]

For the first stage of my research, critical inquiry, I began preliminary interviews with a set of broad research questions and themes pertaining to women's experience within Pentecostalism and their thoughts concerning HIV/AIDS. The women were all Pentecostals, and they readily talked about their faith. Regarding HIV/AIDS I asked women their opinions about what churches are or should be doing. A high degree of stigma surrounds HIV in South Africa, and many women mentioned gossip as a problem within the church. Accordingly, I did not ask anyone to disclose her HIV status, although a few women voluntarily did so.[16] The themes of Pentecostal experience and HIV/AIDS guided my research, but I guarded against imposing my concerns on the participants by implementing a semistructured, open-ended, qualitative interview method.[17]

In explaining my research to participants, I stated my objective as learning about the lives of South African women who went to churches like theirs. I wanted to learn about the problems they face, how their faith helps them, and what their churches do (and can do better) to assist them. Invariably I started out by asking a participant to share "how she came to know the Lord." There are no wrong answers to this question, which anchored the interview in my commitment to listening to women's stories. I also asked general questions, such as, "What problems do women in South Africa face?" "What are your favorite Bible verses?" and "For what do you pray?" I ended interviews with the question, "Is there anything else that I did not ask about that you believe would be important for me to know?" This question reinforced my status as learner and often opened the door for further discussion. Responses to these general questions illuminated the community's concerns and provided the information for framing subsequent focus group discussions. I also identified individuals with whom I would conduct follow-up interviews. Of the fifty women with whom I conducted preliminary interviews, I conducted one or more follow-up interviews with twelve of them.

For the second stage of my research, facilitating deliberative opportunities, I conducted eight focus groups to generate dialogue and ensure a collaborative approach. I endeavored to create safe spaces for women to discuss shared challenges and possible solutions. The women in the focus groups espoused a multiplicity of perspectives, an important sign that the creation of knowledge emerges from participants, rather than being imposed by the researcher. In addition to the focus groups, the one-on-one dialogues with my research assistants provided many other valuable deliberative opportunities.

In each of the two congregations that I studied, more than three-quarters of congregants were women. These women frequently associated (non-Christian) South African masculinity with drug and alcohol abuse, marital infidelity, unsafe sex, domestic abuse, and authoritarian decision-making. The women added that many men reject Pentecostalism because of its behavioral norms that restrict alcohol use and sex outside of marriage.

Of the fifty women with whom I conducted interviews, more than three-quarters were married, divorced, or widowed; more than half of the husbands were non-Christians. In one congregation, more than half of the married women had non-Christian husbands; more than half of the non-Christian husbands committed adultery; and more than a quarter of the non-Christian husbands physically abused their wives.[18] Women are exceedingly more vulnerable to HIV infection when their husbands cheat on them and practice unsafe sex. Given my participants' attestation to the prevalence of adultery and unsafe sex, then, the efficacy of any comprehensive HIV prevention strategy can be measured by the extent to which it protects the faithful wives of unfaithful husbands from HIV infection.

By far the most prevalent approach for addressing HIV/AIDS worldwide has been the A-B-C strategy: Abstain, Be faithful, and/or use Condoms. The A-B-C approach proved especially effective in reducing Uganda's infection rate in the 1990s.[19] However, the congregations in my study only support the A-B-C strategy in part. That is, overwhelmingly they do not think that churches should support condom use. When I asked Pentecostal pastors and other church members what prevention strategies they thought were most relevant, they emphasized abstinence and faithfulness. I heard multiple times that the church's message should be abstinence before marriage, faithfulness in marriage, and then trust Christ, not condoms. Yet this HIV prevention strategy is hardly effective in protecting a sizable cross section of women.

The Limits of Abstinence and Faithfulness

For unmarried individuals, a number of participants promoted abstinence-only HIV prevention as the church's only option. Although people often speak of choosing abstinence, as it turns out, abstinence is not always a choice. The very first interview I conducted in South Africa revealed the limits of abstinence-only strategies. Sofia was a preschool teacher who sang praise and worship in the church. In our interview, Sofia kept referring to several "difficulties" that she had experienced. When I asked if she would explain what she meant by "difficulties," she said that she had been sexually abused as a four-year-old by her stepfather, who was a pastor.

Then Sofia related the following story. When she was eighteen years old, as she was returning home to her mother one evening, a truck full of men drove up beside her. A bunch of guys jumped out of the truck; they beat her with a beer bottle and put her in the truck and drove off. She cried but no one could hear her. They robbed her and drove far outside of town. Then a number of men raped her. They drove along farther and had a wreck, and one of the men led her away because he said the others were going to kill her. But even this man raped her along the way. Eventually Sofia and her rapist/rescuer stumbled onto a funeral. The man left and the funeral goers took care of Sofia by paying her bus fare back home.

Granted Sofia's experience provides an extreme example, but I include her story because it poignantly reveals the limitations of abstinence-only teaching. Abstinence is not always a choice, and those who cite abstinence's 100 percent effectiveness reveal their failure to imagine threats to bodily integrity as well as who is expected to abstain. Along these lines, Musa Dube calls attention to rape and gender inequality, and she says that 100 percent abstinence teaching "borders on an irresponsibility that leads many lives to death."[20] On a more basic level, abstinence teaching does not pertain to married couples, and more than three-quarters of my participants were married.

The B in A-B-C refers to being faithful in marriage. In South Africa, many of the married couples spent considerable time living apart in order to find work. The geographic relationship of housing to jobs spoke to the realities of black South African life, particularly the effects of apartheid policies under which black people worked but could not live in urban centers.[21]

For faithfulness to be effective, both partners must share that commitment. The most common scenario I found was of wives remaining faithful to unfaithful husbands. As I mentioned earlier, in one congregation, more than half of the married women had non-Christian husbands, more than half of the non-Christian husbands committed adultery, and more than a quarter of the non-Christian husbands physically abused their wives.[22]

A woman named Violet married young. Her husband was a police officer who regularly (sometimes daily) beat her with his nightstick, which resulted in many hospitalizations, at least two miscarriages, and permanent disfigurement to her leg. Her entire family and neighborhood knew of the ongoing abuse but no one came to her defense. Violet never reported her husband's abuse to authorities because he was a policeman. She said, "In those days they would just come to our house and talk to us. They would tell us it would look bad if their top officer was abusing his wife. It would just disappear." Violet's husband did not want her to attend her Pentecostal church, and he even burned some of her belongings as punishment for her doing so. Despite her faithfulness to her abusive husband, Violet found out after her husband's death that he had infected her with HIV.

The churches preach faithfulness, and the women hear and adhere to that message. The problem is that their husbands are not in church, do not get the message, and are unfaithful. Simply put, "faithfulness" is not effective enough to prevent HIV infection among the women who participated in my study.

Reinserting Condoms in the A-B-C Approach

The "C" in the A-B-C strategy stands for condoms; that is, use condoms consistently and correctly. As mentioned earlier, though, the churches I studied generally do not promote condom use, and some Pentecostal believers even actively oppose condoms and call attention to failure rates. Pentecostals do not oppose condoms on the grounds of natural law, which, depending on the interpretation in use, may reject birth control as contrary to God's purpose for sexual intercourse.[23] In fact, many Pentecostal women access other forms of birth control such as the pill for the purposes of family planning.

Instead, South African Pentecostals frequently characterize condoms as culturally inappropriate, a "Western" (i.e., not an African) solution. This argument does not ultimately hold. Many South Africans do accept condom use, illustrating Seyla Benhabib's argument that cultures are contested and speak with many voices.[24] Cultures also change through time. By way of example, the birth control pill did not originate in South Africa, but it has come to be widely accepted even among the women I interviewed. By integrating medical advancements in reproductive health, South Africans exemplify Benhabib's point that "tradition is in transition."[25]

Whether the wider South African culture comes to accept condoms is a separate issue from the assertion of some Pentecostals that condoms are unchristian, based on the supposition that condom distribution encourages promiscuity among otherwise chaste individuals. Among Pentecostals there are competing views on condom use. Violet, whose unfaithful husband infected her with HIV, said that she would not recommend condoms for someone in her situation. She said: "The woman can't say that he should use a condom. You have to have sex even knowing that he's cheating; your body is not yours, it is your husband's. You have to be submissive. You also have to ask God to protect you because you can't ask (your husband) to use a condom."

Not every woman shared Violet's opinion. I heard secondhand stories of women who suspected their husbands of unfaithfulness and told their husbands to use a condom. If the husbands would protest, then the women would tell their husbands to get out. However, I do not know the rest of that story. It is possible that the husbands would agree to use a condom; it is also possible that the husbands would leave their wives. More disturbingly, some of my data would suggest that the women could get beaten or raped by their husbands for insinuating infidelity and claiming their right to safe sex.

One male pastor differentiated between what he would say about condoms publicly from the pulpit and what he would say privately to an HIV discordant couple. He said, "As Christians, we believe that condoms are a help to protect people, but you cannot preach condoms. . . . You preach faithfulness and abstinence." From the pulpit, this pastor tells his congregants that the "C" should stand for "Christianize." The pastor qualified, though, that if he were counseling an HIV discordant couple, he would recommend condom use. I find the pastor's recommendation of condoms to be heartening, but it would be better to offer that qualification publicly because many women I interviewed had internalized the teaching that condoms are unchristian.

I did find one female pastor who regularly advocates for condom use from the pulpit. Pastor Felicia preaches that her congregants should abstain, be faithful, and use condoms. She said that she includes teachings about condoms because not everyone in the congregation will be able to choose to abstain and be faithful, and using condoms may save their lives. She said, "If we face the truth, not everyone can abstain. . . . Some, they will go their own way. Now I encourage them they must use condoms so they mustn't get AIDS. . . . I tell them 'if you know you are fooling around you must use a condom.'"

The summary point is that perspectives on condoms are contested among South Africans and Pentecostals. At the time of my fieldwork, the disparaging message that condoms are unchristian was the consensus. Nevertheless, there is potential for the dissenting voices to publicize a pro-condom message that would benefit Pentecostal women whose husbands are unfaithful to them.

The Biblical Ethics of Permissible Divorce

So far I have described the inadequacies of the A-B-C strategy as it pertains to the demographic of faithful Pentecostal wives whose husbands commit adultery. Abstinence does not apply, since the women are married. Faithfulness applies, but my research found women remaining faithful while their husbands do not. Regarding condoms, men are likely to refuse condoms for cultural reasons, and Pentecostals are particularly likely to disparage condoms within the church. Condom use can even be seen as a lack of faith, so to thwart infection women pray for HIV prevention—a disturbing trend my research revealed. Within the churches I studied, then, married women basically have two options: one is simply to pray that they do not contract HIV from their unfaithful husbands; the other is to divorce. Yet the church's teachings on divorce make that option an incredibly difficult choice.

In my time in South African Pentecostal churches, I heard two main teachings on marriage. First was a phrase from the household codes in New Testament epistles attributed to Paul: "Wives, be subject to your husbands . . ." (Eph. 5:22; Col. 3:18); second was a phrase from the Israelite prophet Malachi: "'I hate divorce,' says the Lord God of Israel" (Mal. 2:16). The prevailing understanding is that of absolute prohibition of divorce. Pastors and women generally affirmed their faith that prayer could save troubled marriages, and one participant even shared her own testimony to that effect. According to the participants in my study, adultery and domestic violence constitute the two main strains on marriage. In spite of difficult circumstances, the overwhelming majority of participants upheld the ideal of wifely submission, avoiding divorce, and trusting in prayer. Although this ideal was a consensus position, there was occasional dissent.

Two women offered different perspectives on divorce. Pastor Linda was an associate pastor in one of the congregations, and she herself was a divorcée. The primary factor in her divorce was that her non-Christian husband cheated on her. Pastor Linda said that, because she is a single parent and divorced woman, people will come to her and expect her to recommend divorce. She said, "I don't advise anyone to get divorced. . . . But I say, 'the first thing we need to do is pray.'" She said that even in cases of abuse, she tells couples that "the answer is prayer." Pastor Linda exemplifies the apodictic character of the Pentecostal divorce prohibition: even if I have done it myself, divorce is the wrong thing to do because the general maxim is that married couples ought to remain married.

Another woman, Mrs. Nkabinde, found herself in conflict with her Pentecostal prayer group because she recommended that her daughter separate from and divorce her abusive husband. Mrs. Nkabinde shared that her son-in-law would regularly beat her daughter. He also threatened to kill his wife/her daughter and had even sent his nephews with axes to underscore the seriousness of his threats. Mrs. Nkabinde then told the daughter to come home to her. The daughter did so, and she eventually divorced her abusive husband. When Mrs. Nkabinde told her prayer group of this decision, however, they disapproved. The prayer group recommended that the wife submit and not divorce the husband. These women said instead that the daughter should remain with her husband while they prayed for her safety. Mrs. Nkabinde affirmed her strong belief in the power of prayer, but she disagreed with her prayer group's recommendations. Moreover, Mrs. Nkabinde was uncomfortable that the group disapproved of her course of action, as though she had shown a lack of faith in God and distrust in the efficacy of the group's prayers.

In my study, the Pentecostal congregations treat the Bible as the source for their ethical norms, much in the way James Gustafson describes conservative Protestants' regard for the Bible as "revealed morality" and, thereby, authoritative for beliefs and practices.[26] Again and again, participants paraphrased Malachi as saying that "God hates divorce" (Mal. 2:16). I later found that this phrase comprises only a portion of the verse, in fact, only one-third. The Masoretes, the rabbinic scribes who pointed the consonantal Hebrew text in the Middle Ages, divided the verse in half and then split the first half in two.[27] So the sentence begins, "I hate divorce,' says the Lord God of Israel" (Mal. 2:16aa). The very next phrase reads, "'and I hate a man's covering himself with violence as well as with his garment,' says the Lord Almighty" (Mal. 2:16ab); in a footnote, the NIV translators propose the following rendering: "I hate a man's covering *his wife* with violence" (emphasis mine).[28] The point is that Malachi balances God's hatred of divorce with God's hatred of violence. Given the prevalence of domestic abuse among my participants, my work endeavors to reclaim Malachi's balanced presentation of things God hates with regard to marriage.

When it comes to New Testament teachings on divorce, to my surprise participants did not mention any. There are, though, two key passages, one by Jesus and another by Paul. In the Gospels of Matthew and Mark, the Pharisees ask Jesus about the permissibility of divorce (Mark 10:2–4).[29] Jesus says that divorce results from people's hardheartedness and that divorce transgresses God's original design for marriage (Mark 2:5–8). Jesus then commands, "Therefore, what God has joined together, let no one separate" (Mark 10:9).[30] To explain this prohibition, Jesus says that divorce plus remarriage equals adultery (Mark 10:10–12).[31] By explicitly mentioning remarriage, Jesus presupposes that some couples will divorce. Accordingly, his prohibition of remarriage constitutes an intensification of the Seventh Commandment's prohibition of adultery.[32] Given that so many South African Pentecostal women already have husbands committing adultery, my prevention strategy seeks to reassert Jesus's presupposition that some couples will divorce and to reemphasize the impropriety of adultery.

The apostle Paul provides the earliest interpretation of Jesus's saying, and Paul accentuates the presupposition of divorce: "To the married I give this command—not I but the Lord—that the wife should not separate from her husband (but if she does, let her remain unmarried . . .)" (1 Cor. 7:10–11). Paul then points out that Jesus did not give directives concerning marriages between believers and nonbelievers. So Paul lays down the following guidelines. As long as the unbeliever consents to remain together, the couple should do so (1 Cor. 7:12–13). Conversely, if the unbeliever separates, then Paul says the believer is free to go. Literally, the believer is not to be "enslaved" (δουλεύω), and Paul adds that

"God has called us to peace" (1 Cor. 7:15). I interviewed many women who meet Paul's conditions for divorcing with impunity.

In summary, of the married Pentecostal women who participated in my study, more than half of their husbands were non-Christians. A number of the husbands physically abused their wives; but we learn through the prophet Malachi that God condemns such violence. Many of the husbands committed adultery; but we learn that Jesus's intensification of the seventh commandment implicitly denounces such infidelity. A majority of the nonbelieving husbands did not accept the wives' Christian faith or consent to live peaceably together; then we learn that Paul grants the believer the free choice to divorce. Highlighting the aforementioned biblical passages offers what Sarojini Nadar calls "life affirming rather than life denying interpretations of Scripture."[33] By remaining in dangerous marriages, women are rendered significantly more vulnerable to HIV infection. Therefore, I put forward biblically permissible divorce as a crucial choice for enhancing women's freedom and flourishing.[34]

Conclusion

By way of conclusion, I draw on feminist political theorist Nancy Hirschmann's notion of freedom. According to Hirschmann, freedom is essentially about choice, and choice involves the complicated interaction among internal and external factors. Hirschmann highlights what people prefer when given the choice, whether people are given the choice, and whether they are then able to make it.[35] Enhancing freedom thus requires removing barriers—real and imagined—so that new possibilities can be created.

In outlining the limits of abstinence and faithfulness, the participants in my study have revealed how South African Pentecostal women's choices are constrained. Although abstinence is an important part of HIV prevention, Sofia's story reveals that not everyone can choose abstinence. Similarly, Violet's story shows that for faithfulness to be an effective HIV prevention strategy, both partners must practice this virtue.

Most importantly, some participants show how condoms and divorce can create more choices for women. Pastor Felicia boldly endorses condoms, not only in private counseling but also in preaching from the pulpit. Moreover, Mrs. Nkabinde knows that divorce—albeit regrettably less than ideal—may be necessary to save the life of her daughter. Although they presently voice a minority position among South African Pentecostals, Pastor Felicia and Mrs. Nkabinde expand women's freedom by endorsing condoms and divorce. This expansion, sitting well within the Pentecostal tradition, amounts to the A-B-C-D HIV prevention strategy that emerged from my fieldwork.

Questions for Reflection

1. Given the acute vulnerability among South African women and many other women worldwide to HIV and domestic violence, and the prevalence of patriarchal structures restricting women's and girls' exercise of free choice in matters of sex, marriage, and divorce, it is literally a matter of life and death that ways be found to contribute to women's and girls' empowerment. In your context, how is the culture of patriarchy expressed? How might the church challenge such attitudes and structures so as to foster equality instead?

2. UN Millennium Development Goal 6 intended to halt and begin to reverse the spread of HIV/AIDS and achieve universal access to treatment for HIV/AIDS for all in need by 2015; likewise, the UN Sustainable Development Goal 3 seeks to end the pandemic of AIDS by 2030. What specific recommendations might a theological ethic grounded in equal regard for all contribute to such efforts locally and globally?

3. Institutional Review Board approval is required before any research with human subjects begins. Alongside their vulnerability to the social stigma associated with HIV and AIDS, from what other harms might this researcher need to have to protect her participant collaborators?

Suggestions for Further Reading

Africa Today 56.1 (2009), Special Issue: *Christianity and HIV/AIDS in East and Southern Africa*. Ruth Prince, Philippe Denis, and Rijk van Dijk, "Introduction to Special Issue: Engaging Christianities, Negotiating HIV/AIDS, Health, and Social Relations in East and Southern Africa," v–xviii; Damaris Seleina Parsitau, "Keep Holy Distance and Abstain till He Comes: Interpreting a Pentecostal Church's Engagements with HIV/AIDS and the Youth in Kenya," 45–64.

Browning, Melissa. *Risky Marriage: HIV and Intimate Relationships in Tanzania* (Studies in Body and Religion). Plymouth, UK: Lexington Books, 2014.

Iozzio, Mary Jo. "HIV/AIDS." In *The Oxford Handbook of Theology, Sexuality, and Gender*, Adrian Thatcher, ed., 538–556. Oxford, UK: Oxford University Press, 2015.

Loader, William. "Divorce." In *The New Testament on Sexuality*, 54–61. Grand Rapids, MI: Eerdmans, 2012.

Stivers, Laura A., Christine E. Gudorf, and James B. Martin-Schramm. "Case: What God Has Joined." In *Christian Ethics: A Case Method Approach*, 4th ed, Stivers, Gudorf, and Martin-Schramm, eds., 31–50. Maryknoll, NY: Orbis Press, 2012.

Notes

Special thanks to James Barker for sharing his expertise in biblical studies and for offering encouragement throughout the research and writing processes. Unless otherwise noted, scripture citations are from the New Revised Standard Version Bible, copyright © 1989, Division of Christian Education of the National Council of the Churches of Christ in the USA.

1. According to the 2010 UNAIDS report, globally an estimated 33.3 million people are living with HIV/AIDS; sub-Saharan Africa is home to 22.5 million people living with HIV. Of the 2.6 million new infections worldwide in 2009, 1.8 million (nearly 70 percent) occurred in sub-Saharan Africa. UNAIDS, *Global Report: UNAIDS Report on the Global AIDS Epidemic* (New York: UNAIDS, 2010), 20–21.

2. Ibid., 28.

3. Pew Forum on Public Life, "Spirit and Power: A 10-Country Survey of Pentecostals" (Washington, DC: Pew Research Center, October 2006), 2–3.

4. Ibid., 2–3, 87.

5. In 2008 South African women comprised 3.2 million of South Africa's 4.6 million infected adults. UNAIDS, *Report on the Global AIDS Epidemic* (Geneva: Joint United Nations Programme on HIV/AIDS, 2008), 32.

6. IRB approval #050395, approved annually from 2005 to 2008, Institutional Review Board at Vanderbilt University; in accordance with IRB protocols, I have changed the names of all participants to ensure anonymity.

7. Roughly half of the interviews were in English and the other half in either Setho or Tswana, which my research assistants translated.

8. Early on at my first site, it seemed as though my key informant was directing

me to talk to well-educated women whom she thought would give me the "best" information, and so I reiterated that I was interested in talking to women of different ages, educational backgrounds, and professions.

9. Nancy Tatom Ammerman, *Bible Believers: Fundamentalists in the Modern World* (New Brunswick, NJ: Rutgers, 1987), 11.

10. Led by Jennifer Beste, Melissa Browning, and Todd David Whitmore, the fieldwork and ethics interest group (aka Fieldwork in Christian Ethics) has been part of the SCE's annual meeting since 2008. In 2009 the SCE adopted a policy requiring members to seek institutional review board approval prior to beginning any study involving human subjects.

11. Aana Marie Vigen and Christian Scharen, "The Ethnographic Turn in Theology and Ethics," in *Ethnography as Christian Theology and Ethics*, Aana Marie Vigen and Christian Scharen, eds., 28–46 (New York: Continuum, 2010), at 28.

12. Aana Marie Vigen and Christian Scharen, "Theological Justifications for Turning to Ethnography," in *Ethnography as Christian Theology and Ethics*, Vigen and Scharen, eds., 58–76 (New York: Continuum, 2010), at 66, emphasis original.

13. The strategies that I highlight are by no means the consensus positions in the congregations I studied. In fact, condoms and divorce emerged as exceptional strategies within my relatively small sample group. As a qualitative rather than a quantitative study, my project not only lifts up the voices of those women who broke with the theologically supported norms of their community but also provides biblical and theological support for their actions.

14. Brooke Ackerly, *Political Theory and Feminist Social Criticism* (Cambridge: Cambridge University Press, 2000), 123–31; see also Brooke Ackerly, *Universal Human Rights in a World of Difference* (Cambridge: Cambridge University Press, 2008), 168.

15. My participants did not consider A-B-C language simplistic or paternalistic, contrary to the suggestion by Melissa D. Browning, "HIV/AIDS Prevention and Sexed Bodies: Rethinking Abstinence in Light of the African AIDS Pandemic," *Theology & Sexuality* 15 (2009): 27–46, at 36–38; although English was the language of a colonizer, the majority of my participants embraced English but rejected Afrikaans, which they associated with the oppression of apartheid.

16. For a study focusing exclusively on HIV positive women, see Melissa D. Browning, "Patriarchy, Christianity, and the African AIDS Pandemic: Rethinking Christian Marriage in Light of the Experiences of HIV Positive Women in Tanzania" (PhD diss., Loyola University Chicago, 2011).

17. Vigen and Scharen caution ethnographers that "being in a hurry means that the researcher only wants confirmation of what he thinks she knows—of the themes and issues already chosen as foundational. Proceeding in such a way leads to a tautological circle where one's assumptions substitute for the evidence needed to support them. The aim of ethnography is not merely to confirm or prove false one's hypothesis or theoretical claim. Rather, it is to learn from the scene itself—to

let the questions and knowledge bubble up from the situation—to get a deep reading of what is there—on its own terms." Vigen and Christian Scharen, "What Is Ethnography?," 27.

18. Given the silence that shrouds domestic violence, it is likely that more of my participants had similar experiences. In the second congregation I studied, women were more reticent to discuss adultery and domestic violence. One factor might have been that my research assistant for that congregation was younger and unmarried, whereas in the first congregation my research assistant was older and married; that is, married women may have been more likely to confide in other married women.

19. Edward C. Green, Daniel T. Halperin, Ninand Nantulya, and Janice A. Hogle, "Uganda's HIV Prevention Success: The Role of Sexual Behavior Change and the National Response," *AIDS and Behavior* 10 (2006): 335–46. The authors highlight that the A-B-C message contributes to changes in sexual behaviors, which then leads to a reduction in HIV prevalence.

20. Musa W. Dube, "Theological Challenges: Proclaiming the Fullness of Life in the HIV/AIDS and Global Economic Era," *International Review of Mission* 91 (2003): 535–49, at 541.

21. Leonard M. Thompson, *A History of South Africa*, 2nd ed. (New Haven, CT: Yale University Press, 1995), 193–94.

22. The scenario of wives abusing or cheating on their husbands did not appear in my fieldwork.

23. For example, according to the papal encyclical *Humanae vitae*, the sexual activity of husbands and wives should be intrinsically related to procreation in observance of natural law (§11); birth control is deemed unlawful (§14). Paul VI, *Humanae vitae*, July 25, 1968. www.vatican.va/holy_father/paul_vi/encyclicals/documents/hf_p-vi_enc_25071968_ humanae-vitae_en.html.

24. Seyla Benhabib, *Situating the Self: Gender, Community, and Postmodernism in Contemporary Ethics* (New York: Routledge, 1992), 26–27: "Cultures themselves, as well as societies, are not holistic but polyvocal, multilayered, decentered, and fractured systems of action and signification."

25. Ibid., 116.

26. James Gustafson, *Theology and Christian Ethics* (Philadelphia: United Church Press, 1974), 130–31. Similarly, Philip Jenkins characterizes the purpose of Bible reading in the "global South" as "an authoritative source and a guide for daily living." Philip Jenkins, *The New Faces of Christianity: Believing the Bible in the Global South* (Oxford: Oxford University Press, 2008), 5.

27. See Karl Elliger and Wilhelm Rudolph, eds., *Biblia Hebraica Stuttgartensia* (Stuttgart: Deutsche Bibelgesellschaft, 1967–77).

28. *The Holy Bible*, New International Version (Colorado Springs, CO: International Bible Society, 1973, 1978, 1984).

29. Mark 10:2–12 is paralleled in Matthew 19:3–9. Matthew's qualification in

verse 3, "for any cause," more clearly situates the divorce controversy in its first-century rabbinic context in which R. Hillel was more permissive than R. Shammai. The Gospel of Luke excludes the controversy story but includes the solitary saying about divorce and remarriage constituting adultery (16:18).

30. This is a third-person imperative in Greek (χωριζέτω).

31. Matthew adds a much debated "exception clause," which states, "I tell you that anyone who divorces his wife, except for marital unfaithfulness, and marries another woman commits adultery" (Matt. 19:9).

32. The extent to which contemporary churches should prohibit remarriage after divorce remains contested; e.g., David Instone-Brewer, "What God Has Joined," *Christianity Today* (October 2007): 26–29.

33. Sarojini Nadar, "'The Bible Says!' Feminism, Hermeneutics, and Neo-Pentecostal Challenges," *Journal for Theology of Southern Africa* 134 (2009): 131–46, at 131.

34. The notion of biblically permissible divorce was virtually unheard of among the participants in my study.

35. Nancy J. Hirschmann, *The Subject of Liberty: Toward a Feminist Theory of Freedom* (Princeton, NJ: Princeton University Press, 2003), ix.

6

Brothers in Arms and Brothers in Christ?

The Military and the Catholic Church as Sources for Modern Korean Masculinity

HOON CHOI

In this essay I examine how compulsory military service and the Roman Catholic Church uphold and perpetuate an inadequate notion of masculinity in South Korea. I argue that the militaristic and Catholic definitions of masculinity significantly and pejoratively affect Korean culture. To unlearn these definitions, I propose an educational "readjusting" program that denounces any unjust discrimination on the basis of sex and gender.

Scholars who examine South Korean churches often locate problems of gender inequity in these institutions in an authoritarianism that results from years of Confucian ideological inculcation. Similar to locating the current problem of unjust gender structures in the West in ancient dualisms, locating the origins of this reality in any context requires a multipronged approach for discovering the source of its perpetuation and working toward equity. Many institutions share culpability in this regard, including families, schools, workplaces, religious groups, and the media. While recognizing the importance of these factors, I focus on the ways in which compulsory military service and the Roman Catholic Church in South Korea play major roles in upholding an authoritarian notion of masculinity. Drawing from personal experience and research by others, I argue that militaristic and Catholic definitions of masculinity are two major culprits in the Korean insistence on an authoritarian gendered hierarchy, and that such received definitions of masculinity

---

This essay was published originally in the *Journal of the Society of Christian Ethics* 32.2 (2012): 75–92.

are neither helpful nor Christian for women and men. In pursuing this research, I have the modest objective of proposing readjustment education at or near the end of compulsory military service to foster the process of differentiating the military milieu from society at large, including Korean Roman Catholic settings. Ultimately, my hope is to contribute to the denouncement and rejection of unjust treatment based on gender or sex.

To understand this longstanding tradition of the hegemonic notion of masculinity, I first introduce multiple historical factors that led to the militarization of South Korea. Then I show a hegemonic and authoritarian approach that the Korean Roman Catholic Church eventually adopted. There are many negative effects, I argue, as a consequence of militarism and authoritarianism in the construction of the notion of masculinity in Korea. Finally, I present some positive efforts that some Korean scholars have made to unlearn such a notion and propose an educational "readjusting" program to begin the process of amelioration.[1]

Gendered Attitudes in Korea

Korean culture is multifaceted and a product of myriad influences. It would be impossible—and misleading—to point out a single cause for Koreans' attitudes toward masculinity. The current norms of Korean masculinity are the result of a longstanding tradition of customs, ideology, and inculcation about gender. It would be inaccurate to place the blame solely, or even mostly, on the ancient Korean (neo-Confucian) system of social norms and values for the unjust, unfair, and uneven attitudes toward gender in modern Korean society.[2] One must consider not only where such ideologies and practices originated but also what or who is perpetuating them. Only when I fulfilled my own compulsory military duty did I realize that one of the major reasons for the maintenance of such norms is the relentless encouragement of young Korean men by the military. To understand this phenomenon, a background of the hegemonic construction of compulsory military service in Korea and its culture and effects is in order.

Korean Military Culture

Multiple historical factors led to the militarization of South Korea. First, Korea's experience of Japanese colonization (1910–45) heightened the status of warriors tremendously. Second, the introduction of Western weapons technology fed into the glorification of war. Third, the policies of the US interim government after Korea's independence and during the turmoil leading to and following the Korean War conditioned the nation to desire military strength. Fourth, dictatorial rule and militaristic control of the populace contributed to the militarism of the nation. Finally, and most importantly, the ongoing compulsory military service of all men in Korea has had a great impact on the military mindset of the nation and its subsequent thinking about gender. It is evident that one can easily invoke neo-Confucian notions to achieve a military agenda and vice versa. Indeed, one can see that favoring militarism or neo-Confucianism may be about maintaining power, including interpretive power.

Military culture has a profound influence on many facets of Korean life as a whole. The enormity of the military influence that upholds the traditional neo-Confucian attitude toward men is a curious reality. That is, neo-Confucianism, which was a philosophy of ruling by "cultivated" scholars, claimed that "men of the pen enjoyed political dominance over men of the sword," and "it was a gentleman scholar (sŏnbi), not a martial warrior, who represented 'hegemonic masculinity' under the Confucian order."[3] However after years of colonization by Japan, the model of the patriotic man eventually combined the two, the scholar and the warrior. How, then, did military culture, vis-à-vis the scholarly, infiltrate so deeply into Korean culture and also become the dominant influence on gender?

Later in the Chosŏn period (1392–1910), around the late nineteenth century, there were a series of challenges from foreign powers and native peasants that forced the ruling elite to adopt ideas by kaehwap'a, or the reformist Confucian group. One of the factions from this group thought that whereas the East had the superior mentality, the West was much more materially advanced. Eventually, they adopted the notion of *tongdosŏgi* (Eastern way, Western technology). The legacy of this adoption was that Koreans remained critical of, or downright opposed to, the notion of democracy and its institutions while adopting the materials of democracy—namely technology, arsenals, and weapons manufacturing—to combat the challenges from neighboring countries and uprisings within the country. The acceptance of Western technology gave more weight to military prowess. Pre- and postcolonial Korea continued to adopt and embrace *tongdosŏgi*, blaming colonization on effeminate Koreans and praising and glorifying the military tradition of honor and patriotism.[4]

Another factor contributing to the militarization of the nation was Japanese disciplinary control during the colonial period. The Japanese colonial state campaigned for cutting men's hair short, wearing colored clothes (as opposed to traditional white clothes), saving money, and prohibiting organized movements for public meetings and associations. The Japanese controlled not only the actions but also the minds of their subjects. This systemization of surveillance, monitoring, and use of physical force resulted in a fierce and violent rule, which added to the strong militaristic framework of postcolonial Korea. Although colonial rule left an extensive infrastructure for industrialization during the postcolonial era, it also left many who were deeply affected by, and willing to accept as a norm, its repressive and brutal militarism. Moreover, the interim US military government in Korea (1945–48) used the same people who served in the Japanese colonial government.[5] Hence, the militaristic culture was prolonged.

Hegemonic sentiments may grow after times of national turmoil. When a country is attacked or controlled, its citizens long for a stronger nation. Thus, the Korean War also had a profound impact on the populace for "the paramountcy of militarized national security and therefore the need for a strong military for decades to come."[6] Such a demand was met with the junta led by Park Chung Hee, who ruled from 1961 to 1979. Park formerly served in the Japanese military and was aware of the effects of dominant militarism. He enacted into law the current system of resident registration (*chumindŭng-nokchedo*). That registration enabled him to control the populace by assigning each citizen an unchallengeable number at birth and using it to store records about individuals regarding military service, taxation, and criminal investigations. In the meantime, Park continued to galvanize the nation with anticommunist posters, mottoes, and sentiments to fortify his military rule and to put down any detractors as suspicious communists. He and his successor, Chun Doo Hwan, who ruled from 1980 to 1987, continued militaristic rule and monitoring with the use of residential meetings by regions (*pansanghoe*), propaganda and anticommunist education, and contests in schools and in the mass media.[7]

Well before the Korean War, however, the dominant vehicle for instilling military ideals in the nation was and remains men's compulsory military service. At the end of World War II and the Japanese occupation of Korea, the US government inaugurated a new military system in Korea. However, because this newly US-established military consisted of elite officers who were trained by, and had served in, the Japanese Imperial Army, the final product was a curious mixture of US military structures and Japanese Imperial Army culture and routines.[8] Members of the military endured daily subjection to harsh bodily discipline that was justified by the collective ethos of "sacrifice of the individual for the sake of a larger goal, that is, the military security of a nation."[9]

With national security as a pretext, the military exploited its soldiers into complete obedience and required them to carry out orders without critical thinking. Although disobedience can be fatal during war, using wartime scenarios to instill a culture of complete obedience in non–combat-related situations, without opportunity for reflection, resulted in much abuse within the military. A number of books written by former officers, as well as countless articles that have been published in recent years and my own experience in the military, testify to the fact that much mental and physical abuse is still going on in the military.[10] Such a culture continues to reinforce "macho" mores, justifying the abuse and forcing soldiers to endure like "real" men.

These general features of military culture were accentuated in the South Korean military as shaped, to a great extent, by the fascistic culture of the Japanese Imperial Army. Before the recent gradual change in the military subculture began, strenuous discipline often took the form of repeated physical assault and psychological abuse to break down an individual conscript's will and subject him to the orders of his superiors. For instance, habitual practice of abuse ranged from verbal humiliation and severe beating to depriving subordinate soldiers of meals and sleep. Absolute obedience and the performance of personal services such as washing and ironing clothes or running errands governed the relationship between subordinates and superiors. These routine aspects of the military subculture indicate that popular acceptance of military services as men's national duty was not grounded in any genetic inclination of males to violence but stemmed rather from a "cultural inclination to obedience that would permit integration into the highly hierarchical military system." This process of bodily subjection, though it is designed to promote obedience, is likely to generate resistance toward military service, instead, if it is not accompanied by substantial rewards, a sense of entitlement, or a sense of fairness in bearing this burden.[11]

Notwithstanding the "few good men" who exemplify a "good" soldier and commander who rules without absoluteness and ruthlessness and expects unexamined acceptance, the proliferation of abuse and consequent male gender identity formation continue to burgeon within and beyond the military. The result of these practices is a culture that defines masculinity in a very peculiar and specific way. By studying numerous documents, Cho Sŏng-suk observed three common aspects of the ideal military man: The real man (*chinjja sanai*), (a) via common expressions and indoctrination of male supremacy, endures everything with superhuman toughness and fortitude; (b) via the rationalization of power, he accepts authoritarianism and strives for that power for himself; and (c) via sex as amusement or entertainment, he relieves stress by belittling women or by using demeaning sexual words, gestures, and actions.[12] There are efforts to eliminate these practices from high up in the military, but they are so prevalent and ingrained that they remain common in the Republic of Korea (ROK) Army.

Soldiers who do not fit neatly into, or who do not adhere to, these expectations are often treated abusively. The English equivalents of commonly used phrases in the military are, "At least a real man should," "Why don't you act like a man?," and "If you were born with something between your legs, act like it!" The greatest insult of all is, "Are you a girl?"[13] Guilt is another tactic used in the military to maintain these expectations. Superiors constantly remind subordinates, "Your parents believe in you," "Do it for your parents," and "Think of your parents and endure!" If not, they will be ashamed of you and you will have transgressed not only duty but also familial piety. These statements put tremendous pressure on soldiers to obey without question.[14] Moreover, what is not said is just as powerful as what is. That is, without actually saying that men are superior, these comments reinforce the notion that men, "at least," are not like lowly women.[15]

Those who do bear the painful experiences are eventually rewarded when they are promoted to positions of power. Officers, mostly men in their early twenties, get to experience power, enabling them to move a great number of men with a phrase or a flick of a finger. Wielding great power at such an early age leaves a lasting impression, and many continue to seek that power post service in the workplace and in their households.[16]

Non-officers are also rewarded the freedom and exoneration of any vulgarity by the time they become sergeants (the final rank before being discharged conscripts). Sergeants freely share often-fabricated stories of their sexual lives and make subordinates share their stories. Through this process manhood is measured by how many women a man has slept with, and the stories encourage other soldiers to imagine engaging in similarly exploitive sexual situations. As a result, women are often seen and talked about as objects of sex to be dominated and used at will.[17]

These experiences do not end as soldiers leave the guardhouse of their unit and are discharged. Most are discharged while they are in their early twenties and bring what they learned in the military into society. Because all able Korean men serve in the military and are conscripted at an impressionable age, most bring the gender ideology they acquired during their military service to their schools, families, and workplaces. Furthermore, given that most power positions are occupied by men, their gender ideology permeates all parts of Korean society.

In a sense, military modernity seems to be a stronger influence than neo-Confucianism as far as systematic dissemination of ideas of gender, sex, race, class, and so on. Similarly, the influence of the military at the time of the military coup demonstrated its power over Confucian ideologies. For example, immediately after the 1961 coup d'état, the military junta employed a new way of living by simplifying family rituals and slowly doing away with the Confucian notion of having many children as good luck. To alter this deeply rooted Confucian understanding and practice, the state "made extensive use of hierarchical organizations in administering the family planning policies."[18]

Simultaneously, however, the state used neo-Confucian gender ideology to its advantage when implementing the practice of contraception.[19] It is fair to say, then, that it was not neo-Confucian ideology per se that controlled the populace but the institutions that had the interpretive power of that ideology. The military is one such institution, and the state is another. With this power, the militaristic approach has infiltrated all corners of the society from which "the military mindset can translate into non-warring forms of aggression" in the family, marriage, workplaces, government, and other social institutions.[20] When a man enters a social institution, for example, it becomes a war zone, the circumstances become war situations, and competitors become enemies. "When the warrior male goes into business, business becomes war. . . . The market place is a heartless zone."[21]

Just as the culprit of this masculinity cannot simply be Korean neo-Confucianism, the indictment for unhealthy notions of gender in Korea cannot lie solely with military culture. The military is not the only institution of power and influence. Hence, although military modernity is a stronger influence than neo-Confucianism in indoctrinating specific notions of gender, there are other influential institutions that perpetuate gender norms, including the workplace, media, family, politics, church, schools, and textbooks.[22] I do not cover all of these institutions in Korea here; rather, I consider the Korean Roman Catholic Church.

The Roman Catholic Church in Korea

Catholic missions had positive influences on the Korean peninsula. The missionaries' transmission of Catholic teachings brought the nation new ideas and opportunities. Missions proclaimed radical ideas of equality before God, which was unimaginable in the neo-Confucian Chosŏn society. Korean Catholic women learned the Korean alphabet for the purpose of reading Catechism and prayer books, they became active in the early stages of the Catholic Church in Korea, and they benefited from the Catholic marriage and divorce system; some were even considered "companions and partners rather than submissive wives."[23]

Notwithstanding these positive influences, I cannot overlook the kinds of repression brought about by the Catholic Church.[24] Many setbacks from positive influences of Catholic missions were in the form of gender ideologies, especially those that appealed to Confucian concepts of chastity and womanly virtues. For example, instead of focusing on Mary as the mother of Jesus, the focus was on Mary as a silent and submissive virgin. The consequence of this approach was repetition of the old ways whereby women's obedience was more important than justice.[25]

Consider the Korean women who often were beaten by their anti-Catholic husbands and who ran away. The missionaries told them to go back home and respect the Catholic way by submitting to and obeying their husbands. The French missionary priests did not help the situation by demanding strict obedience from the faithful; they reinforced neo-Confucian notions that made Korean women more willing to be silent and to obey men.[26] Thus, what was an active group in the Catholic Church at its foundation in Korea became a passive group, becoming more restricted upon returning home. Conversely, men became compassionate partners with their counterparts in the early Church in

Korea, only to return to their authoritative and commanding masculinity at home.[27]

Since then a hegemonic and authoritarian approach, as further propagated in the ROK Army, has been the overarching method chosen by many priests in Korea.[28] Because Koreans were accustomed to ideas of hierarchical cosmology and obedience to superiors, and since all able priests have fulfilled compulsory military service, priests had no problems implementing the corresponding militaristic mores.[29] In an emblematic representation of such reality, Korea remains one of the very few parts of the world that still practices head covering (using *misabo* or Mass veils) by its women. Continuing with such a methodology and refusing to listen to the voices of lay (women) within the Church will be detrimental for the future of the Church in Korea. The Korean Catholic Church is using an authoritarian approach dangerously similar to that used in the military. Many priests demand complete loyalty from their parishioners and do so in hegemonic fashion.[30] There is an expectation of sacrifice while very little theological explanation is given for this demand. Priests are comfortable demanding material gifts, and many believers follow and bow to them in the same way they do to the altar; however, many are starting to recognize these problems.

Small but powerful voices of discontent have begun to emerge. Some Catholic scholars have published their dissatisfaction with the authoritarianism of Korean Catholic priests and called for a less authoritative and more loving approach.[31] Other books call for reforms to do away with authoritarianism and give more opportunities to the laity, especially women.[32] Many articles call for more lay and women's participation to eradicate the subserviently obedient and passive images of women and Mary and to replace such models with more inquisitive, conversational, and active images.[33]

Although never directly acknowledging the Church's gender ideology as problematic, the Roman Catholic Church in Korea has taken steps to respond to a growing number of dissenting voices concerning women's issues. In a letter commemorating two hundred years of Catholicism in Korea (1984), the Pastoral Council in Korea included a "separate issue" section in which it admitted that the role of women in the Church had been diminished from what it was when the Church was just beginning to take shape in Korea. The council also stated that it is problematic for the Church's future that women could only participate as helpers, and that more education is needed for and about women and more opportunities must be given to them.[34]

Unfortunately, few improvements have been made in practice.[35] While priests' attitudes toward women and gendered cosmology are not always visible, the prevalence of enforcing the wearing of the *misabo* and the insistence on women's role as helpers for the Church, their family, and their husbands are indicative of where they stand. Consequently, men are on the receiving end of women's help, and the priests benefit most of all.[36] It is difficult not to think of the alarming similarities with militaristic ordering: obedience to absolute authority, expectations of sacrifice for the whole, and differentiated gender expectations.

As in the case of men in the workplace, all able priests have fulfilled compulsory military duties, and they return to the male-dominated hierarchal society of the seminaries. It is almost inevitable that they continue to practice what they became familiar with and were taught to think in the military. There are countless studies of the negative effects these norms have on women.[37] In what follows, I explore the dangers of these Korean (neo-Confucian and militaristic) ideologies for men.

The Dangers

When the economic crisis hit Korea (known as the "IMF crisis" because of the Korean government's acceptance of an International Monetary Fund bailout) in 1997, and again in recent years, many workers lost their jobs. In a country where masculinity is defined by one's performance, the ability to have power over inferiors according to that performance, and status as the breadwinner, many men found themselves in a dire situation. Suddenly, they were not "man enough," and their identities were in jeopardy. For many, it was better to live in the streets or even to commit suicide rather than return to their families to live as powerless men.[38]

Other men were stressed from the pressure to keep their productivity and performance high, from the prospect of losing their jobs, from the demands of superiors, and from not fulfilling familial duties. As a result, many men came to rely on alcohol, cigarettes, and even sexual services to relieve these stresses. Not being able to talk about their feelings (for that would not be "manly") only added to their anxiety.[39]

The ramifications of the hegemonic masculine ideology go beyond men's reaction to it. Korean women, like other members of the society, also respond in a pejorative fashion when these expectations are not met. When men are not fulfilling their roles as breadwinners, it is often acceptable for women to leave the home. One of the lawful reasons for divorce in Korea is a husband's economic incompetence.[40] Faced with possible divorce, men often choose to accommodate their wives in any way they can, sometimes even to the point of allowing their wives to commit adultery.[41] Incidents of domestic violence and battered husbands have reached news and media outlets.[42]

Also, as more Korean women find employment outside the home, more power in the family is allocated to them. Used properly, their economic power brings opportunities for shared power in the family. Used improperly, however, it serves as a tool of revenge for years of being ordered and controlled and even as a way to win money in divorce suits.[43] Men sometimes react by tolerating abuse or even by committing suicide (Koreans are ranked number one in the world for suicide among men in their forties).[44] However, men also react violently. Struggling with abandonment by society and neglect from the family, men resort to verbal abuse and domestic violence to reclaim their throne as the ruler in the family in the hope of recovering the power and control they lost.[45]

When all corners of society—whether the workplace, media, family, political arena, military, church, school, or textbooks—tell men they must embrace authority and power in order to be accepted, men find it difficult to think otherwise. When men cannot find a way to fulfill these expectations, the negative effects on all levels of society are almost inevitable. These "manly" expectations are unhealthy for everyone— whether Korean, Catholic, man, or woman—no matter where they live.

The need for new models and expectations regarding men and masculinity is urgent and cannot wait another generation.

Signs of Hope: Changes in Korea

Despite overwhelming institutional indoctrination, voices of concern have begun to emerge among men, taking cues from earlier feminist movements and calling attention to the existence and enforcing of machismo culture in Korea. In May 1992 a group called the Good Fathers' Gathering (my translation) set out to nurture a happy, safe, and healthy family by respecting all family members, instead of enforcing the paterfamilias approach.[46] Eventually similar groups would unite to form a comprehensive male movement called the National Association of Korean Fathers.[47] Prior to the formulation of these male groups, the men's studies programs in Korea focused only on Western scholarship. Now the men's studies programs have taken on a Korean shape.[48] Unfortunately, the voice of these movements remains small, but there is possibility for growth.

Aside from these men's movements, there have been social and policy changes in Korea. Increasingly more Koreans approve of women in the workforce (eight in ten), place women who are housewives on equal ground as those who work for wages (nine in ten), and do not see the need to prefer sons (one in ten Korean women aged fifteen to forty-four).[49] The 1987 Equal Employment Law, the 1989 New Family Law, the 1991 Infant Protection and Care Law, the 1993 Special Law against Sexual Violence, the 1997 Law Prohibiting Family Violence, and the 1999 Law to Prohibit and Regulate Gender Discrimination are all geared toward gender equality and human rights.[50] At a glance, Korea seems to be on its way to greater gender fairness; however, even a fractional study of these data reveals otherwise.

I do not intend to detract from or belittle the fruits of the efforts of the men and women who fight for justice in Korea. However, it must be noted that the psyche and structures of Korean society have not changed greatly, and much work is yet needed to achieve gender justice. For instance, it is true that Koreans view women in the workforce much more positively than before, but only insofar as they also fulfill their duties as housewives and mothers. That is, a better social status combined with the same traditional gender role expectations in the family yields worse situations for women. These "improvements" often are setbacks for women because mothers are expected to be full-time career women as well as full-time housewives and caregivers.[51] Progress did not redefine gender roles for women and men; it simply added to previous expectations.

More women have opportunities to work than ever before. However, the ratio of women in the workplace is lower than the average for women in nations studied by the Organization for Economic Cooperation and Development (OECD) in 2004 (50.3 percent compared to 60.4 percent) and for Korean men (74.8 percent).[52] Also, women's wages are about 60 percent of what men earn, and women work in service, blue-collar, clerical, and part-time jobs more often than men.[53]

These data mean that perspectives on male roles have stayed essentially the same as well, which is not necessarily good news for men. The more lasting and rigid the gender role expectations, the more men feel pressured to perform, deliver, and achieve power as authorities and as breadwinners. The increase of women in the workforce may be seen as a threat to men's objective to gain control in the workplace. When women earn more money than men, or when wives are forced to work, husbands and fathers may perceive this outside employment by their wives and daughters as their failure as men.[54]

However, the consciousness of Korean men is also changing. According to a 2006 survey of seven hundred Korean men, 68.7 percent approved of the so-called women's quota system (*yŏsung haldangje*, requiring and encouraging women's participation in the workplace) in private and public workplaces, 56.9 percent stated the sex of their only born child did not matter, and only 10.2 percent thought that men must buy the house and women provide the dowry (wedding and household expenses) at the beginning of a marriage, which is traditionally the case in Korea.[55] In a different 2006 survey, which was compared to a 1995 survey in which

37 percent of Korean respondents (male and female) stated a university education is more important for a man than for a woman, there was a significant drop to 23 percent. Some men are even choosing to become nurses, telephone customer service representatives, and weather forecasters—occupations traditionally associated with women in Korea.[56]

Unfortunately, the mindset seems somewhat inconsistent. For example, of the seven hundred surveyed men, only 3.2 percent preferred having a woman as their superior at work, and 70.2 percent said women could work insofar as their jobs do not interfere with their domestic duties. In other words, men permit more women in the workplace but restrict them from being their superiors and require them to fill their normal roles at home, too. The conclusions of the survey were that men, overall, wanted to escape the pressure and the responsibility of a paterfamilias model but did not want to let go of their authority and power, especially over women.[57]

Thus, while Koreans are on the path to improvement, there is still a long way to go. The more institutions become aware of these realities, the better the Korean social situation of justice will be. Policies, organizations, and participation for equality and mutuality are on the rise but must do more. High schools and universities must include awareness programs on their orientation agenda to educate students about the dangers of rigid gender norms. Institutions such as the Korean Roman Catholic Church must also follow suit. Prior to that, however, the ROK military must try to eliminate the overly militaristic male identity before it reaches the society at large.

Readjusting Educational Program

Veterans "who have been injured psychologically and physically" often seek the services of readjustment programs, such as the one offered by the Northeast Veteran Training and Rehabilitation Center, that "give struggling young veterans and their families the tools they need for a life after war."[58] While completing compulsory military service may not necessarily be as traumatic as being in a war, psychological harm incurred in military service can be damaging for young men of an impressionable age and can have effects on society. Even when they do not find their experience unsettling, those who have completed military service must be taught that the ROK military milieu is not transferable and should not be translated into society and its institutions in general. To that end, I propose a readjustment educational program that takes place prior to, or at least soon after, an individual's discharge from compulsory service.

Such education should include lessons about unequal political, economic, and religio-social rights and opportunities for men and women that stem from androcentric ideologies; the individual's participation in an androcentric culture during the duration of his military service; education about the harmful effects for both women and men that result from such ideologies within culture; a just vision of society contra a military ethos that follows a hierarchal model, demands absolute obedience, and puts manhood over and against womanhood; and steps that one can take to curb one's acquired militaristic tendencies and become part of the solution for a more just society outside the military. The aim would be to evoke in the young minds of soldiers an awareness of the realities of injustice and inequality of the world. More importantly, this kind of educational program would demand disconnect and discontinuity of the military (gender) ethos necessary for adjusting to the larger society in a healthy way. In this manner, a young soldier at the end of his duty may realize that if he is not part of the solution, he is perpetuating unjust notions about gender in the institutions to which he must return, which certainly include religious institutions.

Of course, there are discharged men who adjust to society well. There are a few good men with mature minds and attitudes who clearly distinguish the life of military service from the life outside it. They probably do not need such a readjustment educational process to the same extent that some others do, although they might still benefit from it. However, the harmful effects of not having a readjustment process are too detrimental and the chances of being able to make such sound judgments at a young age are too small to have a laissez-faire attitude about the future of those who are discharged from the military. As the military exists today, there is no check on the system. A reflective educational program for soldiers awaiting the end of their compulsory service or for college students who recently completed their military duties would be an important corrective experience.

One of the best ways to help discontinue the militaristic (gender) ethos is to reflect on the times when one was able to act honestly in spite of expectations of the military culture. As a soldier, I lived up to the expectations of the mass. However, there was a moment, after marching up and reaching the peak of a mountainous region of Kangwon Province, when everybody was too exhausted to think about any expectations. When we started our descent—a surprisingly more strenuous task than going up the mountain—some soldiers started to show emotions, and we started to hold each other's hands, a sure sign of weakness. Reminiscent of the male athletes holding hands before attempting the game-winning goal, what would normally be unacceptable became acceptable. The exercise was grueling enough that we were able to act honestly and accept each other without preconceptions because this act of sympathy helped us to endure. Upon reflection, this heuristic moment taught me that, whatever "manliness" or being a "true solider" entailed, it must also include caring, supporting, and accepting human frailty.

Conclusion

I entered the service with a critical view, a mind filled with the hermeneutics of suspicion, and a disapproving attitude regarding the military's language of gender. Moreover, I entered the service as the oldest (thirty years old) of nearly two thousand trainees and likely much less impressionable than many of the soldiers who entered with me. Despite these qualities, I found myself saying, doing, and thinking the very things that I had criticized before I had entered, especially as I neared the end of my service, a time at which I enjoyed a tremendous amount of power as a sergeant. Even with my preparation before entering, I required quite a long period to adjust to the world outside the fences of the military after my discharge. Even at my age, I had unknowingly lived in, and played into, the physical and mental constructions of this military culture. I can imagine the dire consequences for many soldiers who are younger, less prepared, less informed, and less aware. For these young men, not doing anything is not an option. I believe that education regarding gender inequity must happen in all corners of society, including families, workplaces, schools, and churches. Given the situation in Korea, however, the first and perhaps the most important place for the educational program I have proposed is in the military. Given the sociopolitical and religious climate in Korea, this reeducation will not be an easy task. However, improbability has always accompanied Christian missions, starting with Jesus of Nazareth. My hope is that one day the effects of this essay, that is, education, will extend beyond military institutions to the larger Korean society, including the Korean Roman Catholic Church.

Questions for Reflection

1. Choi argues that patriarchal notions of masculinity were readily reinforced by neo-Confucian social structures, militarism, and the Catholic Church in Korea. What institutions and ideologies similarly reinforce patriarchal notions of masculinity in North America? What structures challenge these notions of masculinity?

2. Given the fact that military service is presently voluntary rather than compulsory in the United States and Canada, and that this system "promises" upward mobility, albeit with significant risk for those who might well have chosen alternatives had they been available, how might North American soldiers identify and then think about the way hegemonic norms for class as well as gender are reinforced and/or challenged in and through their military service?

3. Although the essay considers the Catholic reinforcement and appropriation of Korean-styled patriarchy, other Christian denominations have adopted similar patterns for the administrative use of power. What structures in other Christian denominations or world religions concentrate power in ways both obvious and subtle that disproportionately advantage some over others in their communities?

Suggestions for Further Reading

Burke, Kelsy, and Amy Moff Hudec. "Sexual Encounters and Manhood Acts: Evangelicals, Latter-Day Saints, and Religious Masculinities." *Journal for the Scientific Study of Religion* 54.2 (2015): 330–344.

Lee, Na-Young. "Negotiating the Boundaries of Nation, Christianity, and Gender: The Korean Women's Movement against Military Prostitution." *Asian Journal of Women's Studies* 17.1 (2011): 34–66.

Nye, Robert A. "Western Masculinities in War and Peace." *American Historical Review* 112.2 (2007): 417–438.

Pinn, Anthony B. "What to Make of Gendered Bodies?: Adressing the Male Problem" and "Sex(uality) and the (Un)Doping of Bodies." In *Embodiment and the New Shape of Black Theological Thought*, 53–70, 71–100. New York: New York University Press, 2010.

Wilson, Brittany E. "Gender Disrupted: Jesus as a 'Man' in the Fourfold Gospel." *Word and World* 36.1 (2016): 24–35.

Notes

I thank those who came to hear the presentation version of this essay, the anonymous reviewers, and the supportive community from Loyola University Chicago.

1. I used the Revised Romanization for transliterations of the modern and commonly used Korean terms (http://web.archive.org/web/20070916025652 /http://www.korea.net/korea/kor_loca.asp?code=A020303); and the McCune-Reischauer Romanization for the historical or scholarly terms and names (G. M. McCune and E. O. Reischauer, "The Romanization of Korean Language," *Transactions of the Korean Branch of the Royal Asiatic Society* 29 [1939]: 1–55; www.nla .gov.au/librariesaustralia/files/2011/07/ras-1939.pdf).

2. When contemporary Koreans refer to the "old ways" (*gusik*) of the Chosŏn (Yi) Dynasty (1392–1910) or Confucianism, they are often referring to the later version of neo-Confucian (Sŏnglihak) thoughts, with its emphasis on the Four Books by Chu Hsi (1130–1200) from the Song Dynasty in China. Yang Jong-Hoe, "Changing Values Cause Ideological Confusion," in *Social Change in Korea*, vol. 2, ed. Kim Kyong-Dong and the *Korea Herald* (Gyeonggi-do, Korea: Jimoondang, 2008), 86–98. While the limits of this essay do not allow me to explain further, it is my belief that a more genuine Confucian (gender) cosmological interpretation emphasizes harmony rather than unevenness, despite its historical patriarchalism.

3. Seungsook Moon, *Militarized Modernity and Gendered Citizenship in South Korea* (Durham, NC: Duke University Press, 2005), 47.

4. Ibid., 20.

5. Ibid., 22–24. See also Bruce Cummings, *The Origins of the Korean War: Liberation and the Emergence of Separate Regimes, 1945–1947* (Princeton, NJ: Prince-

ton University Press, 1981), 349, 380. The citizens of Korea had already established their own versions of interim governmental commissions, right after their independence on August 15, 1945. Hence, ironically, when the US military decided to appoint the "experienced" people for infrastructural "order," the Korean people were ruled by the same people against whom the nation had just fought and gained independence.

6. Moon, *Militarized Modernity*, 25.

7. Ibid., 28–37.

8. See Sŏ Hyo-il, *Military Reform Must Be Done This Way* [*Kungaehyŏk irŏke haeyahanda, sang/ha*], vol. 2 (Seoul, Korea: Paek'am, 1995), 72; and Moon, *Militarized Modernity*, 49.

9. Moon, *Militarized Modernity*, 48–49.

10. Si-soo Park, "Junior Marines Fall Victim to Abuse," *Korea Times*, March 24, 2011; www.koreatimes.co.kr/www/news/nation/2011/03/113_83801.html. Although some good and benefit resulted from my having compulsorily served in the Republic of Korea (ROK) Army, the negative experiences significantly outweighed the positive. For the increase in the suicide rate in the ROK military in the last six years, despite the efforts to end abuse (popularly known as "Code Red"), see Kim Dae Woo, "Increase in Suicide in the Military," *Herald Business*, July 11, 2011; http://biz.heraldm.com/common/Detail.jsp?newsMLId=20110711000633.

11. Moon, *Militarized Modernity*, 50.

12. Cho Sŏng-suk, "Military Culture and Man," [*Kundaemunhwawa Namsŏng*] in *Man and Korean Society* [*Namsŏngkwa Hankuksahoe*], ed. Center for the Research of Korean Women Society (Seoul, Korea: Sahoemunhwa yŏnkuso, 1997), 159. The negative outcomes resulting from militaristic masculine imagery are not specific to Korea, of course. See Cynthia Enloe's argument that the torture at Abu Ghraib was a technique to show imperial superiority to the subjugated by having them be naked, masturbate, and pretend homosexual acts with each other. Cynthia Enloe, "Feminist Readings on Abu Ghraib: Introduction," *International Feminist Journal of Politics* 9, no. 1 (2007): 37–40. See also Keun-joo Christine Pae, "Western Princesses—A Missing Story: A Christian Feminist Ethical Analysis of US Military Prostitution in South Korea," *Journal of the Society of Christian Ethics* 29, no. 2 (2009): 121–39.

13. The threat of appearing "feminine" may have played a big part, according to Enloe, in much of the immoral decisions in the military, government, and foreign policies. See her discussion of presidents Lyndon Johnson's and Richard Nixon's insistence on military engagements in Vietnam. Enloe, *Globalization and Militarism*, especially 48, 61.

14. Ibid., 160–66; and Cho Sŏng-suk, "Military and Man" [*Kundaewa Namsŏng*] *Hankuk Sahoehak Nonmunchip*, December 1996, 221–22.

15. Much of the reinforcement comes by way of military songs depicting (only)

men as strong, patriotic, and doing the really important work for the country and for their families.

16. Sŏng-suk, "Military Culture and Man," 166–70; and Sŏng-suk, "Military and Man," 223.

17. Sŏng-suk, "Military Culture and Man," 172–75; and Sŏng-suk, "Military and Man," 223–24.

18. Moon, *Militarized Modernity*, 81, 91.

19. Ibid., 88. This implementation was done by highlighting women's domesticity, putting them in charge of childbirth and controlling of it, and by portraying them as being "dutiful" and willing nationals in practicing family planning.

20. Daniel C. Maguire, "The Feminization of God and Ethics," *Annual of the Society of Christian Ethics* 2 (1982), 10.

21. Ibid., 11.

22. For influences from these institutions, see CRKWS, ed., *Man and Korean Society [Namsŏngkwa Hankuksahoe]* (Seoul, Korea: Sahoemunhwa yŏnkuso, 1997). See also Korean Woman Institute, ed., *New Lecture in Feminist Studies [Sae Yŏsŏnghakkangŏi]* (Seoul, Korea: DongNyuk, 1999), 103–312.

23. Jong-rye Gratia Song SPC, "Listening with the Heart to the Echo of Silenced Voice" (PhD diss., Weston Jesuit School of Theology, May 2002), 87–91. Catholic missionary teachings were considered dangerously progressive—introducing ideas such as gender equality, monogamy, the possibility of more autonomous life as virgins, and the possibility of a more active public life—to the point of governmental persecution of Korean Catholics. See Yŏngok Kang, "Korean Catholic Woman's Movement" [Hankuk Gatolik yŏsŏngundongŏi ui hŭruŭm] in *Catholic Church in 100 Years of Modern Korea [Hankuk Kŭn/Hyŏndae ioonyŏn sokŭi Gatolikkyohoe]*, vol. 1 (Seoul, Korea: Gatolik Chulpansa [Catholic Publishers], 2003), 363–73.

24. Some were in the form of "spiritual" ideologies. According to Deberniere Torrey, Catholicism brought about "a limited but significant application of the doctrine of equality and the transcending of traditional gender-based norms" but not without being "constrained by anxiety over spiritual contamination, for which the best recourse is escape from the body through martyrdom." For a fuller discussion, see Deberniere Torrey, "Transcending Nature and Tradition at a Price: The Female in Early Korean Catholic Texts," *International Comparative Literature Association Conference*, Seoul, Korea, August 2010, 2, 12–13.

25. Song, *Listening with the Heart*, 92.

26. Ibid., 92–93.

27. Anselm Hee Sun Byun, SJ, "The Reality of God Is the Subject-Matter of Theology: A Study of Bernard Lonergan's Position" (PhD diss., Boston College, May 1995), 235–41.

28. For more on authoritarianism, see Anselm Kyongsuk Min, *The Korean*

Church 2000: Beyond Authoritarianism and Ecclesiocentrism [*HanKuk Kyohoe 2000*] (Seoul, Korea: Bundo Book [*Bundo Chulpansa*], 2000).

29. A similar method is used in seminaries, making theological education for seminarians indistinguishable from catechist training. In an interview, a diocesan seminarian in Korea told me, "The grass must be even. As soon as there is a leaf of grass longer than the rest, it is cut off right away!" Dissenting voices, advocating a theologically inquisitive and stimulating conversation, are starting to appear. See the product of the symposiums held in Korea on the subject-matter, Kongsŏk Seo and Yangmo Chŏng, *Korean Catholic Church: Is It OK the Way It Is?* [*HanKuk Gatolic KyoHoe Idaero Johŭnka?*] (Seoul, Korea: Bundo Books [*Bundo Chulpansa*], 1999).

30. Min, *Korean Church 2000*, 239–68.

31. Numerous articles published in *KyungHyang Japji* that struggle with authoritarianism in Korean Catholic churches (priests more specifically) can be found in issues published in April 1988, 48–49; September 1988, 125–26; and January 2008, 23.

32. Seo and Chŏng, *Korean Catholic Church: Is It OK the Way It Is?* See also Yŏngok Kang, *Dreaming of an Open Church* [*Yŏllin Kyohoelŭl Kkumkkumyŏ*] (Seoul, Korea: Pauline Press [Paoroŭittal], 2004); cf. Kathryn Reyes Hamrlik, "The Principle of Subsidiarity and Catholic Ecclesiology" (PhD diss., Loyola University Chicago, March 2011).

33. *KyungHyang Japji*, August 1994, 123–26; September 1995; February 1996, 38–40 and 67; and August 2000, 41. There are some Korean Catholic women's groups that formed since the 1950s in an effort to resolve these problems. See Yŏngok Kang, "The Present Status and Characteristics of Korean Catholic Woman's Groups" [Hankuk Gatolik Yŏsŏng danchedŭlŭi Hyŏnhwanggwa Tŭksŏng], in *Catholic Church in 100 Years of Modern Korea*, vol. 2 (Seoul, Korea: Gatolik Chulpansa [Catholic Publishers], 2006): 373–402; also Jung Woo Park, "The Korean Catholic Church and Feminism: A Study of Four Catholic Feminist Groups and Their Members" (PhD diss., Fordham University, May 2004).

34. Yŏngye Jang, "Women Pastoring: A Subject That Cannot Be Ignored Any Longer," *KyungHyang Japji* (August 2000): 41–44.

35. It is significant that these concerns were discussed in a "separate issue" section, as if it should not be included in the main discussions.

36. Seo and Chŏng, *Korean Catholic Church*; and Kang, *Dreaming of an Open Church*.

37. Chŏgmoon Cho, *Love and Sex* [Sarang kwa Sŏng]; and Sŏk-il Ahn, *Sexual Liberation of Men* [Namsŏngŭi SŏngHaepang], quoted in Chŏ moon Cho, "Male Sex According to Men," in *Feminist, Speaking about Men* [*Peminisŭtŭ, Namsŏngŭl Malhada*], ed. Myunghee Song (Seoul: Purŭnsasang, 2000), 99.

38. Masanori Sasaki, JaeTaek Lee, Chae Ki Jung, and JiHwan Han, ed., *Men Studies and Men Movement about Feminism* [*Peminijŭme Taehan Namsŏnghakwa Namsŏngundong*] (WonMiSa: Seoul, Korea, 2007), 293–98; see also a more recent

article in Korean illustrating the increase in suicide rate among baby-boomers (four times that of same age group twenty years ago) and the reason (44.9%) for suicidal thoughts among men: economic hardship. Park Yong Joo, "Increase in Suicide Rate among the Early 50s 'Baby-Boomer,'" *Yonhap News*, September 20, 2011. www.yonhapnews.co.kr/society/2011/09/19/0701000000AKR201109191688 00004.HTML?template=2085.

39. Chŏngmoon Cho, MyungSoo Kwon, ŭiSoo Lee, O K Lee, NaYoung Lee, Chae Ki Jung, Russell Feldmeir, and Paul Kivel, eds., *Men's Studies & Men's Movement* [*Namsŏnghakwa Namsŏngundong*] (Seoul, Korea: Tongmoonsa, 2000), 415–60.

40. Sasaki et al., *Men Studies and Men Movement about Feminism*, 298–99.

41. Cho et al., *Men's Studies & Men's Movement*, 439–40, 452–54.

42. Ibid., 449–51, 458–60. One must be careful, however, in a society mostly ruled by men, that these instances may well be accented much more so than the reality—a way of putting the blame on women. Nevertheless, these wrongdoings do occur and must not be dismissed as minor instances.

43. Ibid., 437–39.

44. Sasaki et al., *Men Studies and Men Movement about Feminism*, 296–97.

45. Cho et al., *Men's Studies & Men's Movement*, 416. Such a phenomenon extends, at the very least, to families that are influenced by the same or similar cultural expectations. For example, see Young I. Song, *Battered Women in Korean Immigrant Families: The Silent Scream* (New York: Garland Press, 1996).

46. Cho et al., *Men's Studies & Men's Movement*, 202–5, 206–11.

47. Sasaki et al., *Men Studies and Men Movement about Feminism*, 48–52. Another group, Fathers Who Love Their Daughters [*Ttalŭl Saranghanun Apŏchidŭlŭi Moim*], established in 2001, tried to broaden the previous groups' "neighborhood" boundaries of influence to a "social" influence.

48. Ibid., 26–27.

49. Kisoo Eun, "Family Values Changing—but Still Conservative," in *Social Change in Korea*, vol. 2, ed. Kim Kyong-Dong and the *Korea Herald* (Gyeonggi-do, Korea: Jimoondang, 2008), 146–56, esp. 151; and Onjook Lee, "More Gender Equality, but Women Still Held Back," in *Social Change in Korea*, vol. 2, ed. Kim Kyong-Dong and the *Korea Herald* (Gyeonggi-do, Korea: Jimoondang, 2008), 167–74, esp. 167.

50. Lee, "More Gender Equality, but Women Still Held Back," 171.

51. Eun, "Family Values Changing—but Still Conservative," 146–52. See also his "Lowest-Low Fertility in the ROK: Causes, Consequences, and Policy Responses," *Asian-Pacific Population Journal* 22, no. 2 (August 2007): 51–72.

52. Lee, "More Gender Equality, but Women Still Held Back," 167–74.

53. The most recent research shows that among thirty-eight OECD countries, South Korea had the greatest wage disparity between men and women and placed third in hiring disparity. See Kim Kitae, "Korea, the Greatest Gender Wage Dis-

parity in OECD Nations," *Hankyoreh Daily*, July 9, 2009; www.hani.co.kr/arti /economy/economy_general/364952.html.

54. For more on Korean "normality" of the family and the anxiety caused by that normality, see Hyejeong Byun's, "Homophobia and the Snail Family in Korea" in *Social Change in Korea*, vol. 2, ed. Kim Kyong-Dong and the *Korea Herald* (Gyeonggi-do, Korea: Jimoondang, 2008), 184–93. Also see CRKWS, ed., *Man and Korean Society*, 9–12; and Korean Woman Institute, ed., *New Lecture in Feminist Studies*, 103–312.

55. *Hankyoreh 21 Monthly*, "[We] Will Not Live Like Our Fathers! [Abŏjich'ŏrum Salji Anketta]," March 14, 2006. 600; especially Sohee Kim's articles, 42–62.

56. Eun, "Family Values Changing—but Still Conservative," 149.

57. *Hankyoreh 21 Monthly*, 48–49. It is noteworthy that Korean men in their late forties showed the highest percentage of affirmation to the statement "Men should not show their weakness in any situations," yet the study found the highest rate of men who had cried recently because of hardship or sadness in the same group of men. This result may be an indication that men who do not fit the norm are more likely to be adamant about that same norm.

58. Brian MacQuarrie, "Readjustment: Gardner Rehab Center Helps Young Veterans to Cope with Life after War," *Boston Globe*, August 23, 2011; www.boston .com/news/local/massachusetts/articles/2011/08/23/training_and_rehab _center_helps_war_veterans_readjust/.

7

Mobile Porn?

Teenage Sexting and Justice for Women

Karen Peterson-Iyer

The practice of sending and receiving sexually explicit images via mobile phones ("sexting") has grown exponentially in recent years with the accessibility of cellular technology. This essay examines this practice, when conducted by teenagers, in light of a Christian feminist approach to justice. Without harmfully exhorting girls' sexual "purity," we must nevertheless develop a moral framework that challenges the practice of sexting while simultaneously empowering young women to claim primary control over their own sexual experience. For Christians, justice, addressed to sexting, must attend to sexual injustice even as it promotes genuine freedom, embodiment, mutuality and relational intimacy, and equality.

In winter of 2010 in Lacey, Washington, a fourteen-year-old named Margarite took out her cell phone and snapped a full-length photo of herself, naked, in her bathroom mirror. She then sent the photo to a potential new boyfriend, Isaiah, at his suggestion. A few weeks later, Isaiah forwarded the photo to another eighth-grade girl, a former friend of Margarite's, who transmitted it (along with the text "Ho Alert!") to dozens of others on her cell phone contact list. Margarite became instantly (in)famous in her middle school; other kids began calling her a "slut" and a "whore," and she received sneers and ogles from peers she barely knew. Her friends were ostracized for associating with her. School officials soon discovered the situation, and the police were notified. Reaction was swift: the county prosecutor chose not to press charges against Margarite herself, but three students involved in the case, including

This essay was published originally in the *Journal of the Society of Christian Ethics* 33.2 (2013): 93–110.

Isaiah and two of the girls who forwarded Margarite's photo, were charged with distributing child pornography—a Class C felony. All these students were in eighth grade.[1]

Stories like this one are by no means an everyday occurrence, in spite of their notoriety. Neither are they a complete anomaly. In recent years, a few well-publicized cases of teen "sexting"—the sending of sexually suggestive images via mobile phones[2]—have inspired widespread fear on the part of parents and educators alike. The dangers of sexting are not limited to middle schoolers like Margarite and Isaiah. In a similar case, Jesse Logan, an eighteen-year-old high school senior from Ohio, sent a nude photo of herself to her boyfriend, who then made the decision to forward it to four other girls. The photo went viral, and Jesse was ostracized by her peers and quickly spun into an emotional depression. Taunted and labeled a "slut," a "whore," and a "porn queen," Jesse Logan hanged herself at her home a few months later.[3] Unlike Margarite, Jesse was not a minor at the time of the incident, so no child pornography charges were raised. But her case is undeniably tragic, and her death reminds us that teen sexting represents a far weightier act than a harmless youthful prank.

The practice of sexting has grown exponentially in recent years. It is particularly troubling when carried out by minors, especially young teenagers—a demographic whose cell phone use has skyrocketed over the past decade.[4] Minors who send or receive sexual images often do not recognize the serious social, legal, emotional, and psychological implications of doing so. A further troubling aspect of sexting is that the images distributed are more commonly of young women, often without their consent. Hence, society's mostly fearful response thus far arguably contributes to the exercise of negative social control over female sexuality. Without reverting to moral evaluations that extol young women's modesty or sexual purity—evaluations often promulgated by Christians and propped up by historical antisexuality themes within Christian thought—we must nevertheless develop a freshly relevant moral and legal framework that discourages the practice of sexting while simultaneously empowering young women to claim primary control over their own sexual experience.

Along these lines, I approach the topic of teen sexting not only as a Christian concerned with what justice requires but also as a feminist. Drawing heavily upon the understanding of justice articulated by feminist ethicist Margaret Farley, I argue that an adequate approach to sexting is governed by an understanding of justice that attends to the concrete reality of the sexter, including his or her social, emotional, and psychosexual experience. Moreover, for Christians, justice—addressed to the practice of sexting—must include attention to the sexual injustice that already structures the lives of so many young women. An adequate understanding of justice promotes freedom, embodiment, mutuality and relational intimacy, and equality of power—qualities that should in fact govern all sexual relations. This essay concludes with brief suggestions of concrete directions for an ecclesial and social response to the practice of teenage sexting.

The Prevalence of Teen Sexting

It is primarily teenagers and young adults who sext. This essay focuses exclusively on teenagers. Analyses of the prevalence of sexting among teens vary dramatically. A 2008 study by the National Campaign to Prevent Teen and Unplanned Pregnancy, in conjunction with Cosmogirl.com, concluded that 20 percent of teens overall (22 percent of girls and 18 percent of boys) have sent or posted nude or seminude pictures or videos of themselves. For young teen girls (aged thirteen to sixteen), the figure was 11 percent. According to the same study, 25 percent of teen girls and 33 percent of teen boys say that they have had nude or seminude images—originally meant for someone else—shared with them.[5] A study conducted by the Pew Research Center in 2009 sampled adolescents ages twelve to seventeen and found the numbers to be more modest: 4 percent of cell phone–owning teens said they had sent sexually suggestive nude or nearly nude images of themselves to someone else via text, and

15 percent said they had received such images.[6] Early in 2012, the American Academy of Pediatrics arrived at an even lower number; according to this study, 2.5 percent of youth had appeared in or created nude or nearly nude images, and 7.1 percent of youth had received them.[7] Finally, a large study published in the July 2012 issue of the *Archives of Pediatrics and Adolescent Medicine* found that a stunning 28 percent of public high school students aged fifteen to seventeen admitted to having sent a naked picture of themselves via text or email, while 31 percent had asked someone else to do so, and a full 57 percent had themselves been asked to send such pictures.[8]

The variance in these numbers should cause us to pause before jumping on a media-fueled bandwagon that depicts sexting as a dominant feature of nearly every American teenager's life. However, even at the more modest figures, "sexting of explicit images involves a low percentage but still a considerable number of youth."[9] Moreover, the larger studies, if correct, reveal that US high school students might consider sexting a relatively common practice and, further, that the majority of fifteen- to seventeen-year-old students have been urged at some point to take part in sexting. We simply cannot dismiss the practice as peripheral to modern teenagers' experience.

While some disagreement exists about how often it is females whose images are sexted, most studies show at least a slightly larger percentage of teen girls have sent or posted nude or seminude pictures of themselves than have teen boys. According to the study by the American Academy of Pediatrics, 61 percent of those who created or appeared in sexted images were female.[10] The latest 2012 study, while finding no significant difference between percentages of males and females who had sent a sext, found that females were far more likely than males to be asked for sexts; almost 70 percent of the girls polled had been asked to send a photo or video of themselves.[11] Both males and females, then, are transmitting sexted images, but it seems that female bodies are more likely to be sought (and appear) as the subject of a sext. Further, according to Danah Boyd, a fellow at Harvard's Berkman Center for Internet and Society, although boys and girls both send sexts, "photos of girls tend to go viral more often, because boys and girls will circulate girls' photos in part to shame them."[12] Because girls and young women appear to be disproportionately impacted by the practice of sexting, it is imperative to examine the practice using the lens of gender analysis.

Legal, Social, and Emotional Ramifications of Sexting

What are the real consequences—legal, social, or emotional—for teenagers who sext? For teens sending or receiving a photo of someone under age eighteen, the legal penalties can be severe. Existing laws tend to address teen sexting under the rubric of child pornography so that the transmitted images fall outside First Amendment protection. While the definitions of child pornography differ from state to state, under federal law it is a felony to produce, possess, or distribute child pornographic materials. Receiving just one picture can carry a mandatory minimum sentence of five years.[13] Overzealous prosecution can lead to criminal charges, imprisonment, fines, and federally mandated sex offender registration—a designation that can drive a teenager from his or her parents' home and haunt that teenager decades into his or her future. Some states have begun statutory reform regarding teen sexting, but most have not.[14]

Many scholars agree that charging minors with child pornography offenses is not an appropriate response to teen sexting, especially for the original sexter and recipient. In numerous cases, these teenagers seem to have had little or no idea of the serious legal implications of their actions. Moreover, a teen sexter's experience is markedly different from victims of traditional child pornography; the intent of child pornography laws as they are written is to protect defenseless victims from being "manipulated and forced to participate in 'graphic sexual [activities]' against their will."[15] Admittedly, teen sexting does take place in a social context that may generally be characterized as exploitative of women and girls, but the level of direct manipulation involved in sexting is lower than in the case of traditional child pornography.

Because penalties for child pornography are severe, there is an obvious mismatch between these laws and the phenomenon of teen sexting.

Legal scholar John A. Humbach points out the ridiculous consequences of applying such laws in blanket fashion:

> On the conservative assumption that, for each teen who photographs herself, an average of two or three classmates receive copies of the pictures, it is a plausible estimate that as many as forty to fifty percent or more of otherwise law-abiding American teenagers are already felony sex offenders under current law and as such are subject to long-term imprisonment followed by "sex offender" registration requirements for decades or for life. . . . There is certainly reason to suspect something is profoundly amiss when the system of laws makes serious felony offenders of such a large proportion of its young people.[16]

Furthermore, these laws can have profoundly negative effects on the broader public. For instance, the crowding of sex offender registries with convicted sexters would diminish the effectiveness of those registries in their original intent of alerting the public to predatory danger. As one legal scholar has argued, "the current system creates negative repercussions for the prosecution of traditional pornography, ruins the lives of the prosecuted children, and provides no long-term benefits for society."[17]

The negative consequences of sexting are not just legal. They also include important social and emotional penalties for many teens who sext. Harassment by peers can be debilitating and can dramatically impact a teenager's psychological well-being. In the American Academy of Pediatrics study, 21 percent of respondents who appeared in or created images reported feeling very or extremely upset, embarrassed, or afraid as a result, as did 25 percent of youth who received such images.[18] Exacerbating the harm for girls who sext, a widely acknowledged sexual double standard too often labels them as "sluts" or "whores." The negative social stigma that results from sexting-gone-awry can remain with the sexter for a very long time, in an age where reputations spread virally and digital footprints seem immortal. Further, threat of parental and school punishment (including suspension or expulsion) can complicate emotional and psychological damage and can severely compromise a teenager's future prospects for school, college, or employment.

Why Teenagers Sext

If we are to take seriously the "concrete reality" of the sexter, it is crucial for us to try to understand: Why do teenagers choose to sext? What is it in a teenager's experience that inspires him or her to take part in an activity that may carry such dangerous legal, social, and emotional consequences? Definite social benefits draw some teens to sext: social cachet and the craving for increased popularity, or the desire to draw closer to a boyfriend or girlfriend with whom one already shares an emotional relationship.

One of the most common reasons that teenagers offer for sexting is simple "flirting." It represents a modern and hightech version of the age-old flirtatious games that young people play as they grow and develop sexually. According to the "Sex and Tech" survey, 66 percent of teen girls and 60 percent of teen boys who have sent sexually suggestive content say that they did so to be "fun and flirtatious."[19] As an experimental stage of exploring and expressing one's sexuality, sexting can represent a playful invitation into not-yet-actualized relational and sexual activity. Sometimes either the sexter or the person asking for the sext is hoping to become romantically or sexually involved with the other party, and sending or requesting nude photos feels like a means to "up the ante" on a budding relationship.

Another reason teens give for why they sext is to meet the requests or demands of a significant other. Of teen girls who sext send sexually suggestive content, 52 percent sent it "as a sexy present" for a boyfriend.[20] The sext might indicate an openness to future sexual experimentation. Couples already sexually active might use sexting as an extension of their physical relationships. In some cases, though, one person might feel uncomfortably strong-armed into sexting; indeed, 23 percent of teen girls and 24 percent of teen boys in the same study said they were pressured by friends to send or post sexual content.[21]

Of course, not all sexters have benign intentions. In an act of hightech bullying, some teenagers who sext do not send their own photos but rather maliciously forward the photos of others. Such "secondary" sexters may be motivated by the desire to mock or intimidate the primary

sexter, or simply by the wish to gain a social "leg up" at the expense
of another. Or perhaps the secondary sexter is merely engaging in a
thoughtless prank—albeit one with potentially serious consequences for
all involved. The judgmental immaturity of many teenagers can have
disastrous consequences when taking hurtful action requires nothing
more than the click of a "send" button on a cell phone.

Regardless of their reasons, many teens do in fact get caught in the
gap between their own intentions and an unforgiving societal response.
Yet it would be incomplete to attribute their actions purely to individual
bad judgment. Teen sexting does not exist in a social vacuum but rather
is a part of a larger, gendered social system in which teen sexters—as
sexual beings—replicate broader social behavior. As such, "when adolescents are taught, largely through the mass media, that sexual experience is a desired good, and these values are then perpetuated among
their peers, it seems clear that portraying oneself as sexual would be a
desirable strategy. Trying to save adolescents from themselves without
understanding the roots of the behavior is misguided at best."[22] Thus, to
better understand the reality of sexting, one must examine its place in the
wider landscape of popular culture.

The Social Context of Sexting: Sexualized Media, Sexual Violence, and Purity Culture

In American popular media and advertising, women's bodies are routinely sexualized, objectified, and demeaned. Even seemingly harmless
advertisements for clothing, food or alcohol, and other consumer products often carry a subtextual message that women's personal identity and
worth depend heavily on how physically attractive and sexy they appear.
In a similar vein, women's sexual identities are frequently trivialized.
Sex is commonly presented as little more than a dirty joke or a titillat-
ing activity, divorced from any authentic human relationship or deeper
personal identity. The idealized image of physical and sexual flawless-
ness—a fantasy that belies the reality of virtually every woman—is far
from harmless. Real women and girls measure themselves against these

images every day, leading to untold (and largely unmeasured) damage to women's self-esteem and psychological well-being.[23]

The images are particularly shocking in the world of music videos, where women are generally presented in a state of perpetual sexual arousal, compliant with male fantasy and what has been termed the male "pornographic imagination."[24] Moreover, retrospective analysis reveals that the images themselves have become progressively explicit over time, with increasingly shocking representations necessary in order to touch an overexposed and desensitized audience. The epidemic of eating disorders, cosmetic surgery, and violence against women and girls must be seen against the backdrop of the toxic media landscape in which women and girls find themselves.

So must the contours of the teen sexting debate. This sexualization of popular culture normalizes a teenager's inclination to send nude or seminude photos of himself or herself to someone else. Indeed, the teen super-idol Miley Cyrus (formerly Disney's tween star "Hannah Montana") posed seminude at age fifteen for a controversial Vanity Fair photo spread in 2008. It is easy to see how many young teens would not hesitate to follow suit in such a culture of exhibitionism.

Along with a sexy media backdrop that demeans the female body and belittles human sexuality, body-related fear and shame are a dominant background experience for many (or arguably most) women and girls. Although accurate rape statistics are notoriously hard to obtain, at a minimum, one out of every six American women report having survived rape or attempted rape in their lifetime. For college women, the number rises to between one in four and one in five.[25] Moreover, of females who are raped, 54 percent report that the rape happened before they were eighteen years old.[26] Girls' developing sense of their sexuality must be set against this disturbing backdrop, one of clear misogynistic and objectifying practices and of violence directed specifically against the female body. Further, "rape culture"—aspects of popular culture that make sexual coercion and violence against women seem normal—does not merely humiliate women vis-à-vis their bodies. Rape culture undermines women's sexual decision making, so that "no means yes," or at least a flirtatious "maybe." Insofar as sexting invites the view that girls and women are the playthings of men, and that women's sexual "yes" can be assumed, the practice should be considered highly damaging and morally problematic.

Finally, an aspect of popular culture that is often overlooked—but should not be, especially by Christians—is what is sometimes termed the "purity culture" that pervades large swaths of North American society. Common especially within evangelical and fundamentalist Christian circles, purity culture responds to the sexualization of American popular culture by retrenching: purity advocates urge girls and women to remain sexually chaste until they are (heterosexually) married. Purity culture is characterized by abstinence-only sexual education, "purity balls" (prom-like events promoting virginity until marriage), and "promise rings" (with which girls pledge—usually to their fathers—to guard their virginity until they are heterosexually married). Purity advocates would like to return to what they see as a better, simpler era, when girls would "save themselves" for marriage—even as a "boys-will-be-boys" mentality often releases teenage boys from similar expectations.[27]

As feminist blogger Jessica Valenti points out, the message of purity culture is, ironically, not so different from our overly sexualized popular media culture: for both, a woman's worth lies in her ability, or her refusal, to be overtly sexual. Both approaches teach American girls that their bodies and their sexuality are what make them valuable.[28] While at times well-intentioned, purity advocates perpetuate the same social rubrics that guide girls to understand their own sexual desire as a source of shame and embarrassment. Rather than encouraging girls to understand themselves as moral agents and sex as a moral and deliberate choice, purity culture encourages girls to think of themselves as moral children, in need of a father's, or a husband's, sexual protection.

In the midst of these social backdrops—an oversexualized, misogynistic culture of assault and rape on the one hand, and a Christian-based purity culture where desire and pleasure are pathologized on the other—we must locate a helpful, life-giving, justice-based response to sexting. Society must empower young women to claim primary responsibility for their own sexuality while also avoiding the dangerous and unhelpful pitfall of treating teenage sexters as if they were adults engaged in child pornography. Yet, even as we seek to do this, we must acknowledge the alienating and debilitating impact that teen sexting too often has upon those who take part in it.

A Christian Anthropological Understanding of Sexting:
Starting Points

How, then, should Christians make sense of the practice of sexting? Put differently, what does justice—understood from Christian sensibilities—require in relation to teen sexting? The classic rendition of justice—as rendering to each party his or her "due"—tells us little until we fill it out with an articulation of what each person is actually due.

In her seminal work *Just Love*, Christian feminist Margaret Farley elaborates on the classic understanding by arguing that justice requires the affirmation of persons according to their "concrete reality, actual and potential"—that is, in their universally shared human qualities as well as in their untidy particularity. To explain what this entails, Farley describes what she terms "obligating features of personhood," features possessed by every human being and that "constitute the basis of a requirement to respect persons . . . sexually or otherwise." She particularly focuses on autonomy and relationality as twin features of personhood that ground moral obligations and provide content for more specific moral norms for sexual ethics.[29]

Rather than replicate each of Farley's norms here, I draw upon them to illuminate the "concrete reality" and the demands of justice for persons who sext. It is imperative to honor the experience of teenagers who sext and also to invite them into a fuller understanding of sexual desire, one that challenges any practice that does not ultimately serve their well-being. In other words, a Christian sexual ethic must take care to challenge sexting where it harms or otherwise disrespects persons in their concrete, embodied realities—in their autonomy and their relationality. But it also must honor the joy and delight of human desire, and the way that human sexuality invites us to a transcendent experience of ourselves, of others, and even of the Divine.

There is another dimension of justice, however, that is vital to an honest analysis of sexting. An adequate account of justice—one that takes concrete reality seriously—must lift up the contextual and structural injustices that characterize a teenage sexter's world. As ethicist Karen Lebacqz has written, "we cannot approach justice directly, because we already live in the midst of injustice."[30] Injustice is central to human experience; as such, sexual injustice frames any theorizing about what justice requires. Moreover, it is insufficient to view injustice as simply a matter of individual or even institutional wrongdoing. As feminist philosopher Iris Marion Young has emphasized, injustice often transcends individual action and takes the form of social structures and processes—perhaps uncoordinated—that nevertheless function together to constrain choice and to produce, for some, vulnerability to domination.[31]

Addressed to teen sexting, this sort of structural lens on justice means that first and foremost we must recall the social context—elaborated earlier—in which teenagers sext. That we live in a culture that disparages human sexuality and demeans the female body should be central to our moral analysis of sexting. Texting nude photos of a girl's body is not merely an individually wrongheaded act; it also plays directly into this wider trivialization of sex and objectification of the female body. Insofar as sexted images function to portray women as "sex objects" who lack agency or self-determination, or as objects whose feelings and genuine experience need not be considered, they support the sort of social injustice and constraint on women's opportunities that Lebacqz and Young call us to resist.[32]

Moreover, the high incidence of teenagers who feel compelled to send or post sexual content should profoundly disturb us in a world with excessive rates of sexual violence. Sexting, when done by actual teenagers in the real world, very often contains a subtle (or not-so-subtle) element of pressure or manipulation that props up sexual injustices (characterized by fear and shame) already a part of our social reality. The fact that both girls and boys apparently experience such pressure at times does not diminish the very real price that sexting specifically exacts upon girls—who already live with some awareness of the possibility of sexual violence. Whatever else a "just" response to sexting entails, it cannot overlook these harmful patterns or imagine that sexting exists in a sexually "neutral" setting.

The remainder of this essay proposes a Christian sexual ethic specific to the practice of sexting. Such an ethic must take the context of injustice seriously even while establishing what justice requires for human sexual flourishing. Drawing upon the earlier insights, this ethic should promote freedom, embodiment, mutuality and relational intimacy, and equality as attributes that govern sexual relations and guide us as we evaluate the practice of sexting.

A "Sexual" Ethic for Christians

Perhaps the most troubling aspect of Margarite's story is that her freedom was completely disregarded by her boyfriend and classmates so that Margarite herself experienced real, tangible harm. As Farley elaborates, freedom is an essential part of our human reality. Our capacity for free consent, for self-determination, is a central part of what it means to be human. Certainly some feminists—myself included—have rightly highlighted the ways in which a Western Enlightenment bias has at times led to the overemphasis of freedom as a defining characteristic of personhood. Recognizing this overemphasis, however, should not cause us to swing too far in the opposite direction, eviscerating the very real importance of freedom, particularly in the sexual realm. For many of us, our ability to choose our actions, our boundaries, and ultimately our loves is deeply connected to our identity and self-understanding.

When a boyfriend, girlfriend, or classmate passes along a sext that was intended as private communication, the freedom of the original sexter is most certainly violated, resulting in potentially deep psychological harm. But our analysis of freedom must also reach deeper than that violation, for freedom is transgressed on much more fundamental levels when one takes into account the manipulative culture in which sexting takes place. While it is important to resist evaluative discourse that re-moves all agency from teenagers who "choose" to sext, it is also insuf-ficient for a justice-oriented ethic to ignore the culture of exhibitionism and patriarchal power relations that structure that very same choice. In other words, many girls sext (or are asked to sext) because our society tells them that their worth is to be found in their sexually desirable bod-ies. Many young teenagers (boys or girls) sext because our society tells them that sexual exhibitionism is a normal and socially acceptable way for adults to express their sexuality.

A choice driven by the desire to appear sexy or to increase one's pop-ularity cannot be considered free in the fullest sense. It is no secret that the teenage years are often characterized by insecurity and the desire to be liked. Teenagers, especially young ones, often do not have the inner strength and long-term judgment to make wise and confident choices. An ethic that promotes freedom in a more robust sense looks beyond mere free choice and embraces instead a vision of bodily self-possession, self-acceptance, and personal agency. This is particularly important for females. Teenage girls must retain primary control over their own sexual experience, refusing to let others—fathers, boyfriends, peers—dictate how they conduct their sexual lives. Sexual choices should be thought-ful, well-considered decisions—not choices made from social pressure, insecurity, or a lack of assertiveness.

While exhorting true and meaningful freedom in sexual decision mak-ing, however, Christian ethics must also promote and encourage a posi-tive vision of sexuality: one in which bodies (of various shapes and sizes) are understood as beautiful, and where human desire—even in teenag-ers—is considered a valuable part of an embodied creation. As crucial as freedom is to an adequate evaluation of sexting, a feminist approach must be quick to remind us that persons are more than free-floating centers of liberty. We are, rather, profoundly embodied creatures, and human sexual experience and sexual self-understanding remain deeply connected to that embodiedness. In other words, "being a body" is in-trinsic to what it means to "be human." My body is most certainly not all there is to me, but I cannot (and should not) understand myself as wholly separate from my body.

If we consider a strong body–self connection as an integral part of a good creation, there can be no doubt that we live under conditions of brokenness—for bodily objectification is a routine part of human, and especially female, experience. Whatever else it achieves, the act of sending sexually explicit photos of oneself encourages women to think of their bodies primarily as objects of male pornographic imagination. In this way, sexting can forge a wedge between the sexter's experience of herself and her body. The practice thus contradicts the intimate link between body and self. Decades ago—and long before the advent of sexting— Christian ethicist James Nelson described this sort of bodily alienation in detail:

> If the mind is alienated from the body, so also is the body from
> the mind. The depersonalization of one's sexuality, in some form
> or degree, inevitably follows. The body becomes a physical object
> possessed and used by the self. Lacking is the sense of unity with the
> spontaneous rhythms of the body. Lacking is the sense of full par-
> ticipation in the body's stresses and pains, its joys and delights. More
> characteristic is the sense of body as machine. . . . When the body
> is experienced as a thing, it has the right to live only as machine or
> slave owned by the self.[33]

Nelson's portrayal captures the bodily objectification that too of-ten describes the experience of sexting. Particularly when sexting takes place between two parties who do not share a high level of trust and emotional intimacy, the image of the sexualized body is essentially depersonalized in a nude photo. It becomes something to be evaluated in terms of socially determined standards of size, shape, or beauty. This depersonalization becomes heightened when the recipient passes along the sext to other unintended recipients, as the original sexter's body is effectively walled off from her larger personality. Sexting of this sort constitutes a clear case of objectification—that is, "the failure to apprehend and re-spect [a] person in her or his whole reality."[34]

A Christian ethic concerned with justice must instead promote an in-tegrated experience of body and self. The theological concept of the in-carnation signifies that God affirms fleshly existence, that our bodies are not incidental to our identities but rather constitute an important part of who we are. As James Nelson has articulated, "Beyond the dualistic alienations we experience the gracious resurrection of the body-self. I really am *one* person. Body and mind are one; my body is me as my mind is me."[35] Our bodies are inseparable from our souls, our spirits, our selves.

In the context of sexting, to affirm the moral value of human embodiment means that we must stop demonizing sexual pleasure while simultaneously challenging practices that segregate body from self. On the one hand, the mentality encapsulated in the various forms of "purity culture" is decidedly anti-body; it promotes shame and embarrassment and ultimately functions to deny the beauty of human sexuality as an instance of incarnation. On the other hand, an ethic advancing human well-being as necessary to justice should also insist on sexual practices that unite rather than divide a person's body from her larger personality. Sexting too often promotes this alienating division. Theologically, it belies human dignity and denies the power of incarnation.

Freedom and embodiment, both key qualities that should govern the practice of sexting, are nevertheless insufficient on their own; these will be enabled by a context of relational intimacy and mutuality. In an insightful depiction of sex through the lens of virtue ethics, Lisa Fullam has characterized intimacy as "the central goal of sex," recognizing that "sex expresses a personal reality, not a bodily one."[36] Intimacy is not simply physical closeness; it is emotional tenderness, an act of being present to the other in such a way as to transcend erotic affection. At least in the context of modern Western understanding, without intimacy, sex seems to lose its "heart," to be emptied of its sacred power and potential to touch the "inner being" of its participants.[37] Fullam cautions, "A person who is unable to achieve emotional intimacy may use promiscuity as a mask, substituting the physical for the deeper body-spirit-soul connection that is the aim of satisfying sexual relationships."[38] This sort of deep connection with the other is indeed a hallmark of "good sex," inviting persons to transcend their own embodied realities and enter into a profound and mysterious connection with another.

Intimacy must also be mutual to truly serve human sexual well-being. Mutuality is a term often used in sexual ethics, though not often well explained. Farley describes it best as entailing "active receptivity and receptive activity—each partner active, each one receptive . . . [in] mutuality of desire, action, and response."[39] A mutual sexual relationship generally avoids the pitfall where one person always plays the role of "giver" and the other "recipient," whether of care, pleasure, or love itself. Mutuality rules out the overall instrumentalizing of one party to serve the other party's needs.

If mutuality and emotional intimacy are to be genuine, they presuppose a high level of trust between the partners. Sex itself has the capacity to tap into profound human vulnerability, and vulnerability demands trust if it is to serve human well-being. As Karen Lebacqz has put it, "Eros, the desire for another, the passion that accompanies the wish for sexual expression, makes one vulnerable. It creates possibilities for great joy but also for great suffering."[40] A high level of trust takes time to develop. It also requires a significant degree of personal involvement with (and investment in) the other, one that surpasses mere emotional attraction or even romantic love.[41] To violate this sort of trust in the context of sex is a supreme violation indeed; few who have experienced such sexual betrayal would deny the profound emotional pain it engenders. The depth of this emotional pain best explains the suffering experienced in cases of secondary sexting.

Yet the moral problem lies not simply in the forwarding of sexual images to unintended recipients; even the initial act of sexting should prompt us to raise hard questions regarding mutuality and relational intimacy. In many cases, sexting itself, even when freely undertaken, violates these norms. As is so often the case, context is crucial to an adequate understanding. Sexting has a very different moral meaning when it takes place in the context of two people (especially two young teenagers) who barely know each other than it does in the context of a mature, emotionally close, mutual relationship. Why? In the first case, there can be little doubt that harmful objectification occurs. The recipient's gaze upon the sexted image is divorced from a deeper appreciation of (or respect for) the sexter's identity. The subject of the sext becomes little more than a physical object to be admired or, in some cases, mocked. When sexting takes place in the context of an emotionally close and mutually fulfilling relationship, it is at least conceivable that the recipient's gaze might be essentially a benevolent one, affirming the sexter's whole personhood. More often, however, such maturity and emotional grounding is noticeably lacking—especially in the case of young teenagers who sext as a means of flirtation or sexual experimentation, or in response to coercion.

A final quality that a Christian sexual ethic must promote vis-à-vis sexting is equal regard. Freedom, embodiment, relational intimacy, and mutuality are arguably best achieved in relationships marked by equality. This is revealed by examining what happens under conditions of relational inequality. That is, when one partner wields a disproportionate amount of power in a relationship, the other is more apt to feel forced or manipulated into sexting, less able to retain a strong sense of the body–self connection, and unlikely to achieve deep relational intimacy, mutuality, or trust.

In a world where girls and women are routinely understood and portrayed in the media as sex objects, true equal regard can be hard to come by. Insofar as sexting is used to harm or further disempower girls or women, it must be denounced. In fact, gender dynamics aside, we should be suspicious of any instance of sexting that takes place within a relational context marked by a power imbalance. When sexting is used to bolster patterns of domination and subordination—either by way of individual bullying and humiliation or by furthering harmful gendered power dynamics—the practice severely compromises human well-being and therefore must be roundly rejected.

Charting a Course Forward

An adequate response to sexting must squarely acknowledge that the practice does not occur in a social vacuum. Rather, sexting as a practice reflects the larger social patterns in which it takes place. Because these patterns are particularly debilitating toward young women's sexuality, we must remain keenly alert to the ways in which our response can unintentionally exacerbate women's social and sexual disempowerment.

Along these lines, we must reject a purity-based response wherein we—intentionally or inadvertently—deny the beauty of sexual desire. Whatever else we do, we must remind ourselves (and our youth) that sexual desire is beautiful, delightful, and sacred. Indeed, it is because of this sacredness that we must not treat sexual expression lightly. Rather than ignoring or denying the beauty and power of human sexuality, our response to sexting must focus on sexual well-being in the context of real human relationships, lifting up the need to respect human freedom, embodiment, mutuality and relational intimacy, and equal regard.

I suggest three directions in which these sexual norms point us as individuals, as churches, and as a broader society concerned with justice and human sexual well-being. First, and most importantly, a social response to sexting must begin with and focus upon education of ourselves and our youth. Such education must include information about the dangers and legal implications of sexting, but it must also extend to broader discussions about gender stereotyping in the media and the cultural devaluation and instrumentalization of female bodies and sexual agency. Without squarely addressing this educational component and broader social context, any response to sexting risks harming the very children whose well-being should be our central concern.

Second, given the antibody and antisexuality tenor of much of Christian public conversation, Christians concerned with justice have a particular obligation to go further: our conversations must incorporate and promote an understanding of embodiment that avoids harmful dualisms and affirms a profound body–self connection. Churches must address the phenomenon of sexting head-on, not by condemning youth who sext but rather through honest conversation about what it means to be sexual, embodied persons. Teens themselves need to be encouraged toward a deeper sexual self-understanding and equipped to identify the profound connections between one's body and one's deepest identity.

Finally, we as a society must revamp our legal approach to sexting. Treating sexting under the rubric of child pornography is thoroughly inadequate. Children are not adults. Child pornography laws were intended to protect children, not to punish them. Thus, federal laws must be revamped to account for the age and maturity of the sexter, the level of volition involved, and the frequency and scope of the sexting event or events. Sex offender registration, in the vast majority of cases, should be taken off the table, and criminal records for sexting should be expunged when minors reach adult status. Furthermore, we must make a distinction between primary sexting and secondary sexting (passing along sexted photos to others). In general, primary sexting, especially when engaged in voluntarily with one other person, should not be considered a legally punishable offense, and secondary sexting is best treated using remedies from civil, not criminal, law.

This response is not intended to suggest that the practice of sexting is morally acceptable in most cases. In fact, this essay has provided examples to show that teen sexting is generally harmful to those who engage in it, particularly those who are young or immature, disempowered or insecure, or those who sext apart from a relationship characterized by mutuality, equal regard, and trust. Moreover, sexting as a practice contributes to a sociocultural context that routinely objectifies and instrumentalizes women's bodies and normalizes sexual exploitation, thus not only harming individuals but also negatively affecting the larger common good.

Yet in our rush to highlight the myriad ways sexting can compromise human well-being, we must not revert to a heavy-handed legalism that treats children as if they were adult criminals. Nor should we embrace an antibody purity approach that negates the sexual agency of young women or portrays women's sexuality as dirty, dangerous, or shameful. Our sexuality is God-given and connects us to a deeper, mysterious reality. In this sense, we might even call sex sacramental: it is a tangible sign of God's invisible grace, a window into the deepest nature of reality.[42] An adequate response to sexting affirms the sacred beauty of the body and of human desire even as it insists that these are best expressed in the context of healthy personal agency and freedom, a well-integrated body–self identity, mutuality and relational intimacy, and equal regard. In this way we can begin to inject a measure of sanity into society's response to sexting, thereby allowing for and encouraging a deeper conversation about the realities of the practice itself and the real impact it has upon today's youth.

Questions for Reflection

1. The precise difference between an erotic and pornographic image is notoriously difficult to define. But some people believe that there are imaginable circumstances—say between spouses who both find the practice delightful—in which a flirtatious sexting exchange of erotic self-portraits ought to be judged not only permissible but morally welcome, even conjugally edifying. Do you agree? Or do you think that all such images, virtual or otherwise, dehumanize sexual intimacy by exposing what is intrinsically private?

2. Though many may believe there is nothing intrinsically immoral about sexting per se, most recognize that the potentially global and lifelong reach of the internet creates for those so erotically imaged truly stunning levels of vulnerability. Regardless of the intention of one who sends the sext, such images can be misused (by a spouse or "friend" who then shows/forwards it to others) to exploit, shame, and/or otherwise abuse the sexter. What kinds of education programs can be developed to protect people from this form of cyberbullying? What practices should be adopted to reduce the harms associated with it? How should an individual to whom a cyberbully has forwarded a sext addressed clearly to another respond? What response should an individual to whom a sext has been addressed but who does not welcome the "come on" offer to the sender?

3. Though some spouses and domestic or "steady" partners feel pressured to participate in sexting activities, higher percentages of middle-school pre-teens and teenagers feel pressured by their peers and those whom they wish to attract to engaging in sexting than their adult counterparts. Is sexting just a new form of flirting? Why do you think sexting should or should not be treated as an ordinary part of the dating game?

Suggestions for Further Reading

Gabriel, Fleur. "Sexting, Selfies and Self-Harm: Young People, Social Media and the Performance of Self-Development." *Media International Australia* 151.1 (2014): 104–112.

Hogue, David A. "The Desiring Brain: Contemporary Neuroscientific Insights into Pleasure and Longing." In *City of Desires—A Place for God? Practical Theological Perspectives*, R. Ruard Ganzevoort, Rein Brouwer, and Bonnie Miller-McLemore, eds., 51–61. Zurich: Lit Verlag GmbH, 2013.

Lunceford, Brett. "The Body and the Sacred in the Digital Age: Thoughts on Posthuman Sexuality." *Theology and Sexuality* 15.1 (2009): 77–96.

Mercer, Joyce Ann. "Pornography and Abuse of Social Media." In *Professional Sexual Ethics: A Holistic Ministry Approach*, Patricia Beattie Jung and Darryl W. Stephens, eds., 193–204. Minneapolis, MN: Fortress Press, 2013.

Temple, Jeff R., Jonathan A. Paul, and Patricia van den Berg. "Teen Sexting and Its Association with Sexual Behaviors." *Archives of Pediatrics and Adolescent Medicine* 166.9 (2012): 828–833.

Notes

1. Jan Hoffman, "A Girl's Nude Photo, and Altered Lives," *New York Times*, March 26, 2011, www.nytimes.com/2011/03/27/us/27sexting.html?pagewanted=all.

2. Sexting may be differentiated from internet pornography, which claims a quasi-permanent web presence. Sexting, as I examine it here, is ordinarily aimed at a "private" audience (at least initially) and, because it is accomplished by use of a cell phone, lends itself to impulsivity.

3. Cindy Kranz, "Nude Photo Led to Suicide," *Cincinnati.com*, March 22, 2009, http://news.cincinnati.com/article/20090322/NEWS01/903220312/Nude-photo-led-suicide.

4. According to the Pew Research Center, 18 percent of US twelve-year-olds owned a cell phone in 2004; this figure rose to 58 percent in 2009. Further, 83 percent of seventeen-year-olds owned a cell phone in 2009. See Amanda Lenhart, "Teens and Sexting," *Pew Research Center*, December 15, 2009, www.pewinternet.org/Reports/2009/Teens-and-Sexting/Overview.aspx. Few studies have been done to examine differences in sexting behavior across lines of race, class, and ethnicity, although it appears to be a practice that crosses racial and ethnic borders. See Melissa Fleschler Peskin, Christine M. Markham, Robert C. Addy, Ross Shegog, Melanie Thiel, and Susan R. Tortolero, "Prevalence and Patterns of Sexting among Ethnic Minority Urban High School Students," *Cyberpsychology, Behavior, and Social Networking* 16, no. 6 (2013): 454–59.

5. "Sex and Tech: Results from a Survey of Teens and Young Adults," *National Campaign to Prevent Teen and Unplanned Pregnancy* and *Cosmogirl.com*, 1–3, accessed December 18, 2012, www.thenationalcampaign.org/sextech/pdf/sextech _summary.pdf.

6. Lenhart, "Teens and Sexting," 5.

7. Kimberly J. Mitchell, David Finkelhor, Lisa M. Jones, and Janis Wolak, "Prevalence and Characteristics of Youth Sexting: A National Study," *Pediatrics* 129, no. 1 (January 2012): 13–20.

8. "'Sexting' Teens Found to Be up to 82 Percent More Likely to Be Having Sex Compared to the Non-Sexting Teens," *New York Daily News*, July 4, 2012, www .nydailynews.com/life-style/health/sexting-teens-found-tos-82-sex-compared -non-sexting-teens-article-1.1107729.

9. Mitchell et al., "Prevalence and Characteristics of Youth Sexting," 19.

10. Ibid., 16.

11. "'Sexting' Teens Found."

12. Hoffman, "A Girl's Nude Photo."

13. John A. Humbach, "Sexting and the First Amendment," *Hastings Constitutional Law Quarterly* 37, no. 3 (Spring 2010): 437.

14. Julie Halloran McLachlan, "Crime and Punishment: Teen Sexting in Context," *Penn State Law Review* 115, no. 1 (Summer 2010): 135–81.

15. Elizabeth M. Ryan, "Sexting: How the States Can Prevent a Moment of Indiscretion from Leading to a Lifetime of Unintended Consequences for Minors and Young Adults," *Iowa Law Review* 96, no. 357 (2010): 371.

16. Humbach, "Sexting and the First Amendment," 437–38.

17. Krupa Shah, "Sexting: Risky or [F]risky? An Examination of the Current and Future Legal Treatment of Sexting in the United States," *Faulkner Law Review* 2, no. 1 (2010): 216.

18. Mitchell, et al., "Prevalence and Characteristics of Youth Sexting," 16.

19. "Sex and Tech," 4.

20. Ibid.

21. Ibid.

22. Brett Lunceford, "The New Pornographers: Legal and Ethical Considerations of Sexting," in *The Ethics of Emerging Media: Information, Social Norms, and New Media Technology*, ed. Bruce E. Drushel and Kathleen German, 113 (New York: Continuum, 2011).

23. Jean Kilbourne brilliantly examines these patterns in advertising in her series of four documentaries, *Killing Us Softly*. See especially *Killing Us Softly 4: Advertising's Image of Women* (Northampton, MA: Media Education Foundation, 2012), DVD. I have chosen to focus here on the portrayal of women's bodies; however, it is crucial to recognize that the media's portrayal of men's bodies (and sexuality) also contributes to the problem by valorizing men's physical power and dominance over women.

24. Sut Jhally, dir., *Dreamworlds 3: Desire, Sex & Power in Music Video* (Northampton, MA: Media Education Foundation, 2007), DVD.

25. Statistics from RAINN: Rape, Abuse & Incest National Network, accessed August 27, 2012, www.rainn.org/statistics.

26. "TeenHelp.com," accessed August 27, 2012, www.teenhelp.com/index.html.

27. Jessica Valenti, *The Purity Myth: How America's Obsession with Virginity Is Hurting Young Women* (Berkeley, CA: Seal Press, 2010).

28. Ibid., 10.

29. Margaret A. Farley, *Just Love: A Framework for Christian Sexual Ethics* (New York: Continuum, 2006), 209–32.

30. Karen Lebacqz, *Justice in an Unjust World: Foundations for a Christian Approach to Justice* (Minneapolis: Augsburg, 1987), 154. See especially chapters 5 and 6.

31. Iris Marion Young, *Responsibility for Justice* (New York: Oxford University Press, 2011), especially chapter 2.

32. Martha C. Nussbaum, "Objectification," *Philosophy and Public Affairs* 24, no. 4 (Autumn 1995): 249–91.

33. James B. Nelson, *Embodiment: An Approach to Sexuality and Christian Theology* (Minneapolis: Augsburg, 1978), 39–41.

34. Farley, *Just Love*, 121. The morality of objectification in a sexual context is a key concept that deserves more treatment than I can offer here. For a provocative treatment of the concept, see Nussbaum, "Objectification." Nussbaum argues that, in the matter of objectification, context is everything—and that sexual objectification may be morally acceptable as a temporary phase in a relationship characterized by mutual regard.

35. Nelson, *Embodiment*, 79.

36. Lisa Fullam, "Thou Shalt: Sex beyond the List of Don'ts," *Commonweal*, April 24, 2009, http://commonwealmagazine.org/thou-shalt-0.

37. It is valid to question whether intimacy plays such a "central" role in human sexuality when examined with a cross-cultural lens. Here, I self-consciously assume a certain modern, Western posture, admittedly influenced by Judeo-Christian values. While this posture is far from universal, even in the modern West, I do believe that the association of sex with emotional intimacy is a widely shared (if not widely practiced) belief held by American teenagers today. Examining the pitfalls of such a posture is beyond the scope of this essay.

38. Fullam, "Thou Shalt."

39. Farley, *Just Love*, 221–22.

40. Karen Lebacqz, "Appropriate Vulnerability: A Sexual Ethic for Singles," in *Sexuality and the Sacred: Sources for Theological Reflection*, 2nd ed., eds. Marvin M. Ellison and Kelly Brown Douglas, 274 (Louisville, KY: Westminster John Knox Press, 2010).

41. See Roger Burggraeve, "From Responsible to Meaningful Sexuality: An Ethics of Growth as an Ethics of Mercy for Young People in This Era of AIDS,"

in *Catholic Ethicists on HIV/AIDS Prevention*, ed. James F. Keenan, SJ, 303–316 (New York: Continuum, 2005).

42. For a fuller discussion of sex as sacrament, see Elizabeth Myer Boulton and Matthew Myer Boulton, "Sacramental Sex," *Christian Century* 128, no. 6 (March 22, 2011): 28–31.

8

Christian Ethics and Human Trafficking Activism
Progressive Christianity and Social Critique

LETITIA M. CAMPBELL AND YVONNE C. ZIMMERMAN

This essay argues that the anti-trafficking movement's dominant rhetorical and conceptual framework of human trafficking as "sold sex" has significant limitations that deserve greater critical moral reflection. This framework overlooks key issues of social and economic injustice, and eclipses the experiences of marginalized people and communities, including immigrants and gay, lesbian, bisexual, transgender, intersex, and queer people, whose welfare and empowerment have been key concerns for progressive people of faith. By asking what insights progressive Christian social ethics might contribute to shaping alternative perspectives on anti-trafficking analysis and activism, we explore progressive Christian critiques of neoliberalism and feminist critiques of the heteronormative family as resources for crafting analyses of and responses to human trafficking that foreground queer, feminist, and antiracist commitments.

Over the last fifteen years, a powerful anti-human trafficking movement has emerged in the United States, achieving wide recognition for this issue and establishing a new legal regime that organizes govern-mental responses to the phenomenon. The political consensus on human trafficking is broad, and the diversity of the constituencies that make up anti-trafficking coalitions has been a key part of successful legislative strategies at local, state, and national levels. At local and grassroots levels, concerns about human trafficking often bring together groups who are at odds on other issues: feminists and evangelicals, business leaders and student activists. Condemnation of human trafficking serves as

---

This essay was published originally in the *Journal of the Society of Christian Ethics* 34.1 (2014): 145–172.

a point of rare moral consensus among Christians across the theological spectrum as well. Alongside committed feminists and human rights activists, Christian conservatives and moderate evangelicals routinely identify human trafficking as an issue of great urgency and concern. Sociologist Elizabeth Bernstein's research shows how this Christian consensus condemning human trafficking has allowed Christian leaders and organizations to exercise considerable political and moral influence on this issue at the national, state, and local levels.[1]

"Human trafficking" is an evocative term that conjures images of human bondage and oppression, indignation at unjust suffering, and the specter of the outlawed institution of chattel slavery. In the United States especially, where discussions about human trafficking have focused disproportionately on sexual trafficking, the term almost inevitably calls to mind images of sexual exploitation, commercial sex, and the sexual abuse and exploitation of children as well. In this essay, we argue that the dominant framing of human trafficking as "sold sex" around which the US anti-trafficking alliance coheres has a number of significant limitations that are particularly problematic for progressive Christians and deserve greater critical moral reflection.[2] Specifically, we show how the spectacle of consensus on this issue and the discourses that maintain this consensus foreclose certain crucial conversations. Because nobody is *for* human trafficking, discussions about what human trafficking is, why it is wrong, and which strategies could most successfully curtail it rarely emerge in meaningful ways.

For example, the dominant anti-trafficking framework mostly overlooks the experiences and concerns of many of the most marginalized communities, including immigrants and gay, lesbian, bisexual, transgender, intersex, and queer (GLBTIQ) people. As Christian ethicists who identify as queer, feminist, and progressive, we have a unique perspective on these silences. When we are invited to speak to churches about our work and expertise on human trafficking, we feel quite keenly the implicit expectation that the "Christian" aspect of our professional identities means that we will condemn commercial sex work; similarly, our "feminist" perspectives on human trafficking are acceptable as long as we reiterate that trafficked women are forced to exchange sex for money, and that sexual activity for any reason other than love is inherently degrading. Critical feminist perspectives that question whether sex work is always necessarily coercive or uniquely exploitative are distinctly unwelcome, and typically we are not expected to talk or think queerly about trafficking at all.

Our personal experiences confirm a broader observation: when progressive Christian organizations take up issues of human trafficking, they typically make use of and circulate the same stories and images, and support the same basic approaches to conceptualizing and remedying human trafficking that characterize the dominant anti-trafficking consensus. Yet given the consistency with which issues of structural injustice and the concerns of queer and immigrant communities (among others) are written out of dominant forms of anti-trafficking activism, we argue that identifying intellectual resources for conceptualizing human trafficking and anti-trafficking interventions in other ways is a moral imperative. To this end, we suggest that the traditions of critique distinctive to progressive Christian social ethics on economic justice, political justice, and gender and sexuality are promising resources for crafting analyses of and responses to human trafficking that foreground queer, feminist, and antiracist commitments. We begin in the first two sections by defining human trafficking and briefly summarizing the history of the dominant consensus around which contemporary anti-trafficking work is organized. These sections are followed by a more extended discussion of the controlling narratives, images, and assumptions that shape the working alliance that propels the contemporary anti-trafficking movement. The final two sections focus critical moral attention on two distinct but interrelated areas: progressive critiques of neoliberalism and feminist critiques of the heteronormative family. In each case, we ask what progressive Christian social ethics might contribute to shaping alternative perspectives on human trafficking and anti-trafficking activism.

Human Trafficking Defined

Human trafficking is defined in international law as "the recruitment, transportation, transfer, harboring or receipt of persons, by means of the threat or use of force or other forms of coercion, of abduction, of fraud, of deception, of the abuse of power or a position of vulnerability or of the giving or receiving of payments of benefits to achieve the consent of a person having control over another person, for the purpose of exploitation."[3] In other words, human trafficking refers to the wide variety of processes by which individuals become enslaved—that is, unable to leave a situation without fear of violence and paid nothing or next to nothing for any duration of time.[4] Estimates of the number of trafficked or enslaved people around the world vary wildly, from 12.3 million people to a figure more than double that, 27 million people.[5]

Like statistics about global rates of trafficking, estimates of the rates of trafficking in the United States are also incredibly broad. For many years the government claimed that 50,000 women and children were trafficked into the United States annually, although this number is now widely regarded as inflated and has been revised to between 14,500 and 17,500 people.[6] A 2004 study by Free the Slaves and the Human Rights Center estimates that at any given time there are approximately 10,000 people in the United States whose situations meet the definition of human trafficking.[7]

Sex trafficking is a crime that the American public loves to hate. The impression that human trafficking primarily concerns the commercial sexual exploitation of women and children is one that is carefully cultivated, widely circulated, and commonly accepted as true. For many Americans, the term "human trafficking" is more likely to evoke the image of a brothel than that of a factory farm or private home. At the same time, there is clear recognition in both US and international law that human trafficking is not a crime that affects only women and girls, nor is it defined by sexual exploitation. US federal law defines as human trafficking any labor that is performed under conditions of force, fraud, or coercion, thus emphasizing issues of exploited labor. People of any age or gender can be trafficked into many different forms of exploitative labor: man-ufacturing, construction, farming, fishing, custodial work, domestic la-bor—not just commercial sex. The International Labor Organization (ILO) estimates that of the 12.3 million persons who are enslaved world-wide, just 1.39 million individuals (about 11 percent of all trafficking vic-tims) are trafficked into the commercial sex industry.[8] There is no type of human trafficking that is not unequivocally wrong; however, despite carefully crafted impressions, commercial sexual exploitation is not the most common form of human trafficking, and condemnation of prosti-tution and commercial sex cannot therefore be the sine qua non of oppo-sition to human trafficking.

History of US Anti-trafficking Activism

To understand the roots of the prevailing images of human trafficking in the anti-trafficking movement, we have to look back more than two decades.[9] In the 1990s American evangelicals who exerted considerable influence in relation to domestic social issues began making forays into US foreign policy. Although they had been involved in international relief and development work since the early 1970s and had established themselves as major players in this arena, evangelical engagement in in-ternational development work was expanding rapidly. This growth re-flected both shifts within American evangelicalism and a more general expansion of the role of nongovernmental organizations (NGO) and the private sector in providing health, education, and other social services that previously had been provided through state institutions.[10] Overseas, as at home, "faith-based initiatives" were increasingly relied upon to fill gaps left by the neoliberal contraction of the state.[11] Evangelical advo-cacy on foreign policy issues emerged against this backdrop of expand-ing global engagement.

   Christian persecution was the first issue to focus the popular atten-tion of evangelicals on matters of foreign policy. For decades, evangeli-cals had been raising concerns about the repression of the church under communism and the risks of proselytizing in "closed" countries and remote regions. In the post–Cold War period, though, newly circulating reports about the suffering of Christians in countries such as China, India, Sudan, and Islamic countries throughout the Middle East stirred fresh concerns about "the persecuted Church." Increasingly comfortable with the secular language of human rights, evangelicals saw these concerns as an opportunity to "redefine . . . the human rights agenda to include the rights of religious believers."[12] The political pressure that evangelical activism created and brought to bear on Congress resulted in the 1998 International Religious Freedom Act, a legislative accomplishment that definitively marked the beginning of evangelical activism on a spate of foreign policy issues.[13]

By the following year, the coalition that had formed around the issue of religious persecution was mobilizing around what was widely seen in evangelical circles as a "follow-up" issue—human trafficking, specifically the sexual trafficking of women.[14] So powerfully did the earlier movement to end religious persecution frame evangelicals' anti-trafficking activism that many of its constituents perceived human trafficking, like Christian persecution, to be a religious issue.[15] As American evangelicals took up the new issue of sex trafficking, they retained and extended one of the core claims of their previous initiative: the idea that in the globalized Christianity of the twenty-first century, the "paradigmatic Christian . . . [is] a poor and brown third-world female."[16] In the transition from organizing around religious persecution to activism on human trafficking, this figure was recast, rhetorically and symbolically, as the quintessential victim of human trafficking.

One of the first pieces of anti-trafficking legislation proposed during this period, the Freedom from Sexual Trafficking Act of 1999, showcased the preoccupation with sex trafficking.[17] One of the concerns of the congressional sponsors of this bill (which did not become law) was "to categorically distinguish sex trafficking from other, nonsexual forms of exploitation." They did not want "low-wage sweatshop issues" to cloud the issue of human trafficking, which, they argued, was essentially about sexual exploitation of women and not about exploited labor more generally.[18] The narrow focus on sexual exploitation was an innovation. A number of secular NGOs had been involved in human trafficking work prior to the late 1990s, but their work tended to focus broadly on labor trafficking and the structural preconditions of the exploitation of labor, rather than exclusively on sex trafficking.[19] Lawmakers informed by this broader analytic frame pushed for a definition of human trafficking that would incorporate issues of labor exploitation alongside concerns about sexual trafficking.

In part because of this political tension, the United States' flagship anti-trafficking legislation, the 2000 Trafficking Victims Protection Act (or TVPA), codified a definition of human trafficking that expanded beyond narrower concerns with commercial sex, clearly stating that "trafficking in persons is not limited to the sex industry" (§102 b[3]). The statute defines any labor or services induced by fraud, force, or coercion as human trafficking (§103[8]). At the same time, a special concern about sex trafficking is impossible to miss, and implementation of the TVPA has tended to focus disproportionate resources on sexual trafficking over other forms.[20] Thus, while the TVPA codified a relatively wide definition of human trafficking as exploited labor, in the vernacular, trafficking remained the sexual exploitation of women and children. At the grassroots level, images of "sold and abducted sexual victims" and "women and children [trafficked] into lives of sexual bondage" persisted as the primary tropes for mobilizing faith-based anti-trafficking campaigns.[21]

This gap between legal and vernacular anti-trafficking discourses is reminiscent of another political episode that shapes the contemporary anti-trafficking movement, the alliance forged between secular feminists and religious conservatives to combat pornography in the 1970s and 1980s.[22] This alliance came to define the anti-pornography movement and, along with the divisions among feminists that it brought to the fore, has had an enduring impact on the women's movement as a whole. In her rich history of the feminist anti-pornography movement, *Battling Pornography*, Carolyn Bronstein describes its origins in grassroots feminist campaigns against images of sexual violence against women in the mainstream media. She charts the development of feminist alliances with social conservatives in the late 1970s and 1980s, showing how these diverse coalitions worked across pronounced political differences to advance anti-pornography agendas at local, state, and national levels. This alliance between feminists and social conservatives on the issue of pornography led to a bitter split in the feminist movement between anti-pornography feminists who understood pornography as violence against women and self-identified "sex-positive" feminists who saw efforts to ban and regulate pornography as part of broader conservative efforts to reinforce repressive sexual norms that were, in their view, incompatible with feminism's commitment to authentic sexual liberation. Alongside debates about pornography, divergent positions on homosexuality, sex work, and the politics of sadomasochistic sexual practices were also major fault lines that came to define these two bitterly divided branches of the women's movement.[23]

The alliance with feminists on the issue of pornography had a lasting impact on the sexual and gender politics of social and religious conservatives as well. Over time these groups adopted some of the rhetoric secular feminists used to make the case against pornography (though often without taking on the underlying analysis). The rhetoric of pornography as "degrading" to women and concerns about violence against women became what Carole Vance calls "crossover terms," central to both groups' public arguments against pornography but used to suggest rather different kinds of harm.[24] Quite apart from the intent of conservative movement leaders, these terms and concepts rapidly diffused within the right wing, and soon rank-and-file members of socially conservative groups were rehearsing arguments about the "degradation" of women, violence against women, and even women's "inequality."[25]

In crucial ways, the feminist anti-pornography alliance was instrumental in setting the stage for the contemporary movement to end human trafficking.[26] The contemporary anti-trafficking movement has inherited not only a great deal of the rhetoric but also many of the tensions of the earlier anti-pornography alliance that Bronstein describes. The rhetoric of "sexual slavery," for instance, which circulates widely in anti-trafficking networks, appears much earlier (and with different meaning) in radical feminist critiques of the sexual dimensions of women's oppression.[27] Similarly, concern about the media's sexualization of ever-younger girls, a prominent feature of anti-pornography activism in the late 1980s, remains a staple of the contemporary anti-trafficking movement.[28] In fact, not only is the current anti-trafficking movement dominated by many of the same images and concerns that fueled the earlier movements to combat pornography and violence against women, it is also organized around some of the same feminist leaders and networks.[29] The trajectories of these earlier splits thus shape the internal politics of the contemporary anti-trafficking movement, with some of the groups that expressed concern about policies championed in the name of ending violence against women in the 1970s and 1980s today expressing opposition to policies advanced under the banner of anti-trafficking initiatives. Similarly, groups whose voices were mostly excluded from the earlier feminist anti-pornography alliances (GLBTIQ groups and sex workers' rights organizations, most prominently) are similarly absent from anti-trafficking alliances.

Given this history, it is no surprise that framing human trafficking as female sexual slavery and male sexual violence against women has helped transform it from an obscure issue, one on which only a few grassroots organizations and NGOs were focused, to a high-profile human rights issue capable of uniting activists across theological, political, and ideological lines.[30] With the established images and rhetoric of the sexual trafficking of women firmly ensconced as point of departure for anti-trafficking activism, evangelicals and a broad swath of the US feminist establishment found a familiar common ground on this issue. Armed with a shared vocabulary of human rights and gender equality (however differently understood), they began to assemble an anti-trafficking movement rooted in shared commitments to an egalitarian, heterosexual conception of family and the conviction that sexual trafficking could be best remedied through legal and carceral state intervention combined with expanded access to the formal labor market.[31]

Current Anti-trafficking Activism

In part because of this complex cultural and political history, feminist anthropologist Carole S. Vance argues, the contemporary movement to end human trafficking is unified less by coherent analysis or shared ideology than by recourse to the narrative genre of melodrama. Melodramatic depictions of trafficking typically focus on "an innocent female victim crying out for rescue from sexual danger and diabolical male villains intent on her violation," or at least supremely indifferent to it.[32] In turn, morally good people are compelled to action. The intervening hero stops bad men from preying on innocent and unsuspecting victims. Told in this way, trafficking stories feature a stable cast of predictable stock characters: clearly identifiable victims, villains, and heroes.

This melodramatic plot is sufficiently flexible to be set in virtually any global location. From the streets of Atlanta to the brothels of India, the variety of settings in which trafficking stories are set reinforces an image of the anti-trafficking movement as cosmopolitan and globally aware. Yet while trafficking narratives frequently refer to structural factors and conditions such as globalization, poverty, migration, immigration, racism, and gender inequality, rarely are the particular political, economic, and social dynamics of specific locations or narratives explored in depth. As Vance explains, "melodrama is about people, not states, institutions or structural conditions."[33] The melodramatic genre dictates a general storyline of "male lust endangering innocent women" that organizes attention and emotion around individual actors and motivations. The invocation of structural conditions of exploitation in the context of trafficking melodramas thus serves primarily as a backdrop for staging the central emotional drama that characterizes anti-trafficking narratives, that of sexual danger and rescue. In this way, the narrative genre of melodrama mutes the broader roles of structural factors as well as their complexity and particularity in specific locations.

Despite the diverse range of constituencies currently involved in anti-trafficking activism, many policy initiatives and projects designed to fight trafficking look remarkably similar. Elizabeth Bernstein and

Janet Jakobsen have argued that Christian conservatives and secular feminists have developed a working alliance to combat trafficking around shared commitments to "a sexual politics that is premised upon amative, egalitarian, heterosexual relations between women and men and enhanced male participation in the domestic sphere, [and ...] a 'masculinist' model of state intervention that is premised upon militarized humanitarianism and carceral paradigms of justice."[34] In practice, this means that most mainstream anti-trafficking initiatives recommend formal market participation (i.e., legal jobs) and family envelopment (i.e., return to family of origin, or the formation of new heterosexual family units through marriage) as remedies for trafficking victims, and for trafficking offenders, criminal prosecution, and incarceration.[35] Because there are few alternatives to the dominant anti-trafficking framework for conceptualizing and analyzing trafficking, when progressive Christians join anti-trafficking coalitions and projects, they often adopt the same rhetoric, images, and approaches to the issues.[36] Thus the monopoly of the melodramatic framework in human trafficking activism and advocacy extends even to progressives, despite the important issues and communities that this framework eclipses. Two examples illustrate this pattern and the contradictions it creates for progressive anti-trafficking efforts.

January 11 is National Human Trafficking Awareness Day in the United States, a day on which Americans are encouraged to educate themselves about human trafficking, express support for anti-trafficking legislation and enforcement efforts, and pledge financial or volunteer support to various anti-trafficking organizations. In January 2011, one email marking the day began with a fairly standard description of human trafficking: "Human trafficking, referred to as modern-day slavery, is the fastest growing and second most profitable criminal industry in the world. More than 27 million women, men, and children have become victims of human trafficking for labor and sexual exploitation. Trafficking can and does occur in all parts of the world, including the US. Large sporting events like the Super Bowl attract human trafficking, especially for sexual exploitation of women."[37] The email also included a section titled "Stories of Human Trafficking," excerpted from the Polaris Project website. Four of the vignettes related some form of exploitative, immoral, or abusive sex. The single vignette that was not about sex trafficking was the third in the sequence of stories, placed between the two sexual vignettes that preceded it and two that followed, echoing the common perception that while human trafficking is *sometimes* labor exploitation, it is *usually* sexual exploitation. Following the stories of human trafficking, the email ended with a "Prayer of Solidarity."[38]

The presentation of human trafficking in this email—the statistics and description as "modern-day slavery," its depiction in the five vignettes, and the concluding Prayer of Solidarity—could have been produced by any of a range of Christian anti-trafficking organizations: the Salvation Army, the International Justice Mission, or even a local church. However, it came from one of the most progressive Christian feminist organizations in the United States, the Women's Alliance for Theology, Ethics and Ritual (WATER). WATER is a feminist, Catholic, lesbian-affirming organization. The way that the dominant framing of human trafficking—what it is, why it is wrong, and what ought to be done about it—shows up in WATER's email illustrates the long reach of the standard framework for understanding human trafficking. The rhetoric, images, characters, emotions, and moral rationales that define the dominant anti-trafficking consensus are extremely persuasive, even emotionally satisfying. For this reason, when progressive Christian organizations take up the issue of human trafficking, they frequently do so in the terms of the mainstream anti-trafficking movement, circulating the same stories and images, supporting the same basic analytical frameworks and remedies.

Another example further illustrates how difficult it is for progressive Christian organizations to move beyond the dominant anti-trafficking framework. In the summer of 2011, a group of progressive religious leaders joined an already existing campaign to shut down the "adult services" section of the classified advertising website Backpage.com.[39] Campaigners maintained that this section of the website had become a lucrative hub for the arrangement of commercial sex acts, including the "sale of children." Working through Groundswell, a social action initiative of Auburn Theological Seminary in New York City, the group took out a full-page advertisement in the *New York Times*, where they published an open letter to Village Voice Media (VVM), the parent company of Backpage.com.[40] The letter and an accompanying media campaign attracted the attention of VVM, the media, and the public. In December representatives from VVM met with clergy at Auburn Seminary, and the following March Groundswell delivered petitions containing the signatures of more than 600 faith leaders and more than 240,000 community members to VVM's offices.[41] While the campaign did not succeed in forcing Backpage.com to shutter the adult sections of its website, it did add momentum to the campaign and raised the profile of the effort.[42] What sets this campaign apart for the purposes of our analysis here is neither its framing of the issue of trafficking nor its stated objective of shutting down Backpage.com's adult services section but the letter's drafters and signers, a group of prominent rabbis, pastors, bishops, and imams generally associated with liberal and progressive congregations, movements, and institutions.

Like WATER's Human Trafficking Awareness Day email, the Groundswell letter incorporates many of the key features of the dominant anti-trafficking narrative. There is slippage between the broad term "trafficking" and the term "sex trafficking," and further confusion of sex trafficking with commercial sex work generally. A reference to young people as "boys and girls" conjures images of childhood and sexual inexperience that sideline questions of sexual agency. Like many other contemporary anti-trafficking initiatives, the open letter emphasizes both the broad consensus about trafficking—a consensus shared by "moral and religious leaders of many creeds and backgrounds"—and maintains a tone of unflinching moral clarity about the harms of trafficking and the urgency of proposed remedies. The letter begins: "It is a basic fact of the moral universe that girls and boys should not be sold for sex." It concludes with a call to action: "We can do something right now to help these girls and boys. Please shut down the Adult section of Backpage.com immediately so that no minor is exploited through advertisements on your Web site."[43]

The progressive organizers and participants involved in the Groundswell campaign against Backpage.com saw clear connections between the issue of child sex trafficking and a broader set of social justice issues with which they were already involved, including domestic violence, gender justice, immigration, and the concerns of GLBTIQ people. The "Groundswell of Responsibility" website describes the campaign with reference to these issues: "Child sex slavery is rooted in nearly every other social injustice. If you care about ending poverty, homelessness, human trafficking, immigrant exploitation, LGBT oppression, racism, and violence against girls, this is your call to action. This is not a conservative issue, or a liberal issue. This is about ending an unconscionable practice."[44] Groundswell's open letter identifies poverty and abuse as root causes of child sex trafficking, and acknowledges that ending the sex trafficking of minors will require much more than eliminating adult ads from online classified sites. Yet the additional strategies mentioned in the letter—educational campaigns and law enforcement—are among the remedies most commonly endorsed by the mainstream anti-trafficking movement; on their own, they offer little in the way of addressing issues of economic justice and structural inequality. In the broader media coverage of the campaign against Backpage.com, these attempts to highlight systemic inequalities and social justice issues were barely visible.

At the same time, VVM and its supporters, including some feminists and groups representing individuals involved in the commercial sex trade, found it easy to misidentify the Groundswell campaign with the long tradition of socially conservative efforts to curtail freedom of speech in order to promote or preserve "traditional" sexual morality. This fit a well-worn script. Alluding to the *Village Voice*'s antiestablishment ethos and reputation for provocation, VVM chief executive officer, Jim Larkin, told the *New York Times*, "We have all these practicing politicians and concerned clergy after us. We must be doing something right."[45] (VVM representatives struck a more respectful tone in their direct correspondence with the Groundswell coalition.) The identification of anti-trafficking activism with conservative sexual politics frustrated Groundswell's leaders, who could point to a range of progressive issues with which they were involved, including especially their pro-GLBTIQ initiatives, as a way of distinguishing themselves from religious conservatives. Nonetheless, they found it difficult to break out of the deeply ingrained expectations for the role of religious voices in public debates about the tightly linked issues of sexuality, sexual freedom, and free speech.[46]

A consultation titled "Human Trafficking, Commercial Sexual Exploitation and Prophetic Leadership," convened by Auburn Seminary in September 2012, put these issues front and center.[47] Organized as a follow-up to the Backpage.com campaign, the consultation brought together a small group of clergy, journalists, NGO leaders, grassroots activists, and academics to discuss building a long-term progressive coalition around issues of human trafficking. Over the course of the day, many participants raised questions about the theologies of gender and sexuality implicit in the dominant anti-trafficking rhetoric; the movement's tendency to fall into a "rescue mentality"; the need for more robust conversations about race, class, and sexual violence; a desire to take seriously the experiences and needs of GLBTIQ youth; and the potential impact of media images that portray trafficking "victims" as passive and without agency. These concerns, along with a corresponding desire to proceed cautiously and deliberately, were met at times with a sense of urgency and even impatience on the part of some clergy and activists who articulated a sincere desire to leave with a course of action that could help to remedy an unconscionable injustice.[48]

The tensions between these two urges are real, and they reflect the genuine difficulties faced by progressive religious leaders and coalitions who are committed to building broad coalitions to take up the cause of human trafficking while resisting the conservative tendencies of much mainstream anti-trafficking activism. Adopting the prevailing rhetoric and imagery of the anti-trafficking movement often eclipses issues, individuals, and communities to which progressives have traditionally been committed. In particular, the experiences of young people, queer people, and immigrants (many of whom may also be young and/or queer) are often written out of the dominant anti-trafficking narrative. Thinking carefully about why these experiences do not fit easily into the dominant understandings of human trafficking can help direct attention to some of the more fundamental analytical oversights of the anti-trafficking movement.

The issues raised by the Groundswell campaign about minors who sell sex and, more narrowly, young people trafficked for sex illustrate a limitation of the dominant anti-trafficking narrative, which has successfully rewritten street children, runaways, and juvenile delinquents as actual or potential "trafficking victims" in recent years. Penelope Saunders writes that the framework of child trafficking "describes a set of behaviors perpetrated against children and youth. . . and locates volition as well as blame squarely in the actions of traffickers," thereby positioning children and youth as casualties of adult sexual misconduct.[49] For all of the ways that the child-trafficking framework permits youth to articulate sexual experiences as exploitation, Saunders highlights how it falters when confronted with nonconforming youth—young people who "do not consider themselves victims or who do not view the harms done to them in the same way as . . . advocates who intend to help them."[50] Young people who sell sex may or may not understand themselves as "trafficking victims." They may or may not feel that exchanging sex for money is the worst harm they suffer. Framing this issue as a problem of sold sex actually ignores the systems that young people who sell sex report as the major sources of oppression and suffering in their lives, including abuse in families, harassment by police, and failures of the foster care system.[51]

In particular, the child-trafficking framework is unable to account for the ways that homophobia shapes the lives of queer and transgender youth, who by most accounts constitute a large portion of homeless youth in major cities.[52] It misses the stories of other young people—homeless, runaway, and other economically marginal youth—who report complex motives for involvement in the sex work economy and a wide variety of experiences in it.[53] This framework is further unable to accommodate youth, especially youth who identify as gay, lesbian, bisexual and transgender, who are "sexually active on their own terms while at the same time experiencing sexual abuse and exploitation in other arenas of their lives, [or] youth who no longer look or act like small, frightened children but wish to speak out about their own lives and construct their own futures"—futures that might or might not include marriage, the nuclear family, or sober middle-class values, and that might involve any number of arrangements (sexual, commercial, or otherwise) that violate the good judgment of social reformers, the sexual mores of religious crusaders, or the letter of the law.[54] Insofar as one of the primary issues at stake in contemporary anti-trafficking campaigns is normative heterosexuality and its sexual arrangements, sexual minorities generally and sexually nonconforming youth in particular fall out of this framework.[55]

The dominant framing of trafficking likewise glosses over issues of agency, empowerment, and structural violence that rise to the surface in the stories of migrant women and men who report that they sometimes choose work in sexual and erotic services because they prefer it to other kinds of work available to them. Anthropologist Laura Agustín argues that the recurring debates in mainstream anti-trafficking advocacy circles about whether prostitution is best understood as violence or work fail to address undocumented migrants who earn money in sex, housework, and caring sectors of the labor market. "Migrants working in the informal sector are treated as passive subjects rather than as normal people looking for conventional opportunities, conditions and pleasures," she writes.[56] Downplaying the significance of their expressed preferences and the issues that migrants who sell sex identify as their primary concerns—for instance, safe and affordable housing, economic livelihoods, and violence at the hands of police—glosses over important questions about the relationship between sexual and nonsexual forms of exploitation, and between exploitation in intimate and non-intimate spheres. It also overlooks the issues of poverty, economic inequality, and violence that shape the choices and constraints faced by transnational migrants, both documented and undocumented.

Although WATER's Human Trafficking Awareness Day email and the Groundswell campaign to shut down the adult section of Backpage. com are two examples of progressive forays into anti-trafficking activism, they illustrate the force of the dominant anti-trafficking refrain. When groups wish to express condemnation of human trafficking, doing so without adopting the existing rhetorical framework of sold sex and the images and moral rationale of the dominant anti-trafficking consensus but at the same time remaining recognizable as part of the anti-trafficking movement is extremely difficult. Consequently, it is not surprising that progressive Christians—including those groups and individuals who might otherwise critique any number of facets of this dominant anti-trafficking framework—take it up when they turn to the topic of trafficking. Articulating a different analytical framework for talking and thinking about human trafficking is a formidable challenge.

Having noted the ways that the melodramatic framing of human trafficking functions to divert attention from larger macro-level structures of exploitation, the remainder of this essay explores some of the insights of a different analysis of trafficking that intentionally attempts to refuse this seductive narrative. In doing so, we suggest that progressive critiques of neoliberal capitalism and its attendant conceptions of family can be resources for the critical reformulation of the dominant anti-trafficking framework.

Neoliberalism and Human Trafficking

Long before human trafficking was recognized as a social and political issue, progressive Christian ethicists were critical of neoliberalism on account of its distinct form of economic reductionism and its role in dismantling the regulatory and social welfare functions of the state.[57] In *Hitting Home: Feminist Ethics, Women's Work and the Betrayal of Family Values*, ethicist Gloria Albrecht describes neoliberalism as a political economic theory within capitalism that aims at economic growth and efficiency as primary social and political goals.[58] Neoliberal economic theory insists that unregulated or "free" markets are the most efficient and reliable means to achieve economic growth and that free markets are uniquely capable of achieving the best solutions to increasingly complex social problems.[59] In other words, neoliberalism posits the free market as basic not only to economic growth but to social and political goods—individual liberties, human rights, environmental protections—as well. In neoliberal terms, political and social goods are, above all, derivatives of economic success inseparable from, if not identical to, economic prosperity and efficiency.[60]

One of the fronts on which progressive Christians have waged their resistance to neoliberalism is through defending a primary role for the government in addressing social and economic inequalities. A related way that progressive Christians resist neoliberalism is by articulating the connections between particular economic and social policies and the material conditions of people's daily lives, showing how the forms of suffering and precarity about which a wide range of people profess concern are tied to specific policies, practices, and ideologies.

A great variety of US-based anti-trafficking activism is currently organized around promoting neoliberal capitalist institutions as the best and most promising anti-trafficking rejoinder. For instance, Kevin Bales, a leading expert on modern slavery and human trafficking, makes the connection between neoliberal capitalist practices and opposition to human trafficking explicitly, arguing, "Freed slaves . . . become what a slave can never be: a consumer."[61] Echoing Bales's perspective, a staff member of the International Justice Mission (IJM), the largest evangelical anti-trafficking organization in the United States, recently gave a similar explanation of the IJM's anti-trafficking work, stating, "Our real goal is to bring people out of slavery into the free market."[62] Here a market component is positioned as essential to, if not constitutive of, freedom from human trafficking. That is, freedom from human trafficking entails (re)positioning people as consumers in the free market.

Not only is freedom from trafficking articulated as participation in the capitalist marketplace as worker and consumer, but virtually every US-based anti-trafficking organization supports a role for the state in anti-trafficking activism that is fully consistent with neoliberalism's limited conception of the state, namely, as an agent of punitive or carceral redress. Thus, more and tougher laws that criminalize trafficking and harsher sentences for traffickers are proposed as an effective way to fight human trafficking. This neoliberal understanding of the state stands in sharp contrast to liberal conceptions of the welfare state, where the state is conceived as an agent of economic redistribution and assistance rather than primarily an agent of punishment.[63] This is not to deny that some individuals abuse others for financial gain, sexual gratification, or both; nor do we claim that incarceration is never an appropriate penalty for trafficking offenses. Our point is that understanding human trafficking in isolation from the social structures, economic policies, and political assumptions and practices in which it is situated and out of which it emerges, insisting instead that the primary cause of human trafficking is "traffickers"—a set of deviant, depraved, and bad individuals—is too thin an account of the types of violence and exploitation that those vulnerable to trafficking must navigate.

Analyses of human trafficking that work to systematically shift the blame for trafficking onto the backs of individuals offer an inadequate perspective on the social sources of trafficking abuses, erasing any sense of the roles played by neoliberal socioeconomic and cultural institutions, including the market and the family.[64] And yet anti-trafficking advocates frequently emphasize some combination of neoliberal institutions— family, state, market—as constituting the (morally) best and (economically) most efficient antidote to human trafficking. Moreover, whether adults or children, and whether by choice or default, many individuals who experience trafficking live outside or on the margins of these institutions anyway. They work in informal sectors of the market that are mostly excluded from government regulation and accounts, they often occupy subaltern categories of citizenship, they are structurally situated outside of even liberal notions of family, and they engage in modes of dwelling besides that of spatially stable households.[65] The real issues at stake are systemic conditions of economic, social, and political precarity; thus, to frame the challenges faced by trafficked persons and those vulnerable to trafficking in terms of threats posed by malevolent men is a case of analytic reductionism. Although beyond the scope of what we can accomplish here, we acknowledge that a fuller analysis of these issues is necessary.

Sexual Politics and Family

Another common theme threading through a great many US-based anti-trafficking efforts is a sexual politics that presumes monogamous heterosex in the context of marriage or committed relationships to be the moral norm for sexuality.[66] Other arrangements and sexual practices are denounced as degrading to men and harmful to women and children.

Elizabeth Bernstein and Janet Jakobsen describe this as "the sexual politics of 'egalitarian heterosexual relations,'" and argue that it is a contemporary reformulation of the "family values" rhetoric that took shape in the 1970s and 1980s.[67] Then, as now, debates about "family values" are concerned with social morality broadly, and in some leftward leaning circles they were seen as evidence of a widespread conservative backlash against advances in public and private sphere gender equality. Religious studies scholar Stephanie May argues, however, that the "family values" debates were about more than sexual morality, and they in fact signaled a critical reworking of the material relationship between the state and the private sphere institutions of home and family. Just as family values rhetoric was lauding married, heterosexual, and at least potentially reproductive sex as the *only* form of moral sexual relationship, state regulatory and social welfare programs were contracting dramatically. By promoting conformity with this narrowly defined sexual norm as the ticket for accessing what meager resources and protections remained at the state's disposal, the rhetoric of "family values" successfully obscured the massive erosion of the state's ability to function as an agent of economic redress.[68]

Progressive Christians resisted both the conservative moral vision of the "family values" rhetoric and the reimagined relationship between state and home that this rhetoric camouflaged. Feminist Christian ethicists led the way by mining Christian virtues, values, and sources for alternative visions of family. Values such as justice, equality, and care provided crucial moral leverage for efforts to secure recognition for a wider variety of family forms, including those headed by same-sex couples.[69]

Although in its original deployment "family values" rhetoric articulated conservative rejection of ideals of gender equality, a significant shift is discernible in the current iteration of this rhetoric. Bearing the clear mark of its encounter with the various social movements comprising second-wave liberal feminism, many current invocations of "family values" now unapologetically espouse and promote egalitarian heterosexual marriage as a private sphere ideal.[70] In the context of anti-trafficking advocacy, this shift is reflected in recurrent critiques of "third world cultures" for their "traditional" (i.e., *not* egalitarian) ideas about gender and sexuality, and the insistence that this "backwardness" is a causal factor in sex trafficking.[71]

Commercial heterosex is a particularly intense flash point in this fray. Heterosexual prostitution and its abolition stand at the center of an "ever-spiraling array of faith-based and secular activist agendas, human rights initiatives and legal instruments" that claim to fight human trafficking.[72] Symbolically and materially, prostitution represents the antithesis of the ideals of private and public sphere gender equality that unite the anti-trafficking alliance.[73] The fight against human trafficking is thus waged primarily as a fight against prostitution. The fight against prostitution, in turn, is waged as a fight for gender equality in both the public sphere and (especially) the private sphere of the home and family.[74]

The private sphere institutions of home and family are frequently recommended to women as the true basis of their freedom from trafficking. Anti-trafficking rhetoric packages this recommendation variously. For example, in the idea that women become vulnerable to human trafficking when they leave home, there is an assumption that trafficked persons want and need to be returned to their families upon extrication from a trafficking relationship, or a presumption that the ideal situation for women is a familial context like marriage. Although counseled in this way more explicitly by some organizations than by others, the formation of (or reentry into) heteronormative nuclear families is treated as a core benchmark of freedom and "recovery" from trafficking by a wide variety of organizations that work with female survivors of sex trafficking.

Joyce Meyer Ministries' short video "Wedding Bells Ring for Human Trafficking Survivors" is illustrative. It reports the work that an organization called International Crisis Aid is doing in an unspecified African country with former sex workers whom Meyer characterizes as "women and children trapped in sexual slavery." Meyer's guest, a representative from International Crisis Aid, gushes, "These girls are coming out, having *new* lives, complete opportunities, to get an education, to find a new job." But at no point are any specifics about the girls' and women's educational achievements or their jobs described for viewers. Instead, as video footage of young African women attired in big, white, American-style wedding dresses rolls in the background, Meyer's guest happily announces, "Three of the girls recently got married!" She explains to viewers, "They've had the opportunity to begin a new life, and it really is amazing because in that culture for them to find a man who would accept them and marry them after their past is quite . . . [remarkable]." She concludes, "So when we talk about total transformation, that is what God is doing in their lives."[75] Neither education nor jobs turn out to be the crux of the "new lives" these women receive assistance in creating; rather, the crowning achievement to which viewers' attention is drawn is their marriages.

Positing home and family as so tightly connected to women's freedom eclipses several critical issues. For one, it implies that home and family are places of safety for women. Violence thus must come from *external* sources. What this assumption misses is that threats of violence and the risk of sexual exploitation are just as prevalent in the private sphere of family and home as they are in the public sphere outside it. Feminists

have long acknowledged that family members are the most common perpetrators of violence against women, thereby making home one of the
most dangerous spaces for women, rather than one of the safest.[76]

Second, this ideological construction of family tends to take for
granted a well-defined public/private sphere separation that imagines
home and family as clearly distinct from the market. Reality is often
far less tidy, with family and home inextricably entangled with market
forces and the forms of precarity, privation, or flourishing they enable.
Family and social networks, including sexual networks, reflect not only
affective bonds but also networks through which individuals access material and financial resources. In a recent national telephone survey of
unmarried African American and white women aged twenty to forty-
five, for example, a full third of white and African American respondents
reported that economic considerations led them to stay in a relationship
longer than they wanted to. Moreover, 22 percent of African American
women and 11 percent of white women reported *starting* a relationship
in response to economic concerns.[77] Individuals use family, social, and
sexual networks not simply to satisfy affective or "private sphere" needs
and desires but also as sites as of access to material resources, including
financial resources.[78]

Home and family are often presumed to be able (and even obligated)
to ameliorate some of the market's more brutal effects—effects that the
separate-spheres gender ideology ascendant through the nineteenth century held as especially unsuited to women's (alleged) gentle, noncompetitive natures. But no matter how thoroughly romanticized or broadly
defined, home and family are not able to fully offset the effects of the
market. Home and family do not solve the problem of economic vulnerability, and they are certainly inadequate institutional rejoinders to
trafficking.

Understanding home and family as internal to the neoliberal capitalist system and, further, as themselves among the sources of violence, exploitation, or just plain misery that trafficked and vulnerable
people need to navigate are issues that raise significant questions about
the adequacy of the sexual politics around which the consensus on hu-

man trafficking has formed. Given that home and family are among the most dangerous settings for women, why are they repeatedly and enthusiastically endorsed as essential components of freedom? Why is (re)integration into family life so essential? Further, while critical feminists and queer activists may have no essential quarrel with "amative, egalitarian heterosexual relations" for those who choose this, such relations are not the primary way that issues of gender equality come to bear in all lives.[79] In fact, we contend that this sexual politics is one of the points at which queer communities and the concerns of other minority and nonconforming perspectives become most clearly disconnected from the dominant anti-trafficking narrative and the remedies it endorses.

Conclusion

The working alliance on trafficking within American Christianity echoes a broader consensus within the US anti-trafficking movement: an enthusiastic endorsement of state-sanctioned criminalization and incarceration for traffickers and, for trafficking victims, integration into the formal "free" market (via wage labor) and reintegration into heteronormative family life. This understanding of human trafficking and, however implicitly, of human freedom reflects dual commitments to a sexual politics of egalitarian heterosexual relations and the foundational institutions of neoliberalism, including a vision of the state as an agent of carceral justice. In this essay, we have argued that such an understanding of trafficking and its remedies falls short because it overlooks the most pressing concerns and experiences of some of the populations most vulnerable to the harms of trafficking. We have shown how the traditions of critique distinctive to feminist Christian social ethics, including critiques of neoliberalism and the heteronormative family, can provide resources for an analysis of human trafficking that addresses some of the gaps and silences in mainstream anti-trafficking activism and advocacy.

Of course, these are not silences that academic Christian ethicists can or should seek to fill alone. Opening up space for genuine conversation and debate about sexuality, justice, and human freedom in the context of the anti-trafficking movement will require resisting the dominant consensus on trafficking at least long enough to let real questions emerge and complex debates unfold. Listening carefully to the stories and experiences—as well as the political, social, and theological analyses—of those most affected by trafficking can help us do that. To be sure, such listening (and genuine hearing) may have its own difficulties since the choices and desires of those who are most vulnerable to the harms of trafficking may or may not conform to the sexual and moral politics of social conservatives, pro-sex feminists, progressive Christians, or any other category of the concerned. Generous listening will require making space for their dreams of freedom and flourishing alongside our own, and allowing our theologies, political ideologies, and practices of solidarity to be shaped by what we hear.

In insisting on making space for these voices and experiences, we follow in the tradition of feminist Christian ethicists such as Emilie Townes, Sharon Welch, and others. Townes observes that the ethical vision of many white, middle-class Americans—the demographic profile of the very group that dominates US Christian anti-trafficking activism—suffers from a distortion that is rooted in the privilege of comfortability. The luxury of not having to hear the voices or understand the perspectives of others results in isolation and segregation.[80] In the case of sex trafficking, such isolation allows relatively privileged anti-trafficking advocates to romanticize marginalized persons and groups, seeing them as innocent victims deserving of rescue but missing much of the context and complexity that shapes their actual experiences. Sharon Welch makes a similar point in *A Feminist Ethic of Risk:* "If we remain in our own communities, doing social ethics only from within one set of socially shared values and behaviors, we do not see the partiality and immorality of those views and behaviors."[81] As applied to trafficking and the moral analyses on which progressive anti-trafficking activism and advocacy might proceed, without critical perspective on the basic narrative presumed by the dominant anti-trafficking framework, we will only ever tout the virtues of home and family; we will never press beyond the goal of fashioning human beings into consumers.

Nearly twenty-five years ago, in the midst of the acrimonious debates about sexuality that engulfed and threatened to completely implode the women's movement, feminist ethicist Beverly Harrison and theologian Carter Heyward observed that a major contribution of feminist theory in the 1980s and early '90s, in spite of the heated conflicts it generated, was its success in "securing . . . the cultural and intellectual space to forge a genuine . . . 'discourse about sexuality.'"[82] Despite the incredible difficulty of many of these debates, they argued, the creation of space for reflection, dialogue, and even argument marked a substantive advance over a time when frank and thoughtful discussions of human sexuality, moral agency, and practices of freedom were closeted or foreclosed altogether. Public discussions of human trafficking and the widespread consensus that characterizes these discussions suggest that such cultural and intellectual space is needed once again.

Questions for Reflection

1. This essay draws our attention to the voices of some involved in the sex trade that Campbell and Zimmerman believe have been ignored. While they concede that all appear to be at least "bruised" by sex work, their analysis highlights the experiences of some adult prostitutes who do not experience sex work as the most exploitative employment option realistically available to them. This lack of unanimity alerts us to the fact that experience is always socially constructed, that is, interpreted and evaluated through a hermeneutic. Abolitionists might well reply to Campbell and Zimmerman that these accounts of prostitution have been distorted by the internalization of scripts that dehumanize sexual encounters and thus should not be given much weight. What do you think, why, and on what ground(s)?

2. Recognizing that narratives and stories often motivate concern for victims, what alternate concerns—for example, access to common goods like clean water and basic nutrition, education, health care, shelter, and non-

exploitive employment—can be engaged to inform a local and global response to the structural violence of the human trafficking economy?

3. What plan of education would you develop to mobilize your community efforts in affecting positive change supportive of safety, healing, and reintegration into the social mainstream of those victimized by all forms of human trafficking? Toward what sort of penalties for individuals and organizations who perpetrate this violence would you mobilize your community?

Suggestions for Further Reading

Doak, Mary. "Trafficked: Sex Slavery and the Reign of God." In *Women, Wisdom, and Witness: Engaging Contexts in Conversation*, Rosemary P. Carbine and Kathleen J. Dolphin, eds., 45–60. Collegeville, MN: Liturgical Press, 2012.

Haker, Hille. "Catholic Feminist Ethics Reconsidered: The Case of Sex Trafficking." *Journal of Religious Ethics* 43, no. 2 (2015): 218–243.

Hathaway, James C. "The Human Rights Quagmire of Human Trafficking." *Virginia Journal of International Law* 49.1 (2008–2009): 1–59.

Pae, Keun-joo Christine. "Western Princesses—a Missing Story: A Christian Feminist Ethical Analysis of U.S. Military Prostitution in South Korea." *Journal of the Society of Christian Ethics* 29.2 (2009): 121–139.

Shelley, Louise. *Human Trafficking: A Global Perspective*. Cambridge, UK: Cambridge University Press, 2010.

Notes

We are grateful for the feedback and editorial suggestions that we received from our anonymous reviewers and from several others who read and responded to earlier drafts of this essay. We also wish to thank those who participated in the post-presentation discussion of our paper at the 2013 Annual Meeting of the Society of Christian ethics for their candid conversation about the complicated and sensitive issues we raise in this piece.

1. Elizabeth Bernstein, "The Sexual Politics of the New Abolitionism," *Differences: A Journal of Feminist Critical Studies* 18 (2007): 128–51; and Bernstein, "Militarized Humanitarianism Meets Carceral Feminism: The Politics of Sex, Rights and Freedom in Contemporary Anti-trafficking Campaigns," *Signs* 36 (2010): 45–71. See also Bernstein and Janet R. Jakobsen, "Sex, Secularism and Religious Influence in US Politics," *Third World Quarterly* 31 (2010): 1027–28; and Letitia Campbell, "Selling Our Children: Atlanta Does Battle against Sex Trafficking of Kids," *Sojourners*, August 2010, 22–26.

2. On progressive Christianity, see, generally, Delwin Brown, *What Does a Progressive Christian Believe? A Guide for the Searching, the Open and the Curious* (New York: Seabury Books, 2008); and Robert P. Jones, *Progressive and Religious: How Christian, Jewish, Muslim, and Buddhist Leaders Are Moving beyond the Culture Wars and Transforming American Life* (Lanham, MD: Rowman & Littlefield, 2008). Both of these authors link the emergence of such "progressive" religious identities (and use of the term) to the aftermath of the 2004 US presidential election, in which religious conservatives played a significant role, and to subsequent efforts to recover space for moderate and liberal religious voices in US political life. Jones argues that "progressive Christian" leaders and institutions are coalescing around issues of poverty, peacemaking, the environment, social justice, and GLB-TIQ equality. We use the term loosely here (Jones, *Progressive and Religious*, 13–17). For a broader historical perspective on liberal and progressive Christian ideas and movements, see Gary Dorrien, *Soul in Society: The Making and Renewal of Social Christianity* (Minneapolis: Fortress Press, 1995).

3. United Nations, *Protocol to Prevent, Suppress and Punish Trafficking in Persons, Especially Women and Children, Supplementing the United Nations Convention against Transnational Organized Crime* (2000), Article 3, www.uncjin.org/Docu ments/Conventions/dcatoc/final_ documents_2/convention_ traff_eng.pdf.

4. Kevin Bales, *Ending Slavery: How We Free Today's Slaves* (Berkeley: University of California Press, 2007), 11–12. See also Kamala Kempadoo, "From Moral Panic to Global Justice: Changing Perspectives on Trafficking," in *Trafficking and Prostitution Reconsidered: New Perspectives on Migration, Sex Work, and Human Rights*, ed. Kamala Kempadoo, Jyoti Sanghera, and Bandana Pattanaik (Boulder, CO: Paradigm Publishers, 2005), viii.

5. ILO, *A Global Alliance against Forced Labor: Global Report under the Follow up to the ILO Declaration on Fundamental Principles of Rights at Work* (Geneva: International Labor Organization, 2005), 12–13; Kevin Bales, *Disposable People: New Slavery in the Global Economy* (Berkeley: University of California Press, 1999). A full discussion of the debates about the methodologies used to produce human trafficking statistics and the accuracy thereof is beyond the scope of this essay, but debates about methodology are a live and contentious issue in anti-trafficking research, activism, and advocacy. And, indeed, one need not be a specially trained statistician to understand that the range of these estimates is so large that the accuracy of both figures is rendered suspect. See, generally, Laura Agustín, "Trafficking Guesses/Estimates/Fantasies, with and without Sex and Slavery," *The Naked Anthropologist*, February 22, 2011, http://www.lauraagustin.com/pictorial-repre sentation-of-trafficking-estimatesguessesfantasies-with-and-without-sex; Rachel Lloyd, "Urban Legends and Hoaxes: How Hyperbole Hurts Trafficking Victims," *Huffington Post*, February 3, 2012, www.huffingtonpost.com/rachel-lloyd/village -voice-escort-ads_b_1250617.html; and Martin Cizmar, Ellis Conklin, and Kristin Hinman, "Real Men Get Their Facts Straight: Ashton and Demi and Sex Traf-

ficking," *Village Voice,* June 29, 2011, www.villagevoice.com/2011-06-29/news
/real-men-get-their-facts-straight-sex-trafficking-ashton-kutcher-demi-moore/.

6. The figure of fifty thousand female victims of human trafficking is based on
data from a 1999 CIA briefing on global trafficking that is now widely regarded as
inaccurate. The US State Department–based Office to Monitor and Combat Trafficking in Persons stopped citing this statistic after 2003 and began using the down-
wardly revised numbers in 2005. See Wendy Chapkis, "Soft Glove Punishing Fist:
The Trafficking Victims Protection Act of 2000," in *Regulating Sex: The Politics of Intimacy and Identity,* ed. Elizabeth Bernstein and Laurie Schaffner (New
York: Routledge, 2005), 51–66; and US Department of State, Office to Monitor
and Combat Trafficking in Persons, *2005 Trafficking in Persons Report* (Washington, DC: Office to Monitor and Combat Trafficking in Persons, 2005).

7. Free the Slaves and the Human Rights Center, *Slaves: Forced Labor in the
United States* (Washington, DC: Free the Slaves; and Berkeley: University of California Press, 2004).

8. ILO, *Global Alliance against Forced Labor,* 12–13.

9. Our discussion of practices clustered under the term "trafficking" and the
debates over trafficking in this essay will be oriented toward the way that debate
has unfolded in the United States in the last decade and a half. Conversations about
trafficking in other contexts presumably have distinctive inflections. We recognize
that local debates about trafficking in the United States have global consequences,
in part because of the United States' role in funding social programs around the
world. For a discussion of some of these consequences, see Marcus Middleburg,
"The Anti-Prostitution Policy in the US HIV/AIDS Program," *Health and Human Rights* 9, no. 1 (2006): 3–15; and Deborah Macfarlane, "Reproductive Health
Policies in President Bush's Second Term: Old Battles and New Fronts in the
United States and Internationally," *Journal of Public Health Policy* 27, no. 4 (2006):
405–26.

10. For an account of some of the relevant shifts within evangelical Christianity, see Melani McAlister, "What Is Your Heart For? Affect and Internationalism
in the Evangelical Public Sphere," *American Literary History* 20, no. 4 (2008): 870–
95; and David King, "The New Internationalists: World Vision and the Revival
of American Evangelical Humanitarian-ism," *Religions* 3, no. 4 (2012): 922–49.

11. In the wake of the Cold War, the so-called Washington Consensus dictated
a smaller role for the state and a correspondingly larger role for NGOs in the provision of social services. In the United States, this was reflected in the "welfare reform" initiatives codified in the Personal Responsibility and Work Opportunity
Act of 1996 and an expanded focus on "faith-based" (and, later, "community") initiatives. In the developing world, this approach, advanced through the policies of
institutions such as the World Bank and the International Monetary Fund (IMF),
led to a contraction of the state and contraction or privatization of state-provided
services like health, education, pension, and other social programs; an expanded

role for international NGOs in these areas; and an increased emphasis on civil society. The restructuring of the welfare state generally, and the globalization of that process as part of the Washington Consensus specifically, led to an explosion in the number of NGOs during the 1990s. These shifts created opportunities for American evangelicals, among other groups. For one account of this shift, see Cecelia Lynch, "Social Movements and the Problem of Globalization," *Alternatives: Global, Local, Political* 23 (1998): 149–73.

12. Michael Horowitz, quoted in Michael Cromartie, "The Jew Who Is Saving Christians," *Christianity Today*, March 1, 1999, 54; and Yvonne C. Zimmerman, *Other Dreams of Freedom: Religion, Sex and Human Trafficking* (New York: Oxford University Press, 2013), 40. For further discussion of the history and rhetoric of evangelical Christian concerns about religious persecution, see also Elizabeth Castelli, "Praying for the Persecuted Church: US Christian Activism in the Global Arena," *Journal of Human Rights* 4 (2005): 321–51; and Melani McAlister, "The Politics of Persecution," *Middle East Report* 249 (2008): 18–27.

13. The International Religious Freedom Act is 22 USC 6401. Available at the US Government Printing Office website, https://www.gpo.gov/fdsys/pkg/US CODE-2010-title22/pdf/USCODE-2010-title22-chap73-sec6401.pdf. See also Allen D. Hertzke, *Freeing God's Children: The Unlikely Alliance for Global Human Rights* (Lanham, MD: Rowman & Littlefield, 2004), 145. For an extended discussion of evangelicals' activism on religious persecution and, later, human trafficking, see Zimmerman, *Other Dreams of Freedom*, 39–51.

14. Hertzke, *Freeing God's Children*, 325; and Zimmerman, *Other Dreams of Freedom*, 47. In fact, the legislation proposed initially to address Christian persecution (the Freedom from Religious Persecution Act of 1997 [H.R. 1685]), and the legislation initially proposed to address human trafficking (the Freedom from Sexual Trafficking Act of 1999 [FFSTA, H.R. 1356]), were both drafted by the same individual, Rep. Christopher Smith's (R-NJ) top congressional aide, Joseph Rees. The similarities between these pieces of legislation were neither coincidental nor difficult to detect. According to Hertzke, Rees intentionally crafted the FFSTA to draw on the "scaffolding and relationships forged in the religious freedom effort." Hertzke, *Freeing God's Children*, 322.

15. Yvonne C. Zimmerman, "Christianity and Human Trafficking," *Religion Compass* 5 (2011): 572; and Zimmerman, *Other Dreams of Freedom*, 47–48.

16. Michael Horowitz, "How to Win Friends and Influence Culture," *Christianity Today* 49, no. 9 (September 2005), 71.

17. The Freedom from Sexual Trafficking Act of 1999. H.R. 1356, 106th Cong. www.gpo.gov/fdsys/pkg/CHRG-106hhrg60798/html/CHRG-106hhrg60798 .htm. This bill did not become law.

18. Hertzke, *Freeing God's Children*, 324. See also Beatrix Siman Zakhari, "Legal Cases Prosecuted under the Victims of Trafficking and Violence Protection Act of 2000," in *Human Traffic and Transnational Crime: Eurasian and American*

Perspectives, ed. Sally Stoecker and Louise Shelley (Lanham, MD: Rowman & Littlefield, 2004), 125–49; and Debbie Nathan, "Oversexed," *Nation*, August 29, 2005, 27–31.

19. Bernstein, "Militarized Humanitarianism," 49.

20. Victims of Trafficking and Violence Protection Act of 2000 (TVPA). Pub. L. 106–386, 106th Cong., October 28, 2000. https://www.gpo.gov/fdsys/pkg /PLAW-106publ386/content-detail.html. Sex trafficking is the first type of human trafficking specified in the TVPA, and the only type whose basic characteristics are described in detail. Moreover, the TVPA identifies the sex industry as the primary culprit in the proliferation of human trafficking. Anthony DeStefano's research indicates that between 2000 and 2006, virtually every federal policy discussion and debate about human trafficking took sex trafficking as the primary rhetorical and conceptual point of departure. See DeStefano, *The War on Human Trafficking: US Policy Assessed* (New Brunswick, NJ: Rutgers University Press, 2008).

21. Michael Horowitz, quoted in Cromartie, "The Jew Who Is Saving Christians," 54.

22. Carole S. Vance, "Thinking Trafficking, Thinking Sex," *GLQ: A Journal of Lesbian and Gay Studies* 17 (2011): 140.

23. Carolyn Bronstein, *Battling Pornography: The American Feminist Anti-Pornography Movement, 1976–1986* (New York: Cambridge University Press, 2011), esp. 269–308, 320–23. The differences in how constituents of this alliance understood the significance of opposition to media violence against women and pornography are notable. Radical feminists tended to understand the issue as an extension of feminist critiques of heterosexuality and male sexual privilege while, by contrast, social conservatives understood it as but one part of a larger effort to restore "decency" and "family values," to "protect" women from dangerous and immoral writings about sex, and to protest what they saw as the sexual libertinism and moral decay brought on by the social movements of the 1960s and '70s.

24. Carole S. Vance, "Negotiating Sex and Gender in the Attorney General's Commission on Pornography," in *Uncertain Times: Negotiating Gender in American Culture*, ed. Faye Ginsburg and Anna Lauenhaupt Tsing (Boston: Beacon Press, 1990), 118–34. See also Vance, "More Danger, More Pleasure: A Decade after the Barnard Sexuality Conference," *New York Law School Review* 289 (1993): 308–9.

25. Bronstein, *Battling Pornography*, 320–23.

26. For example, the first international conference on "Trafficking in Women," held in New York City in 1988, was organized by Women Against Pornography (WAP), the leading feminist anti-pornography organization in the United States at that time, and Women Hurt in Systems of Prostitution Engaged in Revolt (WHISPER), a Minneapolis-based feminist anti-pornography group. The Coalition against Trafficking in Women (CATW) grew out of this gathering as a vehicle for focusing on the international sex industry. Dorchen Leidholdt, "De-

mand and the Debate" (October 2003), www.catwlac.org/en/wp-content/up
loads/2013/10/Demand_and_the_Debate.pdf.

27. See Kathleen Barry, *Female Sexual Slavery* (Englewood Cliffs, NJ: Pren-
tice Hall, 1979).

28. Bronstein, *Battling Pornography*, 263–69.

29. Dorchen Leidholt and Laura Lederer are two of the leaders from the feminist anti-pornography movement who were influential in launching the anti-
trafficking movement. Leidholdt, a veteran of both the feminist anti-pornography
movement and the violence against women / domestic violence movement, went
on to cofound the CATW with Kathleen Barry. Lederer, a coordinator for Women
against Violence in Pornography and the Media (WAVPM) in the late 1970s and
editor of the feminist anti-pornography anthology *Take Back The Night: Women
on Pornography* (1980), in 1994 founded the Protection Project, a legal research institute dedicated to combatting human trafficking based at Johns Hopkins University. She also worked on the first Human Rights Report on Trafficking in Persons
for the US government and helped to set up the Office to Monitor and Combat
Trafficking in Persons in the US State Department under George Bush, where she
also served as a senior advisor on human trafficking. Lederer now heads an NGO
that describes its work as "fighting modern slavery by focusing on demand" and
provides leadership to the Triple S Network ("Stop Sex Slavery"). See Gayle Rubin, "Blood under the Bridge: Reflections on 'Thinking Sex,'" *GLQ: A Journal of
Lesbian and Gay Studies* 17 (2011); and "About Global Centurion" and "Leadership" at www.globalcenturion.org/

30. Bernstein and Jakobsen, "Sex, Secularism and Religious Influence," 1030.
Bernstein and Jakobsen further point out that the NGOs and other grassroots organizations that worked to combat trafficking before its rise to prominence tended
to frame it as an issue of exploited labor, and articulated their concerns about exploited labor broadly, connecting concerns about women trafficked into sexual labor to struggles for workers', migrants', and sex workers' rights. See also, Hertzke,
Freeing God's Children, 324.

31. Bernstein, "Militarized Humanitarianism," 45–71.

32. Vance, "Thinking Trafficking, Thinking Sex," 136.

33. Ibid., 139.

34. Bernstein and Jakobsen, "Sex, Secularism and Religious Influence," 1035.

35. Ibid.

36. For a succinct discussion of the basic ideological premises of the dominant contemporary anti-trafficking discourse see generally, Gayle S. Rubin, "The
Trouble with Trafficking: Afterthoughts on 'The Traffic in Women,'" in *Devia-
tions: A Gayle Rubin Reader*, ed. Gayle S. Rubin (Durham, NC: Duke University
Press, 2011), 66–67.

37. WATER, email message: "Human Trafficking Awareness: Prayer and Resources," January 10, 2012.

38. The Prayer of Solidarity read, "Holy Compassion, you who hear the cries of those in anguish, Be with us now to bring them to safety and to speak out against those who exploit. Holy Love, you who shout with us 'No' to human trafficking in all its forms, Be with us now to restore freedom to the trafficked and their families. Holy Justice, you who rage with us against the injustices of trafficking, Be with us now to take action to prevent and end this violence. Holy Wisdom, you who know the worth of every human being, Be with us as we erase this sinful practice from the face of the earth." Diann L. Neu, co-director of WATER, from the January 10, 2012, WATER email.

39. In August 2011, the National Association of Attorneys General sent a letter to Backpage.com accusing the site of failing to "effectively limit prostitution and sexual trafficking" on the site. (National Association of Attorneys General to Samuel Fifer, August 31, 2011, www.tn.gov/attorneygeneral/cases/backpage/backpageletter.pdf). The focus on Backpage.com followed on a campaign by activists, politicians, and state attorneys general that had successfully pressured Craigslist to shut down its adult services section in 2010, an outcome that was widely seen by anti-trafficking activists as a milestone in the effort to fight domestic minor sex trafficking. Subsequent research suggests caution in assessing the overall impact of the shuttering of Craigslist's adult services section. See, for example, Mark Latonero, "The Rise of Mobile and the Diffusion of Technology-Facilitated Trafficking" (Research Series on Technology and Human Trafficking, Annenberg Center on Communication Leadership & Policy, University of Southern California, Los Angeles, November 2012), 26–28, https://technologyandtrafficking.usc.edu/files/2012/11/HumanTrafficking2012_Nov12.pdf.

40. See, Groundswell, "An Open Letter to Village Voice Media," *New York Times*, October 20, 2011, www.groundswell-movement.org/nyt-ad/ and their overview of the campaign and its successes (www.groundswell-movement.org/gs-of-responsibility-problem-solution-action/). Full disclosure: Campbell served previously on the program staff at Auburn and knows personally a number of the people and institutions involved in the campaign discussed here.

41. As of October 2012, Groundswell's Change.org petition was one of the most popular active petitions on Change.org related to human trafficking, the petition closed with 266,809 supporters (https://www.change.org/p/tell-village-voice-media-to-stop-child-sex-trafficking-on-backpage-com). See "Digital Activism in Anti-Trafficking Efforts," in Latonero, "Rise of Mobile," 19–20.

42. For positive coverage of the campaign in the religious press, see Elizabeth Palmberg, "Responsible Adults," *Sojourners*, March 2012, 9; and for critical coverage, see Kayley Whalen, "A Dangerous Groundswell: Banning Adult Classifieds Is Not a Panacea for Child Sex Trafficking," *Humanist*, December 23, 2001, http://thehumanist.com/magazine/january-february-2012/up-front/a-dangerous-groundswell. Groundswell's participation in the campaign attracted the attention of national and regional newspapers, including the *New York Times*,

Washington Post, *Los Angeles Times*, *Orlando Sentinel*, *Seattle Times*, and others; online media outlets, such as the *Huffington Post* and the *Daily Beast*; and media industry publications, like NPR's *On the Media* and the Poynter Institute's *MediaWire* blog. See, among others, David Carr, "Fighting over Online Sex Ads," *New York Times*, October 30, 2011; James Rainey, "Village Voice Media Defends Its Backpage.com Ad Policy," *Los Angeles Times*, November 28, 2011; Adelle M. Banks, "Clergy Petition Village Voice to Drop Ads Linked to Sex Trafficking," *Huffington Post*, October 25, 2011; Jim Romanesko, "Village Voice Responds to Religious Leaders' Complaints about Backpage.com," *MediaWire Blog*, Poynter Institute, October 26, 2011, www.poynter.org/latest-news/mediawire/151009/village-voice-responds-to-religious-leaders-complaints-about-backpage-com/; Bob Garfield, "The Case against Backpage.com," *On the Media*, November 4, 2011, www.onthemedia.org/2011/nov/04/case-against-backpagecom/; and Matthew Flamm, "Group Calls on Village Voice Media to Drop Sex Ads," *Crain's New York Business*, October 25, 2011, www.crainsnewyork.com/article/20111025/MEDIA_ENTERTAINMENT/111029930.

43. Groundswell, "Open Letter to Village Voice Media."

44. "GS of Responsibility, Problem—Solution—Action," Groundswell Movement website, n.d., www.groundswell-movement.org/gs-of-responsibility-problem-solution-action/.

45. Carr, "Fighting over Online Sex Ads."

46. Carl Ferrer, email to Isaac Luria, October 17, 2011, http://media.phoenixnewtimes.com/7384300.0.jpg. As the controversy over Backpage.com was heating up, the *Village Voice* ran an "editor's note" characterizing the coalitions targeting Craigslist and Backpage.com as "feminists, religious zealots, the well-intentioned, law enforcement, and social-service bureaucrats" and "reformers, the devout and the government-funded." Editor's note accompanying Cizmar, Conklin, and Hinman, "Real Men." For an overview of some of the legal issues at stake in regulation of online content, see John E. D. Larkin, "Criminal and Civil Liability for User Generated Content: Craigslist, A Case Study," *Journal of Technology Law & Policy* 15 (2010): 85–112.

47. "Human Trafficking, Commercial Sexual Exploitation and Prophetic Leadership: Activist and Theological Perspectives and Groundings," September 10, 2012, Auburn Theological Seminary, New York, NY. Campbell participated in the consultation as a panelist.

48. For a discussion of similar dynamics within the movement around religious persecution, see Castelli, "Praying for the Persecuted Church," 324–25.

49. Penelope Saunders, "From Identity to Acronym: How 'Child Prostitution' Became 'CSEC,'" in *Regulating Sex: The Politics of Intimacy and Identity* (New York: Routledge, 2005), 176.

50. Ibid.

51. For accounts of how young people involved in commercial sex describe their

experiences, see, for example, Ric Curtis, Karen Terry, Kirk Dombrowski, Bilal Khan, Amy Muslim, Melissa Labriola, and Michael Rempel, "Commercial Sexual Exploitation of Children in New York City" (New York: Center for Court Innovation, John Jay College, September 2008), https://www.ncjrs.gov/pdffiles1/nij /grants/225082.pdf; Young Women's Empowerment Project, "Bad Encounter Line, 2012: Denied Help! How Youth in the Sex Trade and Street Economy Are Turned Away from Systems Meant to Help Us & What We Are Doing to Fight Back, A Participatory Action Research Project" (Chicago: YWEP, 2012), http://ywepchicago .files.wordpress.com/2011/06/bad-encounter-line-report-20121.pdf; and Young Women's Empowerment Project, "Bad Encounter Line Zine, #1 and #3" (Chicago: YWEP, n.d.), http://ywepchicago.files.wordpress.com/2011/07/bel-zine-13.pdf.

52. Curtis et al., "Commercial Sexual Exploitation of Children"; and Rachel Aviv, "Netherland," *New Yorker*, December 10, 2012, 60.

53. Contrary to dominant descriptions of domestic minor sex trafficking in the anti-trafficking movement, these youth sometimes work without pimps and exercise agency even in situations where their options are radically limited. See Saunders, "From Identity to Acronym," 167–85; Curtis et al., "Commercial Sexual Exploitation of Children"; Native Youth Sexual Health Network, "Indigenous Peoples in the Sex Trade: Speaking for Ourselves," April 11, 2011, http://www .nativeyouthsexualhealth.com/april112011.pdf; and Aviv, "Netherland," 60.

54. Saunders, "From Identity to Acronym," 180.

55. Vance, "Thinking Trafficking, Thinking Sex," 136. Gayle Rubin argues that legitimate concerns for the sexual welfare of the young have been co-opted to advance political mobilizations and policies with consequences that are sometimes quite damaging to the young people they are intended to help. She cites as an example the way the rhetoric of "child protection" has anchored many a conservative agenda with respect to intensifying women's subordinate status, reinforcing hierarchical family structures, curtailing gay citizenship, opposing comprehensive sex education, limiting the availability of contraception, and restricting abortion, especially for young women and girls. As she points out, virtually anything, "from promoting abstinence to banning gay marriage and adoption, can be and has been framed as promoting children's safety and welfare." Rubin, "Blood under the Bridge," 37. The manner in which concerns about the sexual abuse and exploitation of minors fuel a great deal of anti-trafficking activism that is anchored in a conservative gender and sexual politics is at least potentially a case in point of the concern Rubin raises.

56. Laura María Agustín, *Sex at the Margins: Migration, Labour Markets, and the Rescue Industry* (New York: Zed Books, 2007), 5–8.

57. For a history of Christian critiques of market capitalism in the last one hundred years, see Dorrien, *Soul in Society*. See also Traci C. West, "The Policing of Poor Black Women's Sexual Reproduction," in *God Forbid: Religion and Sex in American Public Life*, ed. Kathleen M. Sands, 135–54 (New York: Oxford Uni-

versity Press, 2000); Beverly Wildung Harrison, *Justice in the Making: Feminist Social Ethics,* eds. Elizabeth M. Bounds, Pamela K. Brubaker, Jane E. Hicks, Marilyn J. Legge, Rebecca Todd Peters, and Traci C. West (Louisville: Westminster John Knox Press, 2004), esp. part 3; Pamela K. Brubaker, Rebecca Todd Peters and Laura Stivers, eds. *Justice in a Global Economy: Strategies for a Global Economy* (Louisville: Westminster John Knox Press, 2006); Rebecca Todd Peters, *In Search of the Good Life: The Ethics of Globalization* (New York: Continuum, 2006); Pamela K. Brubaker, *Globalization at What Price? Economic Change and Daily Life,* rev. and exp. ed. (Boston: Pilgrim Press, 2007); and Gary Dorrien, "Breaking the Oligarchy: Globalization, Turbo-Capitalism, Economic Crash, Economic Democracy," in *Economy, Difference, Empire: Social Ethics for Social Justice* (New York: Columbia University Press, 2010), 143–67.

58. Gloria Albrecht, *Hitting Home: Feminist Ethics, Women's Work and the Betrayal of "Family Values"* (New York: Continuum Press, 2002), 13.

59. Dina Francesca Haynes, "Lessons from Bosnia's Arizona Market: Harm to Women in a Neoliberalized Postconflict Reconstruction Process," *University of Pennsylvania Law Review* 158, no. 6 (2010): 130.

60. Albrecht, *Hitting Home,* 13; and Haynes, "Lessons," 149. Neoliberalism does not claim that deregulated and privatized markets eliminate the possibility of abuse (of workers, the environment, etc.), but in general such situations are understood to be episodic and temporary. The market is assumed to be self-correcting in relation to abuses (since abuse falls under the rubric of "inefficiency") and fully capable of eliminating abusive situations without the imposition of external interventions or control.

61. Kevin Bales, *Understanding Global Slavery: A Reader* (Berkeley: University of California Press, 2005), 18.

62. Bernstein, "Sexual Politics of the New Abolitionism," 140.

63. Bernstein and Jakobsen, "Sex, Secularism and Religious Influence," 1035. See also Jakobsen and Bernstein, "Religion, Politics and Gender Equality: Country Report: USA" (United Nations Research Institute for Social Development; Heinrich Böll Stiftung, September 2009), 30, http://www.boell.org/downloads/USA_Final_Research_Report.pdf.

64. Bernstein, "Militarized Humanitarianism," 54–58; and Bernstein, "Sexual Politics," 137.

65. See, generally, Agustín, *Sex at the Margins*; and Bernstein, "Militarized Humanitarianism."

66. We use the term "heterosex" to refer to sex between men and women without making assumptions or claims about the sexual identities of the people involved.

67. Bernstein and Jakobsen, "Religion, Politics and Gender Equality," 30. See also Bernstein, "Carceral Politics as Gender Justice? The 'Traffic in Women' and Neoliberal Circuits of Crime, Sex, and Rights," *Theory and Society* 41 (2012): 245–47.

68. Stephanie May, "Violence in the Home/land: Christian 'Family Values' and

the Politics of 'Homeland Security'" (paper presented at the Annual Meeting for the Society of Christian Ethics, Washington, DC, January 6, 2012).

69. Ibid.

70. Penelope Saunders, "Traffic Violations: Determining the Meaning of Violence in Sexual Trafficking Versus Sex Work," *Journal of Interpersonal Violence* 20 (2005): 351; and Bernstein, "Militarized Humanitarianism."

71. Bernstein, "Militarized Humanitarianism," 47.

72. Bernstein and Jakobsen, "Sex, Secularism and Religious Influence," 1031.

73. Bernstein, "Militarized Humanitarianism."

74. Gayle Rubin reflects insightfully on how for some activists (feminists, antifeminist social conservatives, and evangelical and conservative Christians alike) "trafficking" functions as a banner to wave as a justification for the project to abolish and further criminalize prostitution "rather than to address the conditions that constrain women's economic choices and social power." Rubin, "Trouble with Trafficking," 86.

75. Hand of Hope, "Wedding Bells Ring for Human Trafficking Survivors," accessed May 29, 2013, www.joycemeyer.org/articles/hoh.aspx?article=wedding _bells_ring/.

76. See May, "Violence in the Home/land"; and Bernstein, "Militarized Humanitarianism."

77. Kristin L. Dunkle, Gina M. Wingood, Christina M. Camp, and Ralph J. DiClemente, "Economically Motivated Relationships and Transactional Sex among Unmarried African American and White Women: Results from a US National Telephone Survey," *Public Health Reports* 125, Suppl 4 (2010), www.ncbi .nlm.nih.gov/pmc/articles/PMC2882979/.

78. The social and economic distance of many anti-trafficking advocates from the communities most affected by trafficking allows advocates to romanticize marginalized persons and groups ("the poor") as asexual and therefore deserving of help and rescue. Liberation theologian Marcella Althaus-Reid reminds us that reality is less comfortable and more complex than what romantic depictions convey, because the poor are often anything but "decent" (in conventional terms), and many of the issues that poor women face are precisely sexual. Althaus-Reid, ed., *Liberation Theology and Sexuality* (Burlington, VT: Ashgate, 2006).

79. Bernstein and Jakobsen, "Sex, Secularism and Religious Influence," 30.

80. Emilie Townes, *In a Blaze of Glory: Womanist Spirituality as Social Witness* (Nashville: Abingdon Press, 2009), 72–73.

81. Sharon D. Welch, *A Feminist Ethic of Risk*, rev. ed. (Minneapolis: Fortress Press, 2000), 33.

82. Beverly W. Harrison and Carter Heyward, "Pain and Pleasure: Avoiding the Confusion of Christian Tradition in Feminist Theory," in *Sexuality and the Sacred: Sources for Theological Reflection*, eds. James B. Nelson and Sandra P. Longfellow (Louisville: Westminster John Knox Press, 1994).

9

The Ethics of "Recognition"

Rowan Williams's Approach to Moral Discernment in the Christian Community

Sarah M. Moses

While he was archbishop of Canterbury from 2002 to 2012, the scholar and theologian Rowan Williams faced divisive controversy over ethical issues such as human sexuality, women's ordination, and the treatment of religious minorities. This essay presents a selective retrieval of Williams's approach to communal disagreement as an important contribution of the Anglican tradition to the future of Christian ethics. Williams's concept of ethical discernment as an exercise in "recognition" offers a way for communities to approach differences as fostering constructive engagement and expanding ethical insight. Kathryn Tanner's analysis of culture and tradition in *Theories of Culture* is used to explicate the strengths and limitations of Williams's thought.

This essay offers a contribution to Christian ethics out of the Anglican tradition, as represented by a selective retrieval of Rowan Williams's approach to moral discernment in the Christian community. Thus, this essay is not focused on an Anglican approach to a specific ethical issue but on how Christian communities negotiate communal disagreement over ethical issues while seeking to maintain genuine forms of unity. Christian communities face a particular challenge: They seek to determine what behaviors are consistent with the will of God as revealed in the life and teachings of Jesus while also seeking unity among a diverse community of persons. My purpose is to show that Williams's approach to ethical discernment as an exercise in "recognition" offers Christian ethics a way for communities to embrace internal diversity and difference as

This essay was published originally in the *Journal of the Society of Christian Ethics* 35.1 (2015): 147–165.

fostering constructive engagement. The essay first provides an analysis of Williams's approach to moral discernment, which I term the "ethics of recognition," and then identifies the potential contributions and limitations of his approach via dialogue with the theologian Kathryn Tanner.

Rowan Williams and the "Ethics of Recognition"

Although debates about sexuality go back several decades in the Anglican Communion, observers cite two key events in 2003 that intensified discussion. First, a diocese in the Anglican Church of Canada authorized the use of a public rite of blessing for same-sex couples. Second, the Diocese of New Hampshire in the Episcopal Church elected as bishop Gene Robinson, a divorced, openly gay man living in a domestic partnership with another man. In response to Robinson's election, some provinces of the Anglican Communion broke communion with the Episcopal Church. Furthermore, the 1998 Lambeth Conference, an international gathering of Anglican bishops, had passed a resolution that described "homosexual practice as incompatible with scripture" and stated that it could not "advise the legitimising or blessing of same sex unions nor ordaining those involved in same gender unions."[1] Though Lambeth Conference resolutions do not carry the force of global canon law, many within the Anglican Communion argued that it ought to be respected as the position of Anglicans worldwide.[2]

It was during this tumultuous time that Williams served as archbishop of Canterbury from 2002 to 2012. In addition to presiding as head of the Church of England, the archbishop of Canterbury serves as global leader of the Anglican Communion, but without any formal power over its member provinces. As Williams himself describes, "the Communion is an association of local churches, not a single organisation with a controlling bureaucracy and a universal system of law."[3] Given this ecclesiology, the Anglican scholar Mark Edington describes the challenge of the archbishop's role: "[The archbishop] is a person called on to serve as the global voice for a group of self-governing churches—all of which reserve to themselves the right to make their own pronouncements—in the broader contexts of both ecumenical and interfaith conversations. To the holder of this office falls the unenviable complication of articulating the 'Anglican view' of Christian faith and social ethics."[4]

Despite these challenges, Williams addressed issues such as the nature of Christian unity and the challenges of diversity and disagreement. In fact, Williams argued that the issue underlying more specific debates about the morality of homosexuality or gender equality was a deeper question about communal ethical discernment. In a 2006 letter to the Anglican Communion, Williams argued that the main issue for the Church "is a question, agonisingly difficult for many, as to what kinds of behaviour a Church that seeks to be loyal to the Bible can bless, and what kinds of behaviour it must warn against—and so it is a question about how we make decisions corporately with other Christians, looking together for the mind of Christ as we share the study of the scriptures."[5]

To understand Williams's approach, it is important to first sketch his larger theological understanding of the Christian community as a non-competitive fellowship. In his essay on New Testament ethics, he argued that the central Christian belief in God's justifying grace creates the possibility of a noncompetitive community in which ethical discussion ceases to be an arena for the defense of one's interest against the others.[6] Thus, within the context of Christian belief, the moral agent can experience his or her being as fundamentally "given," or as secured by God's desire for his or her existence, and not as the result of any special action on the human's part.[7] From this perspective, Williams suggested that Christians should realize that "we are reckoned to have a right to be, by God's free determination."[8] For Williams, the narrative of Jesus found in the Gospels dispels the notion that one's being or one's access to the divine is secured by "moral or spiritual privilege"; instead, Christian tradition has understood Jesus as offering access to God for all.[9] This creates conditions for a noncompetitive community because one's belonging or being is not the result of any special action or ultimately threatened by the action of others. As Williams argued in a 2009 public

address to an international Anglican gathering, this noncompetitive environment should liberate the church from "a ceaseless rhetoric of fear
and competition" that often characterizes communal ethical debate.[10]

From this theological vision of a noncompetitive Church, Williams's
understanding of ethical action as edification and witness emerges. Human action can be reconceived when it is no longer understood as securing one's being and interest or as securing privileged access to the
divine.[11] Rather than measuring human action against abstract principles
or rules, Williams suggested that two basic questions ought to be asked
of any action: "Can it serve as a gift that builds up the community" and
"Does it manifest the selfless holiness of God in Christ."[12] Drawing on
Paul, Williams suggests that the New Testament "treats ethics, questions of specific behaviour, as governed by the principle of 'edification':
Good acts are those that build up the Body of Christ."[13] Rather than ap-
proaching ethical disagreement as the assertion of my interest against
another's, the principle of edification means that the Church ought to be
a community in which actions are measured by whether they "build up
a pattern of selfless engagement with the interest of the other."[14] In addition, Williams argued that fundamental to Christian ethical action is
its capacity to witness to the nature of God. As such, he writes: "The
practice of the ethical life by believers is a communicative strategy, a
discourse of some sort."[15] He connected this understanding of action as
witness to the narrative of Jesus: "Thus, the imperative changes its character: We are to act in such a way that the nature of God becomes visible, in the way it was visible in the life and death of Jesus."[16] Further,
the primary aspect of God's nature in Christ to which Christians are to
give witness is "the God whose nature is self-dispossession for the sake
of the life of the other."[17]

For Williams, the noncompetitive nature of the Church and the related concept of ethics as edification and witness change one's perception of communal disagreement. Ethical disagreement and conflict are
no longer fear-inducing challenges to my interests or spiritual purity but
become occasions to grow with others. Williams wrote, "If there is no
anxiety of rivalry in our ethical reflection, no anxiety about the possible

ultimate extinction of our interest in the presence of God, it follows that
every *perceived* conflict of human interest represents a challenge to work,
to negotiate."[18] Such a noncompetitive environment is indispensable for
creating the space in which genuine sharing and listening can occur. He
argued, "The self is free to *grow* ethically (that is, to assimilate what is
strange, to be formed into intelligibility) only when it is not under obligation to defend itself above all else—or to *create* itself, to carve out
its place in a potentially hostile environment."[19] In this framework, the
Church becomes a community in which persons can move beyond com-
petitiveness because all are equally accountable to the self-giving divine
reality made visible in Jesus.

The second defining element of Williams's ecclesiology is that unity
is given and not predicated on communal unanimity with respect to specific ethical questions. For Williams, the unity of the Church is rooted
in the unity of the Triune God, and thus is given prior to any outward
expressions of unity in the human community. Christians are united to
God through what Williams described as "union with Christ." It is this
unity that Williams sees as a pure gift that provides the basis for unity
between Christian persons. Referencing John 15:16, Williams argued
that "our [the Anglican Communion's] unity is something given to us
prior to our choices—let alone our votes. 'You have not chosen me but I
have chosen you', says Jesus to his disciples."[20] Thus, it is never a choice
between unity and truth because a fundamental element of unity exists
prior to any human activity or choices. From this perspective, Williams
wrote that Christians are "held in unity by something more than just the
consensus of the moment."[21] Following from this, Williams argued the
responsibility of members of the Church is to subsequently "work at a
common life" that embodies this unity.

For Williams, this unity serves an important purpose. "In case we've
forgotten," he stated, "it's worth reminding ourselves that the Bible
seems fairly clear that we are given to one another as believers so that we
may know and experience more of God than we would on our own."[22] Included in this knowledge of God is ethical knowledge. Williams argued
that "what we determine together is more likely, in a New Testament

framework, to be in tune with the Holy Spirit than what any one community decides locally."[23] Thus ecclesial communion is the *prerequisite* for reaching shared ethical understanding, not the *result* of such agreement. Williams's practical efforts to hold the global Anglican Communion together can be situated in relation to his argument that "unity is generally a way of coming closer to revealed truth."[24] He used as a practical example Anglican ecclesiology, which consists of a communion of churches in different geographic regions. In his writings and speeches, he argued that a global communion helps local communities avoid being trapped in narrow local cultural surroundings and thus broadens ethical insights.[25] As he stated at the 2008 Lambeth Conference, unity guards against "the natural instinct on all sides to cling to one dimension of the truth revealed."[26] Thus, for Williams, the embodiment of unity is not an end in itself; rather, he insisted that it is important to find tangible structures to hold persons together in communion in order to reach the broadest ethical understanding or, as he put it, to "help us grow in [Christ's] truth."[27]

Williams's theological understanding of the non-competitiveness of Christian community and ecclesial unity as given provides a necessary framework for an analysis of the ethics of recognition. With regard to moral discernment, Williams identifies moments when new questions and potential new practices force communities to determine whether an ethical judgment is "continuous" with the historic tradition.[28] It is in such situations that the exercise of recognition functions as the practice that allows a community to embody communion and to facilitate ethical discernment in the context of disagreement. The concept of recognition encompasses multiple dimensions: individual persons, actions, and shared communal identity. First, recognition involves seeing the other in relation to Christ, that is, "to see in the other person another believer, another redeemed sinner, another person on the way to transformation in Christ."[29] Recognition also involves seeing in others *Christ's* loyalty or faithfulness to them, which then demands loyalty in response.[30] Williams suggested that this Christological identity establishes a basic recognition of persons as sharing membership in the same community, the Body of Christ.[31]

Second, Williams used the language of recognition regarding an action itself and whether a new practice is recognizable to a community and its tradition. He wrote: "In the Christian context, what this means is that an action offered as gift to the life of the Body must be recognizable as an action that in some way or another manifests the character of the God who has called the community."[32] As we saw above, Williams bases the language of gift on Pauline images of Christians acting in such a way as to build up a communal fellowship. When one intends his or her action as a gift, Williams writes, "I have to struggle to make sense of my decision in terms of the common language of the faith, to demonstrate why this might be a way of speaking the language of the historic schema of Christian belief."[33]

Third, the concept of recognition applies to relations between persons and the practices that enable people to see one another as belonging to the same community. For Williams, part of this recognition of the other is rooted in shared habits and practices, what he called "markers of Christian identity."[34] Throughout his writings, Williams points to several key habits and practices that make members of the Anglican Communion recognizable to one another: "habits of attention and devotion to scripture"; shared commitment to "a rule of life and a pattern of prayer"; sharing in Baptism and the Eucharist; global mission and ministry; and sharing in the threefold ministry of bishops, priests, and deacons.[35] For Williams, it is through such shared markers—and not primarily through explicit agreement on specific ethical issues— that one is able to recognize another as someone to whom I am bound through a given, identifiable fellowship.

In addition to habits and practices, Williams identified obedience as part of communal identity. Obedience fosters recognition, in that what a person sees in the other is a common desire for obedience, what Williams referred to as the "grammar of obedience." In an essay on moral decision making, he defined it thus: "We watch to see if our partners take the same kind of time, sense that they are under the same sort of judgment or scrutiny, and approach the issue with the same attempt to be dispossessed by the truth with which they are engaging. This will not guarantee agreement, but it might explain why we should always first be hesitant and attentive to each other."[36]

The connection between Williams's vision of moral discernment and concrete communal practices is clear; it is impossible to recognize the grammar of obedience outside communal worship and spiritual practices, such as prayer and scripture reading, in which one sees the other seeking to be obedient to a reality beyond themselves. For instance, in an ecclesial letter in 2006, Williams suggested that belonging to such a "global sacramental fellowship" provides "a chance to rediscover a positive common obedience to the mystery of God's gift that was not a matter of coercion from above but of that 'waiting for each other' that Saint Paul commends to the Corinthians."[37] He acknowledged that this is extremely challenging when community members disagree over what are considered to be fundamental moral issues; nonetheless, he urged the possibility: "I can dimly see that the intention of my colleagues who see differently is also a kind of obedience, by their lights, to what we are all trying to discern."[38] In the recognition of a common obedience, persons see that all are bound to something more decisive than personal interests, and people can be vulnerable to one another when they uncover "a sense and a practice of common answerability."[39]

In his essay on moral decision making, Williams provided a practical example of the ethics of recognition with discussion of an issue to which he gave much attention before becoming archbishop: the creation and possession of weapons of mass destruction by nations. He explained that he reached an ethical judgment that it was "impossible for a Christian to tolerate, let alone bless or defend" such weapons.[40] At the same time, he stated that he could not ignore that Christians do in fact do so; and further, that he recognized in such persons shared habits and practices such as reading the Bible, Eucharistic practice, and subjection to the same "central truths of our faith." Because of such recognition, Williams considered himself responsible for listening deeply to the other side's explanation of its position. And though he did not agree with the specific conclusions, he acknowledged that its argument posed the important question of how people take care of one another in a violent world, and he rightly insisted that there could be no casual "withdrawal" from this responsibility. Although he remained committed to his own ethical position on the matter, he also wrote that because of the exercise of recognition, "it seems I am forced to ask what there is in this position that I might recognize as a gift, as a showing of Christ."[41] Furthermore, consistent with his view of the positive benefit of diversity within the Christian community, he suggested that the debate allowed him to gain insight that he would not be able to obtain alone.

Applied to the moral debates while archbishop, Williams argued that Anglicans could not easily dismiss one another as totally wrong or separate from others in the process of ethical disagreement. In a public address on Anglican disagreement over homosexuality, Williams urged: "We have not yet got to the point where we can no longer recognise one another as seeking to obey the same Lord. . . . If we recognise this much, we have to recognise that the other person or community or tradition is not simply going to go away. They are near enough to be capable of conversation, shared prayer and shared discernment with us. They are not just going to be defeated and silenced. For the foreseeable future, they are going to be there, recognisably doing something like what we are doing."[42]

For Williams, recognition is both an aspect of moral discernment and an important spiritual exercise within the Church. In a public address in 2009, Williams in fact explained that the Anglican Communion was doing all that it was precisely "because we hoped that through all these procedures, Christian people would be able to recognise each other a bit more fully, a bit more generously, and a bit more hopefully."[43] For Williams, the ethics of recognition provided a genuine basis for remaining in communion with others, even in the context of fierce disagreement over specific moral issues.

Williams is realistically practical in his insistence that a community capable of practicing the ethics of recognition demands intentionality, effort, and the creation of structures and processes, which he refers to as the "labour of ethics."[44] Members of the community must actually see it as part of the responsibility they owe to one another to continue "efforts to make sense of one another."⁴⁵ His use of "efforts" here is intentional. Recognition does not happen automatically but is an "exercise" of recognition, in the sense of an activity that requires work on my part. As archbishop, Williams saw part of his role as creating spaces for conversation and engagement between members of the Anglican Communion.⁴⁶ For example, at the Lambeth Conference over which Williams presided in 2008, small discussion groups were created to foster a process of sharing and listening between the bishops separate from the formal parliamentary procedures related to voting on resolutions.⁴⁷

It should be noted that Williams explicitly distinguished his approach from forms of ethical relativism or mere toleration. In an address to the General Synod of the Church of England regarding women's ordination to the episcopate, Williams stated that his vision of a Church able to contain "a difficult plurality of conviction" is not "simply a matter of tolerating private views."⁴⁸ For one, both the ordination of female bishops and the ordination of practicing homosexuals are actions that affect the *public* life of the community. Mutual recognition also requires active efforts to understand and make oneself understood; an effort to reach a deeper, shared ethical understanding; and an openness to one's own position being challenged. Williams wrote: "If another Christian comes to a different conclusion and decides in different ways from myself, and if I can still recognize his or her discipline and practice as sufficiently like mine to sustain a conversation, this leaves my own decisions to some extent under question."⁴⁹ He argued such relinquishing of "absolute certainty" is not relativism but rather the kind of "putting oneself at risk" necessary in any genuine effort at moral discernment. Far from a community defined by a relativistic mentality, Williams pictured a community in which people actively "struggle to make recognizable sense" to one another.⁵⁰ And, as seen in his discussion of weapons of mass destruction, this kind of ethical discernment is based upon a belief that genuine ethical insight or moral truth does exist and can be accessed.

Although Williams clearly thought the ethics of recognition fosters genuine unity and moral discernment amid strong disagreement, he also entertained the possibility that persons may reach a point beyond which recognition is not possible. In his writings and public speeches, he stated that it is possible for the Church to reach "points when recognition fails."[51] In fact, for Williams, part of the Church "becoming a discerning community" is the ability to identify limits to recognition, though he warns against "the dangers of deciding well in advance where the nonnegotiable boundaries lie."[52] He offered as a historical example of such a point the decision of Dietrich Bonhoeffer and others to break the communion of the German Protestant churches of the Confessing Church over opposition to anti-Jewish Nazi legislation. In such situations, Williams maintained that certain actions can put a Church "across the central stream of the life they have shared with other Churches."[53] In his own context, Williams suggested in a 2010 Pentecost letter that within the Anglican Communion, there are in fact "acceptable limits of diversity in its practice."[54] As general markers, Williams suggested such limits include when persons no longer "bring acts and projects before the criterion we look to together" and if someone's actions "systematically undermine the unconditionality of the Gospel's offer."[55] In such situations, Williams warned that Christians and their actions can become unrecognizable to others.[56]

Strengths and Limitations of the Ethics of Recognition

Having analyzed Rowan Williams's approach to communal ethical discernment, I turn now to an assessment of the potential contributions that the ethics of recognition offers to the future of Christian ethics in dealing with diversity within communities. For this purpose, Kathryn Tanner proves a fruitful dialogue partner for Williams because her book *Theories of Culture: A New Agenda for Theology* also offers an approach to situations of diversity and disagreement in the Church, one that explicitly appropriates insights from contemporary culture theory.[57] Putting Tanner and Williams in conversation helps illustrate the strengths of Williams's approach and raises constructive challenges.

One insight from contemporary culture theory that Tanner embraced is that differences and disagreements should no longer be seen to exist only on the boundaries *between* cultures and communities but rather "change, conflict, and contradiction" are contained *within* cultures and the communities that shape them.[58] From this perspective, a consensus on the meaning of cultural materials cannot be taken for granted; rather, differences in the interpretation of these materials becomes the norm. Part of the reason for such diversity is the flexibility inherent to cultural materials, a vagueness and indeterminacy that allow different interpretations across different historical moments and situations.[59] Tanner summarized postmodern critiques of previous theories of culture as follows: "It seems less and less plausible to presume that cultures are self-contained and clearly bounded units, internally consistent and unified wholes of beliefs and values simply transmitted to every member of the respective groups as principles of social order."[60] Tanner's analysis is helpful for our consideration of communal moral discernment because in one sense ethics can be seen as the effort of the members of a community to situate their actions in relation to their understanding of the materials of their tradition, such as the Bible, the sacraments, and Church doctrine. As in other human communities, one should expect to find great diversity in this effort rather than a static consensus. Thus, Tanner urged Christian theologians to view internal diversity as the reality within which the Church lives and not as a problem to be overcome.

Similarly, I have shown that Williams's theological understanding of Christian unity does not prevent him from acknowledging the reality and importance of diversity and disagreement within the Church throughout Christian history. For instance, he framed the debate about homosexuality within the Church's long history of negotiating disagreement. In a 2010 Pentecost letter, Williams reminded Anglicans that the New Testament itself records the reality of "internal hostilities" from the beginning of the Church.[61] Furthermore, rather than viewing internal diversity and disagreement merely as an inevitability to be tolerated, Williams argued that such realities provide a potentially wider access to ethical insights. For, in the context of a noncompetitive community, Christians can engage one another, even amid differences, for the sake of ethical growth. Although Williams insisted on the value of a universal or global perspective as a check on parochial narrowness, he also affirms the gift of local perspectives.[62] For Williams, local particularity can enrich the wider community, including knowledge of God and the practice of Christianity. Preferring the language of particularity to autonomy when thinking about the global Anglican community, Williams stated: "Talk about particularity and you're talking about the gift you have to share."[63]

Related to the dynamic of internal diversity, Tanner also suggested that even when a wide consensus may exist within a culture or tradition, contemporary culture theory has shown that such a consensus is always in the process of being contested by some party within the same culture or tradition.[64] For Tanner, the reality of dissent necessitates examining whether a perceived consensus may be the result of power over others, particularly dissenting minorities.[65] On this point, it is important to note that Williams's approach makes room for the prophetic voice of dissent, lest it seem that his vision of ecclesial unity is a subtle argument for conformity to the tradition as it has existed or as the most powerful voices proclaim it. He argued that there is a "debt we always owe to those who ask unfamiliar questions, because they prompt us to explore our tradition more deeply."[66] For instance, in his essay on making moral decisions, Williams acknowledged important developments within the Christian tradition, such as the renunciation of slavery and acceptance of democratic forms of government rather than monarchies.[67] Concerning those who seek to offer the Church "fresh insights," Williams argued, "a healthy church gives space for such exchanges."[68] In the ethics of recognition, a dissenting or prophetic action, like all action, can be beneficial to the community's moral discernment when offered as a potential gift and with respect for the unity of the community in which it is offered.

A second insight from contemporary culture theory that Tanner's approach incorporated is that cultures are products of historical processes in which interpretation and meaning are always in flux and changing. Consequently, rather than viewing cultures as given realities of nature, attention should be paid to the way in which cultures come to be in a certain historical period, how they compare and contrast with earlier periods, and the role of human agency in the shaping of culture.[69] Related to this is the reversal of a commonly held assumption: Change and development within communities are not negative departures from a standard of constancy and stability; rather, periods of a wide consensus within a culture are seen as temporary moments in an unfolding, continuous process of historical change. Following from this, Tanner urged Christian thinkers to see as part of their task the affirmation and explication of necessary development and change within the tradition.

In this regard, Williams's approach is valuable to Christian ethics because his response to the recent crisis within the Anglican Communion represents an effort to guide a process of changing ethical understanding rather than an effort to halt it. As we have seen, for Williams a change in a community's ethical understanding is not inherently a sign of disloyalty to tradition when such a change occurs in a way that "discernment continues *together*."[70] One way to view the ethics of recognition is as a process whereby this can occur as persons submit their practices and thoughts to one another, seeking to listen to and find insights from the other. For Williams, change is not a problem per se; what is important is the process by which it occurs. For instance, Williams suggested that discernment about new insights takes time and that it is a very weighty matter for a new development to receive the authority of the whole Anglican Communion through developments in public liturgy and practice. As noted in the previous section, Williams sought to guide the process of change and evolution in the Church's understanding of what actions are compatible with Christian life in a way that preserved fellowship within the community.

A third insight from contemporary culture theory that Tanner appropriated is the potential of cultural materials and practices to bind persons together in an identifiable community, even without a specific consensus or agreement. Drawing from contemporary anthropology, Tanner wrote, "Whether or not culture is a common focus of *agreement*, culture binds people together as a common focus for *engagement*."[71] In this view, participants within a particular culture or tradition are bound together by their common sense that certain materials and practices are valuable and by their "attachment" to them. But this attachment and engagement do not equal agreement, for shared culture or tradition provides "the basis for conflict as much as it provides the basis for shared beliefs and sentiments."[72] However, the positive side of this insight is that disagreement need not equal community dissolution. It can be reconceived as the site of binding interaction. Williams's approach practically demonstrates this insight by outlining how a community can engage together around shared materials and practices, even when their interpretation of these elements differs. For, as my analysis in the previous section showed, Williams argued that recognition does not equal having the same opinion about a particular action. Rather, recognition of the other is possible because of a shared life. Examples of this include attention to scripture and the practice of prayer. Furthermore, the concept of obedience was not about following the same specific rule of action but rather a mutually recognized attitude of seeking to be obedient to a truth that unfolds through shared life and habits.

Related to these dynamics, Williams's thought also represents an important Anglican contribution to the larger Christian moral tradition because it offers an alternative to ecclesial models that seek to bind shared communal identity around ethical agreement based on hierarchical enforcement or sectarian purity. Williams's understanding of the Church as a community whose diversity of interpretation is the basis from which truth and insight develop is consistent with his support for an ecclesiology that outwardly is neither hierarchically centralized nor sectarian. As archbishop, Williams clearly argued for the retention of what he saw as the Anglican model against calls for a more centralized authority: "The reason Anglicanism is worth bothering with is because it has tried to find a way of being a Church that is neither tightly centralised nor just a loose federation of essentially independent bodies—a Church that is seeking to be a coherent family of communities."[73] For Williams, finding a constructive approach to moral discernment is crucial for "a Church in which a difficult plurality of conviction will not simply be done away with by decree."[74] Based on his understanding of unity as a given and not something created by a human consensus, Williams rejected a sectarian ecclesiology. He argued that Anglicans must "turn away from the temptation to seek the purity and assurance of a community speaking with only one voice and to embrace the reality of living in a communion that is fallible and divided."[75] For Williams, genuine ethical discernment means accepting the reality and potential value of differences, a challenge to both traditionalists and liberals because everyone has "a bit of us that is in love with purity, that wants to find in the other a perfect echo of ourselves and to be able to present to the world outside a united face."[76] Given his embrace of the internal diversity of the Christian community, Williams warned against "trying to create a church of the 'perfect'—people like us."[77]

Thus far, my retrieval of Williams's thought has emphasized potential contributions to Christian ethics, but I conclude this section by raising constructive challenges to his approach. First, Williams's vision of the non-competitiveness of Christian community and his description of the process of recognition could be accused of naïveté regarding human motivations and biases. Here, Tanner's reminder that a seeming consensus is often achieved through domination or exclusion is vital. Although Williams often spoke of the brokenness of Christian community, he neglected the language of sin in the Christian tradition that helps unmask the human capacity for the willful exclusion of others. For instance, during Williams's tenure as archbishop many argued that the consensus of members of the Communion was reflected in the resolution passed at the 1998 Lambeth Conference, which, while commending continued study, stated that homosexual practice was "incompatible with scripture" and discouraged formal blessings of same-sex relationships and the ordination of practicing homosexuals. Yet one must ask whether such a resolution can truly be seen as reflective of a consensus in the wider community when passed by an organizational body consisting exclusively of bishops who are predominantly male and heterosexual. Likewise, one could ask why homosexual practice was singled out when diversity was accepted about other equally, if not more, important moral issues such as war and international economic practices. In his defense, Williams did repeatedly denounce flagrantly homophobic statements by church leaders throughout his tenure.[78] But Tanner's approach suggests that perhaps Williams should have raised sharper questions about the possible homophobic biases of those reserving their strongest moral condemnations for developments within the Episcopal Church and the Anglican Church of Canada. Instead, in his descriptions of ethical discernment and deliberation during discussions of homosexuality, he appears to assume that all parties are proceeding with admirable motives of obedience to Christ.[79]

A second potential limitation of Williams's approach is the burden of justification he placed on those who question the existing tradition. Although he affirmed the prophetic role of dissent, he seemed to place the weight of moral justification on the prophet. For instance, he argued that the biblical role of the prophet was to proclaim a "truth shared with the community of which he was a part, the community that gave him his identity in a number of basic respects."[80] For that reason, he concluded that within the Church, persons or groups offering what they see as prophetic insights must submit their actions and beliefs to the moral discernment of the whole community, particularly when it represents a radical innovation in the tradition. In his concluding speech to the Lambeth Conference in 2008, Williams stated that with regard to the public liturgy and practice of the Church, "the onus of proof is on those who seek a new understanding."[81] And, though admiring examples of twentieth-century prophets who took action despite effects on the visible unity of the Church, Williams wrote: "The nature of prophetic action is that you do not have a cast-iron guarantee that you're right."[82] Thus, while Williams urged the Anglican Communion to create clear ecclesial avenues for the expression of prophetic dissent, Tanner's analysis of power within communities asks whether a more robust critique of entrenched institutional interests and biases is not also necessary.

Third, Tanner's insistence on the value of internal diversity poses questions for Williams's proposal of a process to identify those "beyond recognition." Williams argued that there are situations where the actions of some cross a line in which they become unrecognizable to "the central stream" of Christian life or are outside the bounds of what can be understood as an acceptable development of the tradition. He suggested that groups introducing new insights and developments may put themselves beyond recognition by ceasing to offer their actions for the consideration of the larger community. Consistent with this position, during his tenure as archbishop, Williams urged the Anglican Communion to come up with explicit, clear structures and processes whereby local churches could bring their actions and understanding before the global body so that ethical discernment about controversial issues could take place in a transparent and constructive manner. The most controversial proposal considered in this regard was the adoption of an "Anglican Covenant," an official document describing the structures and mechanisms of global communion.[83] This document included a process by which the actions of certain churches or provinces could be declared "incompatible" with the consensus of the wider Communion, and "consequences" proposed for that provincial body in terms of its participation in the life of the wider Communion.[84] Williams himself supported the adoption of the Covenant as a way forward for the Anglican Communion to express and maintain its bonds and reasonably process serious disagreement such as that surrounding homosexuality.[85]

But in her book, Tanner raised insightful questions about efforts to identify a clear consensus and draw boundaries of recognizable membership. For instance, Tanner asked whether trying to shape a consensus where much disagreement already exists can actually do more harm to unity than help.[86] In such situations, where diversity of practice already exists Tanner suggested that efforts to achieve agreement about a particular norm run the risk of destroying an already fragile fellowship. Furthermore, she urged that the process by which a community determines that "some things [are] out of bound[s]" should proceed very "cautiously" and slowly, especially when new practices and ideas are first being introduced.[87] Otherwise, she argued, it is hard to create the time and space it takes for a community to exercise "good judgment" and conduct a careful analysis of new proposals. And in fact, her concerns have been visible in the mixed reaction of Anglicans to the Covenant proposal. For though the Covenant continues to be considered in provinces of the Anglican Communion, it has also received sharp critiques, and many now consider it without a future given its rejection by a majority of the dioceses of the Church of England.[88]

And yet, though Williams did argue for some form of accountability, through which a community could deem certain ethical actions beyond recognition, he also insisted that even in such situations, a form of communion and engagement ought to continue. Furthermore, though he was unabashedly critical of what he perceived as the preemptive, unilateral actions of some members of the Communion, he also warned against those who in his judgment too quickly decided where the boundaries of recognition lay on the issue of sexuality. As he wrote, the first priority in situations where persons can see that they are still speaking a recognizable language "is to stay in engagement with those who decide differently."[89] Furthermore, he suggested that a form of responsibility still persists, even in contexts of broken communion. This is what he referred to as the requirement of "staying alongside" one another. Such staying alongside is done, according to Williams, out of the acknowledgment of a shared brokenness in the community; this brokenness does not just belong to those with whom I disagree, but are also "my wounds." Thus, Williams argued that Christians should stay alongside one another "in the hope that we may still be exchanging gifts—the gift of Christ—in some ways, for one another's healing."[90] Given this emphasis on genuine engagement despite serious disagreement, the ethics of recognition can be useful for Christian ethics in seeking to articulate a form of global moral solidarity as opposed to isolation and fragmentation.

Conclusion

Most secondary scholarly analysis of Rowan Williams has focused on his systematic theology. This essay has sought to begin a retrieval of Williams's thought for the field of Christian ethics, drawing on both published material and the ecclesial writings and speeches he produced while archbishop. There, a distinct ethical approach is evident—what I have termed "the ethics of recognition." In conclusion, I highlight fruitful avenues for future research that would deepen and expand the retrieval of Williams's thought for Christian ethics, avenues that were beyond the scope of this essay. First, Williams's vision of the Church as a moral community and the nature of Christian ethics is clearly shaped by scripture. In his essay on the New Testament and ethics, Williams focused on the Jesus tradition in Matthew and on the Pauline epistles. Thus, an extensive study of the scriptural basis for Williams's approach would enhance an understanding of his ethics. Second, more remains to be done to explicate the relationship between his theology and spirituality and his ethics. The first section of this essay identified two relevant aspects of his larger theological framework that are related to ecclesiology: the possibility of noncompetitive fellowship and the givenness of Christian unity. But the texts examined for this project point to other potentially important themes in his theology, such as the Trinity, God's indiscriminate grace, and the role of the sacraments.[91] Third, Williams is also an important figure for those interested in retrieving the connection between systematic theology and ethics and between liturgy and ethics in the Christian tradition. Fourth and finally, an analysis of Williams's ethics would benefit from ecumenical contributions from other Christian traditions, particularly on the relationship between ecclesiology and models of moral discernment. As noted in the second section, Williams is himself quite conscious that his ethical approach reflects an ecclesiology rooted in Anglican history and tradition. Thus, a detailed comparison with distinctly alternative ecclesiologies, such as the Roman Catholic and Mennonite traditions, would further illuminate the connection between ecclesiology and ethics.

Based both on the analysis presented here and avenues still to be explored, Williams's thought represents an important contribution of the Anglican tradition to the future of Christian ethics. In particular, the retrieval of the ethics of recognition is important because it reflects a nuanced, realistic understanding of human community and tradition by acknowledging internal diversity, disagreement, and change as given and, more important, by proposing a process whereby such dynamics become vehicles for constructive ethical dialogue and engagement. Such an approach is valuable to the future of Christian ethics because the reality of global diversity and ethical disagreement promises to challenge the Church and academic ethics for the foreseeable future.

Questions for Reflection

1. How might Williams' "ethics of recognition" serve as a strategy for ecumenical and/or interfaith discussions of divisive sexual issues of concern to the commonweal, such as gender equality, gender identity, responsible parenthood, divorce, homosexuality, and heterosexism?

2. The creation of "safe spaces" for the discussion of complex and deeply personal convictions about human sexuality is critical to bridging the distance between competing narratives about it. How specifically might churches facilitate the development of such "safe spaces" for moral discernment within and beyond our communities?

3. With Tanner's assistance, Moses asks several difficult questions about our traditions. She asks: might some aspects of our traditions be deeply sinful and thereby not merely in need only of minor refinement and tweaking? If so, why should those who question tradition or seek change necessarily bear the burden of proof? Is this burden not an example of unrecognized and unjustified privilege? What is to be done if what we disagree about are the common criteria by which we test proposed changes in our shared traditions?

Suggestions for Further Reading

Catholic Common Ground Initiative. "Principles of Dialogue." Chicago: Catholic Theological Union: The Bernardin Center. Accessed October 13, 2016. http://www.catholiccommonground.org/principles-dialogue.

Farley, Margaret A. "Something New under the Sun." *Journal of Religious Ethics* 44.1 (2016): 186–194.

Gumbleton, Thomas. "A Call to Listen: The Church's Pastoral and Theological Response to Gays and Lesbians." In Christine Firer Hinze and J. Patrick Hornbeck II, eds., *More Than a Monologue: Sexual Diversity and the Catholic Church*, 55–69. New York: Fordham University Press, 2014.

Palmer, Parker J. *Healing the Heart of Democracy: The Courage to Create a Politics Worthy of the Human Spirit*. San Francisco: Jossey-Bass, 2011.

"Seeking to Be Faithful Together: Guidelines for Presbyterians during Times of Disagreement." Louisville, KY: Presbyterian Mission, June 4, 2010. http://www.presbyterianmission.org/wp-content/uploads/guidelines.pdf.

Notes

1. Lambeth Commission, Resolution I.10, "Human Sexuality," *The Windsor Report 2004* (London: Anglican Communion Office, 2004), §78.

2. Ibid., §17.

3. Rowan Williams, "The Challenge and Hope of Being an Anglican Today: A Reflection for the Bishops, Clergy, and Faithful of the Anglican Communion," June 27, 2006, http://rowanwilliams.archbishopofcanterbury.org/articles .php/1478/the-challenge-and-hope-of-being-an-anglican-today-a-reflection -for-the-bishops-clergy-and-faithful-0.

4. Mark D. W. Edington, "The Elusive Identity," *Anglican Theological Review* 92, no. 2 (Spring 2010): 381.

5. Williams, "Challenge and Hope."

6. Rowan Williams, "Interiority and Epiphany: A Reading in New Testament Ethics," in *Spirituality and Social Embodiment*, ed. L. Gregory Jones and James J. Buckley (Oxford: Blackwell, 1997), 38.

7. Ibid., 37.

8. Ibid., 38.

9. Ibid., 36.

10. Rowan Williams, "Archbishop's Presidential Address to the 14th Meeting of the ACC," 104th Archbishop of Canterbury, May 11, 2009, http://rowanwil liams.archbishopofcanterbury.org/articles.php/1510/archbishops-presidential -address-to -the-14th-meeting-of-the-acc.

11. Williams, "Interiority and Epiphany," 49.

12. Rowan Williams, "On Making Moral Decisions," *Anglican Theological Review* 81, no. 2 (Spring 1999): 306.

13. Williams, "Interiority and Epiphany," 48. In his writings, Williams focuses his Pauline interpretation on the following texts: Rom. 14 and 15; 1 Cor. 10; and II Cor. 9. See Williams, "On Making Moral Decisions," 299; and Williams, "Interiority and Epiphany," 42. For his specific discussion of the Pauline and deutero-Pauline corpus, see pp. 13–17.

14. Williams, "On Making Moral Decisions," 300.

15. Williams, "Interiority and Epiphany," 44.

16. Ibid., 42.

17. Ibid., 49.

18. Ibid., 38.

19. Ibid., 38.

20. Williams, "Challenge and Hope."

21. Ibid.

22. Williams, "Archbishop's Presidential Address."

23. Rowan Williams, "Communion, Covenant, and Our Anglican Future,"

Anglican Communion News Service, July 27, 2009, §13, www.anglicannews.org /news/2009/07/communion,-covenant-and-our-anglican-future.aspx.

24. Williams, "Challenge and Hope."

25. See Williams, "Concluding Presidential Address to the Lambeth Conference," 104th archbishop of Canterbury, August 3, 2008, http://rowanwilliams .archbishopofcanterbury.org/ articles.php/1350/concluding-presidential-address -to-the-lambeth-conference; Williams, "Communion, Covenant, and Our Anglican Future," §14.

26. Rowan Williams, "Archbishop's Second Presidential Address at Lambeth Conference," 104th archbishop of Canterbury, July 29, 2008, http://rowan williams.archbishopofcanterbury.org/articles.php/1352/archbishops-second -presidential-address-at-lambeth-conference.

27. Rowan Williams, "Renewal in the Spirit: The Archbishop of Canterbury's Pentecost Letter to the Bishops, Clergy and Faithful of the Anglican Communion," 104th archbishop of Canterbury, May 28, 2010, §3, http://rowanwilliams .archbishopofcanterbury.org/articles.php/749/archbishop-of-canterburys-pente cost-letter-to-the-anglican-communion.

28. Williams, "Communion, Covenant, and Our Anglican Future," §17.

29. Rowan Williams, "Archbishop's First Presidential Address to Lambeth Conference," 104th archbishop of Canterbury, July 20, 2008, http://rowanwilliams .archbishopofcanterbury.org/articles.php/1353/archbishops-first-presidential -address-at-lambeth-conference.

30. Rowan Williams, "Archbishop's Presidential Address, General Synod 2010," 104th archbishop of Canterbury, February 9, 2010, http://rowanwilliams .archbishopofcanterbury.org/articles.php/590/the-archbishops-presidential-ad dress -general-synod-february-2010.

31. Williams, "Renewal in the Spirit," §1.

32. Williams, "On Making Moral Decisions," 301.

33. Ibid., 306.

34. Ibid., 303.

35. See Rowan Williams, "The Archbishop's Presidential Address, General Synod 2009," 104th archbishop of Canterbury, February 10, 2009, http://rowan williams.archbishopofcanterbury.org/articles.php/831/the-archbishops-presi dential-address-general-synod-february-2009; Williams, "Archbishop's First Presidential Address"; Williams, "Archbishop's Presidential Address, General Synod 2010;" Williams, "Challenge and Hope."

36. Williams, "On Making Moral Decisions," 304.

37. Williams, "Challenge and Hope."

38. Williams, "On Making Moral Decisions," 303.

39. Williams, "Interiority and Epiphany," 34.

40. Williams, "On Making Moral Decisions," 302.

41. Ibid., 303.

42. Williams, "Archbishop's Presidential Address, General Synod 2009."

43. Williams, "Archbishop's Presidential Address to the 14th Meeting of the ACC."

44. Williams, "Interiority and Epiphany," 38.

45. Williams, "Renewal in the Spirit," §5.

46. Williams, "Archbishop's Presidential Address to the 14th Meeting of the ACC"; Rowan Williams, "Keeping the Faith," *Time International* 169, issue 25 (June 18, 2007): 26–27.

47. This process was called "Indaba groups"; see "Continuing Indaba–Indaba at Lambeth 2008," Anglican Communion Office, December 23, 2013, www.aco .org/ministry/continuingindaba/whatis/atlambeth2008.cfm.

48. Williams, "Archbishop's Presidential Address, General Synod 2009."

49. Williams, "On Making Moral Decisions," 304.

50. Ibid., 308.

51. Ibid., 306.

52. Ibid., 303.

53. Williams, "Challenge and Hope."

54. Williams, "Renewal in the Spirit," §4.

55. Williams, "On Making Moral Decisions," 306–7.

56. Williams, "Challenge and Hope"; Williams, "Renewal in the Spirit," §4.

57. Kathryn Tanner, *Theories of Culture: A New Agenda for Theology* (Minneapolis: Fortress Press, 1997).

58. Ibid., 53.

59. Ibid., 46, 122, 171.

60. Ibid., 38.

61. Williams, "Renewal in the Spirit," §2; see also Williams, "Archbishop's First Presidential Address."

62. See Williams, "On Making Moral Decisions," 298, 301.

63. Williams, "Archbishop's Presidential Address to the 14th Meeting of the ACC."

64. Tanner, *Theories of Culture*, 56.

65. Ibid., 164.

66. Williams, "Concluding Presidential Address."

67. Williams, "On Making Moral Decisions," 306.

68. Williams, "Concluding Presidential Address."

69. Tanner, *Theories of Culture*, 40–41.

70. Williams, "Concluding Presidential Address."

71. Tanner, *Theories of Culture*, 57.

72. Ibid.

73. Williams, "Challenge and Hope"; see also Rowan Williams, "Archbishop: 'Beware the Danger of Becoming Less Than We Aspire to Be as a Communion,'"

Presidential Address to the Anglican Consultative Council, 104th Archbishop of Canterbury, November 4, 2012, http://rowanwilliams.archbishopofcanterbury .org/articles.php/2676/archbishop-beware-the-danger-of-becoming-less-than -we-aspire-to-be-as-a-communion.

74. Williams, "Archbishop's Presidential Address, General Synod 2009."

75. Williams, "On Making Moral Decisions," 304.

76. Williams, "Archbishop's Presidential Address, General Synod 2009."

77. Williams, "Renewal in the Spirit," §3.

78. Williams, "Communion, Covenant, and Our Anglican Future," §5, 10.

79. Williams, "Archbishop's Second Presidential Address." See also Williams, "On Making Moral Decisions," 301.

80. Williams, "On Making Moral Decisions," 299.

81. Williams, "Concluding Presidential Address."

82. Williams, "Challenge and Hope."

83. For the complete document, see "The Anglican Communion Covenant," Anglican Communion Office, December 27, 2013, www.anglicancommunion.org /commission/covenant/final/text.cfm.

84. Ibid., §4.2; for a discussion of this provision, see Edington, "Elusive Identity," 384–87.

85. Rowan Williams, "Archbishop: Why the Covenant Matters," 104th archbishop of Canterbury, March 5, 2012, http://rowanwilliams.archbishopofcanter bury.org/articles.php/2380/archbishop-why-the-covenant-matters.

86. Tanner, *Theories of Culture*, 172.

87. Ibid., 174.

88. Kevin Eckstrom, "'Covenant' to Bind Anglican Communion Appears Dead," *USA Today*, March 27, 2012, http://usatoday30.usatoday.com/news/re ligion/story/2012-03-27/anglican-covenant/53808972/1.

89. Williams, "On Making Moral Decisions," 307.

90. Ibid.

91. See, e.g., Williams, "Interiority and Epiphany," 44; ibid., 38–39; and Williams, "Challenge and Hope."

Contributors

KATHERINE ATTANASI has taught recently at Regent University in Virginia Beach and Luther College in Decorah, Iowa. She coedited a volume with Amos Yong titled, *Pentecostalism and Prosperity: The Socio-economics of the Global Charismatic Movement.*

LETITIA M. CAMPBELL is the director of Contextual Education I and Clinical Pastoral Education at the Candler School of Theology at Emory University. She also serves as the senior program coordinator for the Laney Legacy in Moral Leadership Program.

HOON CHOI is an assistant professor in the Theology Department at Bellarmine University in Louisville, Kentucky. His specialty is World Christianity.

DAVID P. GUSHEE is Distinguished University Professor of Christian Ethics and the director of the Center for Theology and Public Life at Mercer University.

MARY JO IOZZIO is a professor of moral theology at Boston College, School of Theology and Ministry, and the director of the Masters in Theological Studies program.

PATRICIA BEATTIE JUNG is a visiting professor of Christian ethics at the Saint Paul School of Theology in Kansas City, Kansas.

KAREN LEBACQZ is an emerita professor of Christian ethics in the Graduate Theological Union of the Pacific School of Religion. She is based in Berkeley, California.

SARAH M. MOSES is an assistant professor in the Department of Philosophy and Religion at the University of Mississippi.

KAREN PETERSON-IYER is a lecturer in the Department of Religious Studies at Santa Clara University.

JEAN PORTER is the John A. O'Brien Professor of Moral Theology at the University of Notre Dame.

TRACI C. WEST is a professor of ethics and African American studies at the Drew University Theological School in Madison, New Jersey.

YVONNE C. ZIMMERMAN is an associate professor of Christian ethics at the Methodist Theological School in Ohio.

Index

CPSIA information can be obtained
at www.ICGtesting.com
Printed in the USA
BVOW09s1555220917

495386BV00002B/7/P